The Kurds and the State

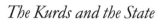

Modern Intellectual and Political History of the Middle East
Mehrzad Boroujerdi, *Series Editor*

Other titles in Modern Intellectual and Political History of the Middle East

The KURDS *and the* STATE

Evolving National Identity in Iraq, Turkey, and Iran

Denise Natali

Syracuse University Press

Library of Congress Cataloging-in-Publication Data

Natali, Denise.
The Kurds and the state : evolving national identity in Iraq, Turkey, and Iran / Denise
Natali.—1st ed.
p. cm.—(Modern intellectual and political history of the Middle East)
Includes bibliographical references and index.
ISBN 0–8156–3084–0 (hardcover : alk. paper)
1. Kurds—Politics and government. 2. Kurds—Iraq—Politics and government.
3. Kurds—Turkey—Politics and government. 4. Kurds—Iran—Politics and
government. 5. Iraq—Ethnic relations. 6. Turkey—Ethnic relations. 7. Iran—Ethnic
relations. I. Title. II. Series.
DS59.K86N38 2005
320.54'089'91597—dc22   2005019612

Manufactured in the United States of America

For Ali

Denise Natali is a professor and researcher at the College of Political Science, University of Salahaddin, Arbil (Hawlêr), Kurdistan region of Iraq. Over the past thirteen years she has lived, worked, and conducted independent field research in the Kurdish regions of Iraq, Turkey, and Iran, publishing numerous articles on Kurdish politics and identity within and beyond Iraq. Her expertise in Kurdish affairs has won her postings as information officer for the U.S. Office of Foreign Disaster Assistance in northern Iraq, the American Red Cross International Disaster Relief Services, and the Center for Strategic and International Studies. For sixteen months, she also worked with Afghan refugees in Pakistan, where she served as liaison to the Afghan interim government's Ministry of Public Health and as director of cross-border operations for a nongovernmental organization set up to train health-care workers.

Contents

Illustrations

Abbreviations

AKP	Adalet ve Kalkinma Partisi
CHF	Cumhuriyet Halk Firkasi
CHP	Cumhuriyet Halk Partisi
CPA	Coalition Provisional Authority
CUP	Committee for Union and Progress
DEHAP	Demokratik Halk Partisi
HADEP	Halken Demokrasi Partisi
ICP	Iraqi Communist Party
IRP	Islamic Republican Party
JK	Komeley-i Jineweh-i Kurdistan
KAJYK	Komeley Azadî Jiyanawey Yekitî Kurd
KDP	Kurdish Democratic Party (Iraq)
KDPI	Kurdish Democratic Party of Iran
KRG	Kurdistan Regional Government
PKK	Partiya Karkerên Kurdistanê
PUK	Patriotic Union of Kurdistan
SHP	Sosyaldemokrat Halk Partisi
TİP	Türkiye İşçi Partisi

Preface

This book took root in emergent political processes in post-Gulf War Iraqi Kurdistan and evolved into a comprehensive analysis of the similarities, variances, and changes in Kurdish national identity across space and time. It was driven by my intention to change misperceptions of "wild Koordistan" and misleading images of Kurds as one large tribal community. The more time I spent in Kurdistan in Iraq, Turkey, and Iran, the more I realized the need to explain the asymmetrical nature of nation-state-building processes, their consequences on national-identity formation, and the complexities of the Kurdish issue outside its tribal component.

Edward N. Luttwak encouraged me to pursue this project from the outset in 1991, after I returned from sixteen months of working with Afghan refugees in Peshawar, Pakistan, and turned toward the Persian Gulf War refugee crisis. Alongside the humanitarian relief demands of two million Iraqi Kurds stranded in the mountainous regions of Iraq, Turkey, and Iran was the unexpected outcome of the first democratic election in Iraqi Kurdistan in 1992. Massoud Barzani's Kurdistan Democratic Party (KDP) and Jelal Talabani's Patriotic Union of Kurdistan (PUK) unexpectedly created a fifty-fifty power-sharing agreement.

The very idea that two traditional antagonists decided to share power and construct a democratic government was fascinating from a political science and conflict resolution perspective. Where there should have been hostility there was compromise. Where dictatorship had ruled for decades a commitment to democratic institutions arose. These unexplained outcomes, as well as Edward's provocative insights, fed my curiosity and quest for further understanding the Kurdish issue. After several research trips, I returned to Iraqi Kurdistan as information officer for the U.S. Office of Foreign Disaster Assistance for fourteen months, when most Iraqi Kurdish refugees had returned from the mountains and were just commencing their experiment in democracy. Upon completing my post, I was more convinced than ever of the need for a book that examined the complexities of the contemporary Kurdish problem.

During my subsequent doctoral work at the University of Pennsylvania I had the benefit of working with Ian S. Lustick, whose constructive criticism and encouragement helped turn the Iraqi Kurdish power-sharing project into a comparative political analysis of Kurdish national identity in Iraq, Turkey, and Iran. I am especially grateful to Ian for his vigorous theoretical guidance, as well as the critiques made on later drafts or articles by Thomas Callaghy, Rudra Sil, Vali Nasr, Henri Barkey, Hamit Bozarslan, Daniele Conversi, Brendan O'Leary, Eric Hooglund, Arif Engin, and two anonymous readers.

Most of the fieldwork, archival research, and writing could not have been completed without the support of the U.S. Institute of Peace, which provided me with two important research grants, one as a Jennings Randolph Peace Scholar and another as part of its Solicited Grant program. I thank the University of Pennsylvania, including its Department of Political Science and Middle East Center, and the U.S. Department of Education for fellowships to conduct fieldwork and language training while this project was still part of my doctoral work.

During my numerous trips to Iraq, Turkey, Iran, Syria, and the Kurdish regions over the past thirteen years, dozens of families and friends assisted me, and I can only thank them anonymously for their nonending hospitality. At a moment's notice, they took me in, often for indeterminate time periods, fed me, served me chai, and ensured my personal security. I am grateful to Massoud Barzani and Jelal Talabani and their political party representatives for offering me housing, contacts, transportation, documents, security assistance, and interviews, all of which facilitated my research in Iraqi Kurdistan. Hoshyr Zibari, Muhammed Tawfik, Hussein Sinjari, Muhammed Ihsan, Avin Faiq, Barham Salih, Pershing Kareem, and Shaykh Muhammed Sargalo gave me detailed information and background histories during different conversations from 1992 to 2003. The villagers of Qishlaqh, Iraqi Kurdistan, and in particular Baji Miriem received me as one of their own during my fieldwork in the summer of 1995. I will never forget their generosity, nor the lessons learned from that experience.

I thank L'Institut Français de Recherche en Iran and its excellent library and administrative staff, which made every effort to accommodate my research demands during my several months' stay in Iran. I am also grateful to an anonymous friend who gave me access to his personal library, contacts, and insights, which proved invaluable for the research.

As I moved the project to Europe to follow Kurdish diasporic communities, the Washington Kurdish Institute and L'Institut Kurde de Paris (IKP) offered administrative and technical support that enabled me to conduct extensive interviews with Kurds in different host-country settings. Dr. Kendal Nezan, president of IKP, and the IKP staff ensured me easy access to the institute's resources during my seven years in Paris. Metin Achard and Arif Engin provided thorough research and translation assistance with Turkish texts. Halkawt Hakim offered valuable insight, encyclopedic knowledge, and fascinating discussions of Iraqi Kurdish political thought. I am also grateful to Joyce Blau, Abdulla Mardukh Kurdistany, Barzan Faraj Abdulla, Verya Nasri, Nezand Begikhani, Ibrahim Mamle, Mehmet Bağiş, Khosro Abdollahi, Salih Yillik, and Michael Chyet.

I thank Oxford University Press, Taylor and Francis, and Blackwell Publishers for permitting me to reprint parts of chapters previously published.

Finally, I thank Ali Ayverdi for his patience, moral support, and nonending assistance in locating texts, arranging necessary contacts, and supporting my travel needs, all of which enabled me to remain deeply engaged in this project despite our family demands. Even when I was not in Kurdistan, Ali ensured that I was in touch with the political realities of the region, as well as the human components of being Kurdish in the homeland and in exile.

This book follows the transliteration style used by the *International Journal of Middle East Studies*. The ayn and hamza are used for Arabic and Farsi words, as well as necessary diacritics for Turkish works. Locations in Kurdistan are designated by the more commonly used Arabic, Turkish, and Farsi names, with Kurdish names in parentheses.

Introduction

Reassessing Ethnonationalism

Although some Kurds trace Kurdish civilization to the seventh millennium, the majority date their origins to the Median Empire in the sixth century B.C. Oral and written historiography shows how Kurds have attempted to preserve their culture, language, and territory despite efforts of central governments to prohibit or deny their identity. Bitlisi's *Sharafname,* Khani's *Mem-u-Zin,* Chamo's *Dimdim,* and Kurdo's *Kurdish Civilization* emphasize the uniqueness of Kurdish identity; Kurds are the conquerors of Xenophon's forces, survivors of Zohhak's cannibalism, and children of the Jinn. Even after the demise of the Ottoman and Persian Empires and division of Kurdish territories into four main states, Kurds have tried to protect their identity by differentiating themselves from the dominant ethnic group. Kurds are Kurds because they are not Arabs, Persians, or Turks. Given their deeply rooted notions of Kurdishness, why then have Kurds expressed their unique ethnic identity at different time frames and in various ways?

This book explains why Kurdayetî, or Kurdish national identity, becomes ethnicized and the similarities and variations in its manifestation across space and time. It shows that given the repertoire of an ethnic group's identities, politics affects how national identity becomes institutionalized and the various forms nationalism may assume. That is, although Kurdish communities have maintained some shared sense of nationalism, Kurdayetî has become part of a larger repertoire of identities based on the nature of the political space in each state. Shaped by the discourse and policies of the state elite, political space is a consequence of nation-state-building strategies that create different notions of inclusion and exclusion. It refers to the political and cultural opportunities for groups to express their ethnic identity and the possibilities to assume alternative identities over time. Whether Kurdayetî becomes ethnicized and salient depends upon the positive and negative incentives offered by central governments and the actions and reactions of Kurdish groups to these incentive structures. What it means to be a Kurd, therefore, must be considered in relation to what it means to be a citizen of Iraq, Turkey, and Iran.

The notion of political space addresses the uneven and changing nature of Kurdish nationalism by examining the larger political contexts that have given Kurdayetî its form and meaning. That is to say, whereas the content of Kurdayetî is based on objective group features, historical experiences, and collective memories, its character, or whether it is directed by urban or tribal leadership, highly organized or weak, ethnicized or Islamized, or compromising or violent, is determined by the political boundaries and opportunity structures that emerge in each state over time.

For instance, the transition from an imperial to state system helped reshape Kurdayetî because it created a new type of political space in which Kurdish identities could unfold. One important change in the postimperial milieu was the shift from religion to ethnicity in the categorization of group identity. Even though the Kurds may have defined themselves as an ethnic, tribal, or national group within their empires, Ottoman and Persian authorities distinguished minority populations according to religious affiliation: Muslims and non-Muslims. Ethnic categorizations may have existed, but they did not define the boundaries of inclusion and exclusion in the imperial system. Rather, Kurds were considered and considered themselves part of the dominant Muslim majority group.

By the mid-1920s the transition from empire to Middle Eastern states altered categorizations of political identity. Although most Muslim communities continued to identify with Islam, the nationalist tendencies that stimulated Arabs, Persians, and Turks also affected the Kurds, who were vying for a position in the new state system. Most important, after the state-formation period Middle Eastern leaders initiated their own nation-building projects to construct unified official state national identities. At different moments in each nation-state-formation project the political elite in Iraq, Turkey, and Iran emphasized ethnicity as a prominent identity marker, underlining differences among the dominant and minority ethnic communities. They promoted myths of cultural authenticity by invoking the greatness of Arab, Turkish, and Persian heritages. These political discourses and policies shaped environments in which new political, social, and economic boundaries were created and old ones were redrawn. Exclusions based on ethnicity created a we-they dichotomy in which Kurdish national identity was framed (Bulloch and Morris 1992; Entessar 1992, 8–12; Nagel 1980, 280–81; Vali 1994a; Kreyenbroek and Allison 1996).

Certainly, the new state system provided opportunities for Kurdish groups. In Iraq some of the wealthiest landowners were Kurds. Kurds from Turkey became prominent businessmen and politicians. In Iran they attained high-level religious and professional posts. Yet in each state Kurds could become fully integrated into the state only by denouncing some aspect of their ethnic identity. As a result, Kurds intentionally created, to different degrees, political, territorial, and cultural subdivisions that did not coincide with state-engineered nationalist programs. Instead of being homogenized into the political center, they differentiated themselves as a distinct ethnic community.

Yet the nature of the political space varied in each state, creating different opportunity structures for Kurdish communities over time. Different founding-state doctrines recognized and denied Kurdish ethnicity, enabling some Kurds to assimilate more easily than others into their political center. State elites also co-opted and controlled different subgroups of landowners, tribes, working classes, leftists, military factions, and religious communities, elevating some while disfranchising others. Variations in nation-state-building policies created structural changes in the Kurdish periphery, which in turn altered political relationships and influenced the form that Kurdayetî could assume (McDowall 1997, 343–56; Koohi-Kamali 1992, 171).

As a result, different forms of Kurdish nationalisms emerged according to the political spaces that became dominant in each state. In Iraq the political space that elevated tribal communities alongside urban groups, and varied between normative and repressive means of compliance, created a semilegal, influential, and fluctuating nationalist movement that became highly ethnicized with the Arabization of Iraqi identity after 1958 and fractured between two main political groupings. In Turkey the highly restrictive and unchanging political space weakened tribal structures and closed all opportunities for Kurds to express their ethnic identity. What resulted was a highly ethnicized, illegal, diversified, urban-based nationalist movement whereby tribal leaders played no significant role as the nationalist elite. In Iran the ethnicized and ambiguous political space that was partially inclusive for Kurdish and Shi'a communities created a more accommodating form of Kurdish nationalism that was directed by a secular, left-leaning Sunni Kurdish community in which the relationship between the state and nationalist elite fluctuated between hostility and compromise.

It can be argued that Kurdish nationalism would have ethnicized and fragmented anyway, despite the political spaces that emerged in Iraq, Turkey, and Iran. Political, linguistic, religious, and regional dichotomies between Sorani and Badinani Kurds in Iraq, Alevi and Sunni Kurds in Turkey, and Sunni and Shi'a Kurds in Iran were added to, and not created by, the politics of exclusion in the modern Middle Eastern state system. Additionally, although political spaces may have shaped certain types of center-periphery relationships, internal power rivalries and personal jealousies within the heterogeneous Kurdish society are likely to have continued anyway, reflecting the dichotomous relations among tribal groups, urban intellectuals and tribal chiefs, and *aghas* and tillers of the land.

Still, if contemporary Kurdish nationalism is a function of traditional social structures, then it becomes increasingly difficult to explain variations in Kurdayetî in states that have undergone social, political, and economic transformations over time. In the early twentieth century, for example, the Kurds were largely a rural and tribal society. Central-government strategies elevated the shaykhly establishment and encouraged tribal and local identities to become salient alongside a budding Kurdish nationalism. However, detribalizations, urbanization trends, refugee movements, and ongoing wars have altered the structure of each state since then. Even if Kurdish society has retribalized, tribal networks operate in a different environment at present than some fifty years ago. The emphasis on the old patron-client networks based on tribal loyalties or the reemergence of Kurdish tribal politics in different forms still leaves us questioning why Kurdish nationalism differs across space and time. If neotribalism has actually reappeared in the form of Kurdish political parties, then what explains the behavior of non-tribal groups in the manifestation of Kurdish nationalism?

In addressing these questions this book challenges views of Kurdish nationalism that focus on essentialist features of Kurdishness—inherent rivalries, unruly tribal behavior, and fixed sociopolitical structures—all of which have less to do with national-identity formation than with pejorative and misleading cultural stereotypes. Kurds have been characterized as "shedders of blood, raisers of strife, seekers after turmoil and uproar, robbers and brigands, and evildoers of depraved habits" (Pelletiere 1984, 11, 16). These images have reinforced the preoccupation with authenticating Kurdish national identity with philological proof: tribal configuration, geographic location, clothing, and rituals. Variations in ascriptive group features are used to explain different types of nationalist expression. Some Kurds are considered more essentially Kurdish than others, which accounts for their salient sense of ethnonationalism and high mobilization potential.

Kurds themselves use essentialist claims to explain variations in Kurdayetî. They argue that pure Kurds come from the Medes, they speak Kurdish, they wear Kurdish clothing, they sing Kurdish songs, they make Kurdish food, and they carry on Kurdish traditions. Those Kurds who differentiate themselves from Arabs, Turks, and Persians are considered good Kurds, conscious of their nationalist identity. Diasporic Kurds who integrate into Western societies are referred to as not being truly Kurdish even if they consider themselves as Kurds first. Groups born of Kurdish origin and who ally with state governments have no sense of nationalism. Unconscious of Kurdishness, they are considered bad Kurds, tribes, and traitors: *gunda, ileyet,* and *jash.*

Group classifications may account for distinctions among Kurds; however, they do not differentiate among the causes and consequences of variations in Kurdayetî. Good or real Kurds are likely to manifest Kurdish ethnonationalism, whereas bad Kurds are not. Determining differences based on subjectively created categories also removes the definitional basis for comparative purposes. Political outcomes are used as evidence to explain nationalist behavior; continued internal Kurdish fighting proves that Kurds have an inchoate sense of national consciousness. Without a systematic analysis of identity formation over time we can offer only ad hoc explanations of changes in national identity. Even when nationalism proves to be real, why does it wake up and then fall dormant again? What explains the periods of quiet between Kurdish nationalist mobilizations?

Ethnicizing National Identity

The study of nationalism has become further complicated with the rise of ethnonationalism, the idea of making nationalist claims based on blood descent. Ethnonationalism is a form of racial nationalism whereby a group differentiates itself according to its genealogical origins. One of the key questions in the ethnonationalist debate is why a group's national identity turns ethnic over time. Because each group has a distinct ethnie it has the potential to mobilize on an ethnonationalist level.

Yet not all nationalisms are ethnically oriented, at least not in their origins. Early European nationalisms were tied not to ethnonationalist sentiment but, rather, to religion. The foundation of the early stages of nationalism in Muslim countries was Islam. Grassroots nationalisms in some Muslim frontier societies such as Russia, Bosnia, Bulgaria, and Cyprus are tied to Islamic political consciousness, which has overlapping symbolism for an individual's ethnic identity (Coakley 2002; Yavuz 1995, 348–50). When the Malays started to make claims as an ethnic group in 1948 their demands were to defeat the Malay Union, and not to create their own ethnically exclusive Malay state. It was only after the 1960s, alongside tensions caused in the posttraditional socioeconomic order, that Malay identity became ethnicized (Shamsul 1997; Esman 1994, 51–53).

Additionally, even when nationalism becomes ethnicized it can be manifested differently at another point in time, and not necessarily for all group members. Basque ethnonationalism became salient in Spain in the late nineteenth century; however, it waited until the 1930s to emerge in a milder form in France. The problematic, therefore, is not the origins or assumptions of a preexisting foundation of ethnonationalist identity such as historical memories, sense of suffering, and shared group traits, but the circumstances, timing, and nature of ethnonationalist revivals. The key question is not what is a nation, but how is a nation at which period in time?

One can avoid periodization problems by treating ethnicity and nationalism as the same phenomenon and regarding ethnonationalism as a natural part of a group's self-awakening. The cognitive force of ethnicity plays such an essential role in mobilizing nationalist groups that its absence can lead to fragmentation even after a nation awakens. Nationalist trajectories are irregular because most of the world's ethnic groups have simply achieved national awareness at different points in history (Connor 2002).

One can further argue that all nationalisms are not necessarily ethnicized but depend on particular circumstances that awaken a group's preexisting ethnie. All groups may have the capacity to ethnicize their national identity; however, their mobilization potential is linked to institutional components, such as the structure of governance and its degree of legitimacy, which may not necessarily be tied to the modern period (Hechter 2000, 28–30; Connor 1994, 44; Connor 1978; Moynihan 1993, 99; Smith 2002, 1987).

Indeed, an essential component of nationalism is the legitimacy of the governing body. Illegitimate states or governments, through policies of repression and exclusion, can awaken a group's ethnie and encourage ethnonationalist revivals. Absence of state legitimacy can also cause quiescence in a nationalist movement. In illegitimate, highly centralized systems the political elite can create a combination of fear, habit, isolation, and disorganization that encourages group docility, even when a national group is conscious of its ethnic identity. Still, even in illegitimate centralized states, why do some group members support the political center, crossing ethnic boundaries for religious, civic, or linguistic ones?

By conflating ethnicity and nationalism into one variable and focusing on the emotional aspects of nationalism it is difficult to account for variations in nationalism within the periphery, especially in transitional societies in the developing world. The emotive aspect of nationalism may help account for its persistence over time; however, it neglects other political identities beyond the psychological sense of belonging. Nationalists are more than emotional freedom fighters. They can also be members of economically active transborder communities, villagers in underdeveloped and isolated regions, or tribal chiefs with large landowning interests. Encompassing localist allegiances is a citizenship regime, which can serve as a primary identity for some peripheral groups (William 1995, 585–87). Depending upon the circumstances and political opportunity structures, even the most die-hard nationalists may choose to emphasize their socioeconomic status, civic identity, or religious affiliation over their distinct ethnonationalism.

Particularly puzzling is the Iranian Kurdish situation. Most agree that Kurds and Persians share overlapping histories and cultures. Archaeological leftovers from the Sassanid and Achemenid periods have been used to prove that Kurds and Iranians come from the same stock. Both groups point to the findings in the mountains of Taq Bostan in Kermanshah as evidence of their shared histories. Persians refer to Howremani Kurds as the purest Iranians. Kurds make similar claims to racial purity. However, when trying to explain variations in Kurdayetî among Iranian Kurds the focus changes to religion; Shi'ism naturally brings Shi'a Kurds from Kermanshah closer to Persian culture than the Sunnism practiced in the Kurdish regions of Sanandaj and Mahabad. If Kurdayetî is explained by religious affiliation, then we should see similar group identification in Iraq. Yet this has not been the case. Sunni Kurds have not bonded with Sunni Arabs as a common Muslim community. Rather, the distinct *Naqshbandiyya* and *Qadiriyya* brotherhoods have coexisted within the same Kurdish society.

Analyzing nationalism as a function of complex political space requires a conceptual shift in the way we think about national-identity formation and change. Instead of assuming that ethnicity and nationalism are the same phenomenon, looking for successful or failed nationalisms, or seeking the existence of a single equilibrium point of national self-expression, the notion of political space shows that nationalism is part of a contextually contingent process whereby a nation can follow multiple paths over long periods. The uneven evolution of Kurdayetî across space and time means that nationalism is not tied to any fixed pattern of political development whereby ethnonationalist mobilizations are part of a cumulative process that has been under way for centuries, a function of particular levels of development, or a phase that will be replaced by a postnational era (Connor 1994, 169; Hobsbawm 1994, 10–11; Tiryakian and Nevitte 1985, 70; Gellner 1983, 48–62). The movement toward an ethnicized nationalism is neither a continuous nor a one-directional process.

Assuming the fluidity of national-identity formation does not mean, however, that we cannot discern a patterned sequence or timing of ethnonationalism. By examining how a nation becomes ethnicized instead of when an ethnic group becomes a nation, we can account for the periodizations of ethnonationalist revivals in a systematic manner. Irregular manifestations are more than part of the "paradox of history and ideas that evolves in fits and starts" (Connor 2002, 33). Rather, they are by-products of particular political spaces that provide different incentives for various subgroups within an ethnic community. As a group's interests change within a given preference structure, so too do the opportunities to manifest national identity, which may or may not be ethnicized (Verdery 1993; Máiz 2003).

For example, in northern Thailand a Thai refers to a Ban Ping trader as Chinese when engaged in commerce and as Thai when involved in politics. In Somalia the Oromos see themselves as Arabs, Somalis, and Amharas, depending upon the circumstances. Burmese populations started calling themselves Christian Karens with the arrival of Western missionaries in Burma in the late nineteenth century (Fearon and Laitin 2000, 853; Williams 1989, 425; Laitin 1983, 331–45; Petry 1993; Tapper 1983, 28). During the imperial period the majority of Kurds identified themselves as Muslims (Sunnis in Persia), landowners, tribal chiefs, peasants, or people inhabiting the Zagros Mountains. One hundred years later Kurdish nationalism became ethnicized alongside modernization processes that created working classes, an intellectual bourgeoisie, and diasporic communities.

Yet if national-identity formation is a function of changing political-opportunity structures, then why have Kurdish groups often chosen not to mobilize on behalf of Kurdayetî even when it was advantageous to do so? Paying attention to contextual change should not reduce identity formation to a mechanical process of symbol manipulation or interest maximization. Choosing identities is not the same type of choice as selecting friends. It can involve a multitude of contexts and levels of identities that become salient in different circumstances or at the same time (Horowitz 1985, 118).

The notion of political space avoids institutional determinism and its tautological outcomes by according agency to national groups. Kurds are not just helpless victims responding to an overpowering political center or its bureaucratic procedures. They act according to their own traditions, charismatic leadership, and local institutions. Alongside structural and institutional capabilities are the cognitive aspects of collective action, such as culture, ideas, and framing processes, which stimulate nationalist sentiment. Social-psychological dynamics and shared meanings that groups bring to their situations facilitate the manifestation of nationalism by offering a common set of symbolic references. Collective action can reconfigure the meanings of situations and shape new identities among national groups (McAdam, McCarthy, and Zald 1996; McAdam, Tarrow, and Tilly 1997, 152–58; Máiz 2003).

Nor can particular types of nationalism be created at the will of the political elite and their institutional mechanisms (Conversi 2002, 278). National identity may be constructed, but it is bounded by the historical, cultural, political, and economic realities of each group's past. National groups have their own distinct historical trajectories and objective group characteristics such as language and religious affiliations that provide a pre-existing basis for national identity. These trajectories and traits limit the appeals that elites can make toward ethnic groups and the choices groups have in expressing their national identities. To claim that a group can choose any identity it wants removes the definitional base upon which nationalism stands. It also disregards ethnicity as an unchanging foundation of group identity.

Thus, we cannot entirely dismiss primordialist ideas. Although the ethnic component of nationalism can be made more or less salient over time, it cannot be interchanged with other ethnic identities in any political context. Ethnicity is an ascriptive identity linked to the gene pool of every individual, and it cannot be transferred to nongroup members. Most group members believe that membership in an ethnic group may be acquired only biologically (Horowitz 2002, 78). A Canadian cannot become a Pakistani, nor can an Iranian become Japanese. A Kurd may be able to become a Turkish citizen, but he or she still cannot become a Turk. Given the existence of inherent ethnic differences, loyalty to the nation and loyalty to the state are not naturally harmonious.

Yet they are not inherently contentious, either. A deeply rooted ethnie may form the basis of the modern sense of nationhood; however, it is not a natural link to modern nations. Rather, ethnonationalism should be regarded as part of the environment, processes, official state ideologies, and policies that legitimate inequalities within a single political unit and in relation to other groups (Esman 1994, 13; Eickleman 1989, 179–227; Weaver 1986; Kedourie 1988, 26; Tapper 1988a, 22). National identity becomes ethnicized when a group senses it is not part of the dominant culture or when it considers itself distinct in regard to the notion of citizenship. Ethnicity became the basis of Kurdish identity not because it was rooted in some premodern past, but because it was the category of political identities used by central governments to determine inclusion and exclusion in the modern state system. Kurdish nationalism varies, therefore, because Kurds are divided among three different ethnically defined political communities—Arabs, Persians, and Turks—in differently endowed political spaces modified by external influences. Thus, as a political identity ethnicity cannot exist prior to some other exclusivist nationalist project. For the Kurds this project commenced in the state-formation period.

It is not enough to identify the state-formation period as a key juncture in the identity-formation process without recontextualizing the analysis after this point. That is, political space matters, but it is never completely set. Middle Eastern states were created in a rapidly changing and chaotic environment influenced by European models. Kurdish nationalist identity that emerged during the early state-formation period was part of a different political space than that which became prominent at later points in time, such as during the cold war years or the onset of globalization and transnationalization processes. Contextual shifts, including modernization, urbanization, and detribalization, can propel or impede certain transformations of the political space and the nation-state-building projects (Conversi 2002, 278; Khoury and Kostiner 1990, 14–17). And as the nature of the state changes, so too do the political boundaries and opportunity structures that can reshape Kurdayetî.

The argument that the expression of Kurdayetî is a function of political space is teased out in three comparative case studies of Kurdish nationalism in Iraq, Turkey, and Iran from the late imperial period to the present (as discussed in chapters 1–7). Each case history is divided into two main transformation periods, or moments when the nature of the political system changed from the previous order. These periods may include regime changes, but they are more significantly marked by alterations in the ideology, organization, and administration of the political apparatus. They include the transition from empire to a colonial, semicolonial, or independent state and the transition from independent statehood to particular types of regimes: republicanism, constitutional monarchy, quasi democracy, and Islamic republic. Although the time periods differ across states, they reflect similar processes that uprooted one system of rule and replaced it with another.

In each case history changes and continuity in the political space over time will be determined by asking: What kind of myth was the center promoting about the official state national identity (that is, the idea of state citizenship)? What strategies did the state elite pursue to make this myth appear real? Which groups benefited and which lost from these nation-state-building policies? Was there a gap between the discourse and reality?

And what alternative opportunities did the state elite make available for Kurdish groups to express their political identities? Although each transformation period does not necessarily lead to a Kurdish ethnonationalist revival, it is likely to reshape the political space and, in turn, the expression of Kurdayetî. The indicators used to measure Kurdayetî are the nature of the nationalist elite and organizations, nationalist sentiment, and the relationship between the Kurdish nationalist and state elite.[1]

Some political spaces, for instance, may support traditional elites such as tribal chiefs and religious shaykhs, others can encourage urban-educated professionals, whereas others may elevate a combination of leadership types. Large political spaces with high resource-mobilization potential tied to political parties, financial resources (domestic and foreign), and institutional support can enhance the significance and legitimacy of the nationalist elite, even though its representation may be limited across Kurdish society. Timing also matters. Some Kurdish communities can have relatively similar spaces that are generous in opportunities but different in time. Kurds may be permitted legal political and cultural space; however, they may not have continuous access to it. In some circumstances Kurds can manifest their national identity to a certain point before the state elite closes the political space again, preventing the institutionalization of the Kurdish nationalist leadership and organizations. Similarly, continuous support of the nationalist elite can help create a large nationalist party, reinforcing Kurdayetî's influence and representation among local populations.

Additionally, Kurdish communities adapt and respond to their political spaces in various ways, establishing particular relationships with the political center that shape their nationalist behavior. In some situations the state elite can choose to consolidate power by employing a political formula that appeals to the Kurdish masses and limits the state's power. Political spaces that enable national groups to participate and administer their own communal affairs encourage constructive center-periphery relationships, allowing for the development of legal nationalist political organizations, internal cohesion, and compromise. Restrictive spaces, on the other hand, stifle opportunities for political growth and negotiation between the nationalist and state elite. Whereby institutional barriers to collective action are high, few

1. These indicators will be assessed by their influence, representation, and significance across Kurdish society.

legal strategies are available to nationalist groups, which can encourage recourse to clandestine, illegal, or violent activities (Moore 1970, 34–36; Hechter 2000, 129).

In other cases, the relationship between the nationalist and state elite may not be so clear. Ambiguous spaces, characterized by the presence of normative and utilitarian means of compliance alongside coercion and control, often create enough uncertainties in the political space to encourage both compromise and hostility between the center and periphery. In Iraq and Iran, for instance, the state elite continuously opened and closed the opportunities for Kurds, and in doing so it created an ambivalent political climate for Kurdish nationalists. Ambiguity resulted in a greater variability in the expression of Kurdayetî than, say, for Turkey, where there was virtually no alteration in the political space over time.

One way to think about the relationship between the nationalist and state elite is to examine state policies as part of the attempt to consolidate political power. Kurdish nationalist relations with the political center become tied to the pushes and pulls of balancing government factions and managing the Kurds. If, for example, military factions win out over civilian groups, or if leftists assume control over conservative nationalist challengers, political power becomes cohesive. Some groups are likely to benefit over others, aggravating the divisions among Kurdish communities. If, however, political power is more evenly divided among the various factions, the chances of political compromise between Kurds and the state elite may increase. Kurds are more likely to support the center during these periods since political accommodation is more conducive under a decentralized state than it is under a highly centralized form of political rule. Internal power plays are important in understanding shifts in Kurdish nationalist behavior because they represent changes in the distribution of power. They are part of regime consolidation and centralization processes that define the boundaries of group membership in the state (Lustick 1993, 42).

The relationship between political space and Kurdayetî started to alter, however, in the early 1990s, with the onset of transnational processes and the creation of influential diasporic communities. Access to international nongovernmental organizations (NGOs) and externally based opportunity structures, shifts in international norms, and advanced telecommunications systems have given Kurdish communities new opportunities to express their ethnonational identity outside the states' territorial borders.

chapter 8 reexamines these developments and their impact on Kurdayetî in the different homelands. The conclusion provides the theoretical and empirical groundwork from which international guidelines for managing the Kurdish problem can be developed.

By regarding nationalism as a consequence of complex political spaces tied to nation-state-building processes, this book presents an image of center-periphery and intra-Kurdish relations that is not inherently hostile across space and time. Variations in Kurdayetî reveal that contrary to popular theories, there is nothing natural about Kurdish national identity, Kurdish political behavior, or the relationships between Kurds and their central governments. Shi'a, Sunni, Christian, and Alevi groups do not have a natural hatred for one another, Kurdish nationalists are not inherently defiant toward the state, and Kurds have not consistently differentiated themselves from Arabs, Turks, or Persians.

The Kurds and the State

1

Late Imperial Period

Large Political Space

One of the key features of the Ottoman and Qajar Empires was the role of religion in determining group identity. Islam differentiated populations according to religious affiliation, Muslim and non-Muslim, giving most Kurds a favored position in politics and society. The political space that elevated the traditional stratum also benefited Kurdish landowners, tribesmen, and warriors, reinforcing tribal, provincial, and religious identities over nationalism. Even as modernization and centralization trends encouraged nationalist mobilizations in the Balkans and Caucasus, by the late nineteenth century Kurdayetî was relatively undeveloped in the Ottoman Empire, and barely existent in Qajar Iran.

Ottoman Empire: Sunni Islamized Political Space

During the imperial period it was religion, not ethnicity, that defined group identity. Based on the *Şaria* code of Sunni Islam the Ottoman Empire was ruled by the sultan-caliph, who served as the spiritual leader of the empire's Muslim communities. Sunni Muslim ideology assumed a central role in the centrally administered Ottoman institutions. The educational system was defined by Islamic jurisprudence, not the doctrine of nationalism. Ottoman authorities used the *millet* system to organize the various ethnic, linguistic, religious, and tribal populations into a single political community. Although they recognized all groups as Ottomans, the millets

1

differentiated populations according to religious affiliation (Bozarslan 1988, 76–85; Braude and Lewis 1982, 5–18; Karpat 1982, 142).[1]

Indeed, ethnicity mattered. Muslim rulers were identified as either Ottoman Turks or Arabs. The Muslim millet regrouped populations according to ethnic and linguistic distinctions: Turkish, Arab, Kurdish, Albanian, or speakers of Balkan-Caucasian languages. In the Ottoman censuses taken from 1881 to 1893 Alep, Damas, and Baghdad were categorized as Muslim provinces with Arab territories. Ottoman Turks promoted the idea of a Turkish Anatolia. Turkish nationalists referred to the Mosul frontier as the zone of Turkishness. To distinguish the ethnolinguistic particularities of Muslim communities the Ottoman elite formally recognized the Kurds as the *boz millet* (gray nation) and the Turkomen as the *kara millet* (black nation). Within the millet system, Christian groups used ethnicity to identify distinctions between orthodox groups (Yavuz 1995, 351; Karpat 1985, 45; Karpat 1978, 1988; Georgeon 1991, 39).

Still, the Ottoman elite stressed the religious aspects of identity to generate a sense of group solidarity in the empire. Mosul Province comprised Kurdish, Arab, and Turkoman groups; however, it was referred to as a Muslim *vilayet*. Kurdish-run and independent *medreses* that advanced Kurdish literature had mosques attached to them (van Bruinessen 1998). The objective was to prepare students for the highly valued position as *meleti*, or office of the *mullah*, in the villages of Kurdistan, not to become politicized nationalists.

This system of sociopolitical identification, formalized in the Akdi Zimmet, privileged the dominant Sunni Muslims *(millet-i hakime)* over dominated non-Muslim groups *(millet-i mahkume)*. Orthodox Greeks, Slavs, Catholics, Armenians, and Jews were given *dhimmi* status as protected minorities, but they could enjoy semiautonomy within their millets only if they recognized the primacy of Islam and the supremacy of Muslim communities.[2] Depending on the internal laws of the millet, non-Muslims

---

1. Bozarslan (1988) states that even though there was a caliph, Ottoman leaders made their decisions based not on Islamic dogmas but on the needs of the moment. They also employed the *hil-ye şeriye,* or law that does not conform to the Şaria.

2. Karpat (1982) notes that it was only in the nineteenth century that dhimmi status commenced and Ottoman populations started to divide among themselves. It is also when the Christians started to be called *re'aya,* denoting their inferiority.

could obtain high positions in the bureaucracy and receive the same salary as Muslims.

Yet they were still discriminated against as a religious community. The political elite imposed various policies to determine who was a real Muslim and who was not. Jews were labeled as *dhull* and had to wear a yellow badge publicly to distinguish themselves. Non-Muslims were prohibited from wearing certain types of clothing and hats that were reserved for Muslims (Les Archives 1885, Sept. 29, no. 838; Unal 2000, 7–9).[3] Even though the Ottoman Constitution of 1876 introduced the idea of representation on the basis of religious communities, Sunni Islam was still considered the millet-i hakime by the Porte (the government of the Ottoman Empire) and local populations. Consequently, the adherence to Sunni Muslim orthodoxy created a dichotomy between the *umma* and the Other that formed the basis of inclusion and exclusion in Ottoman affairs. Identifying as a Greek or Bulgarian or Kurd was largely based on one's religious affiliation.

Group identification was also influenced by one's position in a professional system based on the dominant military class, the bureaucracy, and the court, reinforcing the tacit contract between the center and periphery. According to Kemal Karpat, it was not only religious identity but also the administrative role of the individual that determined tax status, which in turn determined social standing in Ottoman society and within the millet. Christian and Jewish merchants were exempt from paying taxes depending on the services they rendered to the Porte. The taxation system, based on the agrarian economic structure, benefited the landowners while discriminating against the peasants. It distinguished townspeople from the countryside, tillers of the land from warriors, and tribal leaders from other rural groups (Frey 1979, 44–45; Dadrian 1995, 4; Moutafchieva 1988, 143–96; Bozarslan 1988, 76–85; van Bruinessen 1992, 154–55; Karpat 1982, 147–52; Unal 2000, 7–9).

Still, socioeconomic positions were usually tied to one's religious identity. Sunni Muslims were part of the peasant populations, particularly in the Fertile Crescent, Anatolia, and Mesopotamia; however, the majority in the Balkans, Caucasus, and certain Ottoman lands were Christians under the authority of Muslim landlords. Although non-Muslims were integrated

---

3. Muslim identity was also confirmed by the ritual of circumcision; uncircumcised Hungarian officers who took refuge in Europe were not considered real Muslims.

into the power hierarchy as local notables and bureaucrats, only Sunni Muslim groups could gain high ranks in the military.

Certainly, non-Muslims benefited as part of the millet-i mahkume. Distinctions between Muslim and non-Muslims were not necessarily clear. Ottoman officials viewed orthodox groups as part of the millet system while considering western Catholics as foreigners who had to negotiate individual *firmans* with the Porte to regulate their status. The system of *devşirme,* or the periodic levy on unmarried male children from the Christian peasantry, applied to Slavs, Albanians, and Armenians but rarely to Greeks and Jews. Some Christian communities even profited from being part of the non-Muslim millet. The Galata bankers, a group of Levantines, Jews, Armenians, and Greeks, controlled the local banking industry. In 1919 73 percent of factories and workshops belonged to the Greeks, while 85 percent of their employees were Muslims (Frazee 1983, 7; Issawi 1980, 14–15; Karpat 1982, 150–52; Braude and Lewis 1982, 12–13, 339–40).

Further, not all Muslim groups were treated equally. Varying degrees of "Muslimness" existed within the Kurdish Sufi *tariqa* orders, which affected group status and its relationship with the Ottoman Porte. Certain brotherhoods, such as the more orthodox Naqshbandiyya that emphasized the Şaria, occupied a key place in the empire's religious and political affairs. The fixed curriculum and career patterns of the state-supported medreses also encouraged integration of Sunni Naqshbandiyya Kurds into Ottoman professional life. Kurds educated in the Kurdish medreses, such as the eminent Kurdish Naqshbandiyya Shaykh Mawlana Khalid al-Kurdî (1773–1826), maintained an interchange with counterparts in Istanbul, Damascus, and Baghdad (Zarcone 1998, 109–10). Other groups were not as fortunate. Although non-Sunni communities had a tacit contract with the Porte and the Druze (a religious sect) enjoyed a privileged status in Lebanon, heterodox Muslim communities such as the Alevis, the Yezidis, and the Ismailis were subject to discriminatory taxation and employment policies. Sunni Kurds attained prestigious military and political positions; however, Alevi *dedes* were neglected in Ottoman affairs.

Indeed, until the early nineteenth century some Alevi subgroups enjoyed a special relationship with the Porte and were permitted, like other minorities, to regulate their internal affairs at the local level, with the state intervening as a mediator. The Kurdish Alevi region of Dersim did not have to pay taxes or provide soldiers for military service. Bektaşi groups, who composed a large part of the Janissary Corps, enjoyed a special status over rural Anatolian Alevis. Yet these privileges ended in 1826, after the Porte massacred the Janissaries and the Bektaşi brotherhood. Further, unlike Christians and Jews who were protected within their millets and supported by Europeans, non-Sunni Muslims had no such institutionalized legal protection against the dominant Sunni Muslim millet. Some Bektaşis even demanded to join the Protestant millet to seek refuge against Sunni government policies (Poujol 1999, 38, 51).

Sunni Kurdish tribal communities also enjoyed special privileges tied to the caliphate. To be sure, to prevent the downfall of the empire, overhaul the Ottoman system, and reestablish order the Porte asserted control over the tribes and terminated local hereditary rulers, replacing them with Porte-appointed governors. By the time the Tanzimat reforms (1829–1879) commenced the Kurds had lost most of the power and prestige tied to their principalities, the last of which had fallen in 1850. Yet they continued to enjoy a modicum of autonomy in their regions. In contrast to the non-Kurdish provinces, the Ottoman elite did not replace Kurdish emirs with state-appointed governors, creating even greater chaos in Kurdistan and the opportunity for Kurdish shaykhs to fill the void as conflict mediators. The power vacuum created by the decline of the last Kurdish principalities, the religious reverence held by the *sadah* families, and the absence of a clerical hierarchy in the Sunni establishment strengthened the Kurdish shaykhly establishment. Kurdish tribal chiefs retained their local power despite centralization processes occurring in the rest of the empire (Nezan 1993, 15–26; van Bruinessen 1992, 182–84).[4]

Even after the Tanzimat reforms the Porte made no serious effort to alter the traditional power structure in Kurdistan. In the segmented, agrarian-based Kurdish society the roles of agha, shaykh, and tribal chief were often held by the same individual, increasing the influence of local communities bound to the central government. Abdulhamid's uneven centralization policies reinforced the role of Kurdish shaykhs and tribal chiefs by ensuring that the Kurdish traditional stratum, and not an urban bourgeoisie, would remain prominent in Kurdish society. In most parts of the

---

4. The consolidation of shaykhly families was also influenced by the change in land registration, the proselytizing activities of Mawlana Khalid's followers, and the fear of European-supported Christian domination.

empire Abdulhamid strengthened the cities while weakening rural areas. He gained control of tribal groups and landowners by breaking up big estates, creating small landowners, and leasing land under *tapu* grants.

In Kurdistan, however, the situation was different. Although other regions were placed under greater central governmental control, Kurdistan remained relatively autonomous until the early twentieth century. The Ottoman *qadi* and *mufti* had jurisdiction over religious law in most western and central provinces but not in certain Kurdish regions. Some districts were placed under the sultan's control, some retained their quasi autonomy, while others fell under Russian influence. Situated in the far eastern and southern mountain regions of the empire and lacking a developed transportation and communications system, the Kurdish vilayets were often inaccessible to the state's agents. It therefore became necessary for the Porte to negotiate tacit agreements with Kurdish tribal chiefs, further authenticating their political power.

Also, despite the government's attempts to remove collective landownership, by the late nineteenth century large landowners were still predominant in Macedonia, Kurdistan, and some Arab provinces. Some Kurdish and Armenian cultivators lost their traditional land rights; however, most enriched themselves by registering large tracts of land in their family names. Kurdish landlords assumed territory from defaulted borrowers and became land and grain lenders, or *selefdars* (Issawi 1980, 201–19). Although much of the eastern countryside was ravaged, certain Kurdish regions actually benefited from the food shortages and increased transportation costs caused by the wars.

For example, during the reform period the value of land increased by 75 percent, benefiting the cotton growers in Adana and Izmir, and the Kurdish wheat-growing regions of Erzurum and Diyarbakir, referred to as the granary of Kurdistan. When the harvest in Mosul or Baghdad was short, merchants looked to Diyarbakir to compensate for deficiencies, which yielded a higher price for the surplus in average years of export. The Kurdish granaries were also used to store corn. In 1907 some thirty thousand Turkish liras' worth of corn was exported to the Kurdish regions of Bitlis and Van, in spite of the large transportation costs that doubled the price of corn when it arrived in the markets. Kurdish areas in the fertile Mosul plains further profited from the growth in cereal production such as wheat and barley, which were shipped to southern Iraq, Syria, Anatolia, and Persia

(Owen 1981, 274–79). As a result, some Kurdish farmers became part of the new urban-based landlord class where they assumed leading roles in provincial and local affairs.

Thus, whether as leaders of Sufi brotherhoods, tribal militias, or peasant groups, the Kurdish agha and shaykh had much to gain from the traditional Ottoman power structure. Some Kurdish notables may have gained access to the court, but it was the aghas, shaykhs, and tribal chiefs who profited from Abdulhamid's pan-Islamist ideology, his Ottoman Kurdish cavalry (or Hamidiyan forces), and his taxation policies for large landowners (Olson 1989, 7–15; McDowall 1997, 62). The Ottoman elite supported tribal schools in Istanbul and Baghdad, housed Kurdish chiefs in exile, and bestowed nontribal Kurds with honors and privileges. They treated the Kurdish brigand Moussa Bey as royalty when he arrived in Constantinople after massacring Christian groups in the Kurdish regions. Abdulhamid gave the descendants of Kurdish notables such as Bedir Khan, Abdurahman Paşa Baban, and Ubdullah Abdul Qader high posts in the administration, the military, and universities. Said Paşa, the Ottoman premier, ambassador to Berlin, and minister of foreign affairs, was a Sunni Kurd. In this large political space most Kurds coexisted with Turks, Arabs, and some Albanians and had little reason to differentiate from the political center.

Shifting Political Space

Although the content and size of the political space were large, they did not remain constant. Ottoman reforms, the Porte's centralizing tendencies, and foreign penetrations called for new policies that reshaped the opportunity structures in Ottoman society. Some Kurdish regions retained autonomy; however, centralization policies altered the traditional system of regional administration and created new smaller political units within the vilayet that were administered only by Muslim *ayans,* who assumed local authority over Christian millet leaders. The ayans, in turn, elevated Sunni Islam by constructing mosques and using Islamic symbols in schools and public buildings. By placing the universalism of religion next to the local parochialism of ethnic communities the vilayet system reinforced the dominance of the Sunni Muslim ruling groups and heightened tensions between local communities. Over time pockets of ethnic communities identified with their administrative units, which placed greater attention on ethnic distinctions (Karpat 1988, 46). As a result, lines among religion, ethnicity, and socioeconomic status became increasingly blurred.

Territorial transformations and demographic changes reconfigured the political geography of the empire, strengthening religious, ethnic, and linguistic dichotomies. After the conclusion of the Crimean wars and the 1878 Berlin Congress, the Ottomans lost nearly 80 percent of their European domains. Most of the Christian populations were no longer under Ottoman control, which increased the Muslim community to 74 percent of the population (Karpat 1985, 28; Issawi 1980, 18). This loss created an even greater imbalance between the Muslim majority and non-Muslim minorities. Also, the migration of Turkish-speaking Muslim Tatar refugees from Russia to the big cities in the Ottoman Empire pushed non-Muslims into the valleys and towns. What resulted were more pressures on the local administration, land-claim disputes between Muslims and Christians, and demands for independence by the various ethnic groups.

External penetration contributed to the processes of ethnic unbalancing and fanned internal divisions within the millets, between Muslims and non-Muslims, and local groups and foreigners (Les Archives 1874, Oct. 7; 1885, May 17; Dadrian 1995, 26–28). Despite its complaints about the loss of political independence the Istanbul elite desperately needed revenue. They welcomed external penetration into the empire, negotiating commercial treaties with foreign powers and offering capitulations to their agents. Dependence on international markets and foreign exchange brought new economic advantages to foreign powers and their Christian client communities. It also privileged certain groups at local levels and stirred new conflicts between Muslims and Christians. For example, the Russians protected the Greeks, Slavs, and Serbs; the French supported the Catholics; and the British and Americans backed the Armenians, Nestorians, Chaldeans, and Assyrians. Christian missionary activities heightened jealousies simmering among religious, ethnic, and socioeconomic groups. Missionary groups often acted as the liberators of the Armenians and protectors of the Protestants in Beirut, which encouraged local communities to act against their Muslim oppressors.[5]

---

5. The real schism between the churches occurred in 1755, when the Greeks questioned the validity of the sacrament of baptism in the Latin faith and publicized it in their patriarchal decree. Other antagonisms were tied to internal power struggles. The Orthodox Chris-

Moreover, by the late nineteenth century the idea of Ottoman citizenship and the millet system had changed. Christian Balkan groups were awarded national group status by European powers, making it increasingly difficult for Abdulhamid to market his notion of an Islam-first identity. The citizenship issue peaked with the implementation of various Ottoman nationality laws prohibiting the practice of naturalizing foreigners without the authority of the government (Les Archives 1875, May 12, no. 570; May 19, no. 601).[6] Consequently, although the millets existed in principle, by the late nineteenth century the meaning of the minority group had changed. Sunni Muslims may have been the religious majority, but their dominance had come into question by the tide of European penetrations and their support for self-determination movements.

The boundaries of inclusion and exclusion were further challenged by political groups seeking to save the empire. Liberal reformers within the Committee for Union and Progress (CUP) tried to replace Abdulhamid's pan-Islamist ideology with a universally shared Ottoman-first identity that recognized all groups as equal before the law (Sugar 1997; Shaw and Shaw 1997, 186–89; Güzel 1975, 23–40; Belarbi 1983, 251–52). Although Ottomanism did not gain popular support and Abdulhamid continued to favor Muslim groups, the attempt to redefine Ottoman identity persisted, particularly by the Turkish nationalist current affected by the Slavization and Christianization of the Russian Empire. After assuming political control in 1908, Young Turk leaders Enver Paşa, Cemal Paşa, and Talat Paşa asserted a radical form of Turkish national identity, closing Ottoman associations and non-Turkish schools.

---

tian millet had a Greek patriarch, which caused problems with the lower echelons that were also Russian and did not want to be Hellenized or referred to as Greek. The sultan's decision to grant Russian demands for a new religious authority called an exarchate that was independent from the Greek patriarch in Constantinople antagonized the Greeks, who claimed responsibility for the Serbs. This issue became a thorny part of Greek-Bulgarian relations. Similarly, the Catholic millet was beset by Hapsburg turmoil, which fractured the Eastern and Western (Latin) churches and prevented a unified Catholic millet from forming.

6. The 1830 London protocols allowed individuals born in the Ottoman Empire to emigrate to Greece for naturalization and, after three years, to receive a new nationality in the empire as Greeks. From 1837 to 1860 some youths went to Greece to study and obtained Hellenic nationality. When they returned to Ottoman Turkey, however, state officials did not recognize their Greek citizenship and treated them as Ottoman subjects.

The Turkish nationalist current attempted to redraw the boundaries of inclusion and exclusion in the empire based on ethnicity. Pan-Turkish nationalists promoted a view of Turkish identity as a political nationality founded on race, though in the sense of an ethnic-cultural group (Georgeon 1980, 28–35; Ağaoğulları 1987, 180–81; Dadrian 1995, 196–98). New studies of Turkism reinterpreted Turkish history and Turkish identity. As opposed to Ottoman myths that considered the Tatars and Mongols as barbarians, Turanists elevated the role of Genghis Khan and Mongol history as part of the Turkish past. They also used a different set of symbols to represent the Turkish national identity, placing the Turkish step wolf on the covers of pan-Turkish journals (Georgeon 1980, 53). As the movement radicalized, the political space for non-Turkish communities, particularly Armenians, Kurds, and Lazes, was significantly restricted. From 1895 to 1915 the CUP, particularly Teşkilat-i Mahsusa, resettled Kurds, Lazes, and Armenians from their homes to western Turkish villages and implemented genocide campaigns against up to one million Armenians.

Segmented Dissidence and Tribal Resistance

Socioeconomic and political trends challenged the opportunities for Kurds within the traditional power structure. With the arrival of European consuls in Van, Christian ascendancy, and competing territorial claims made by the Armenians, Kurdish leaders started to mobilize against the Porte as a national group. In the Hakkâri region, mixed with Kurds and Nestorian Christians, some Kurds thought the U.S. mission house was to be used as a fortress against them or as a bazaar to draw away business from Kurdish centers (Jwaideh 1960, 197–202). This perceived threat heightened personal jealousies between the Kurdish mir of Hakkâri, Nuzarallah Beg, and the Christian patriarch. The Kurdish Shaykh Ubaydullah of Nehri reacted to the signing of the Treaty of Berlin, which promised the Armenians political autonomy, by vowing to resist and arm the women. Using his charismatic influence and backing from the shaykhly establishment, Ubaydullah revolted on behalf of Kurdish nationalism and Islam (Jwaideh 1960, 223, 297–300; Olson 1989, 17).[7]

7. Some of the demands of the Kurdish shaykhs included a Kurdish administration, Kurdish language instruction, and reinstitution of the Şaria law.

Still, in contrast to Christian communities demanding independence and emancipation at this time, Kurdayetî was relatively weak across Kurdish society. Most Kurds turned to Armenian, Arab, and Turkish groups to make nationalist claims, not to cohesive Kurdish organizations. What accounts for the relative quiet in Kurdish nationalism, particularly as the Turkish nationalist current started to pronounce exclusionary discourse and policies?

Given the nature of the political space, which privileged the traditional stratum, Kurdish shaykhs and tribal chiefs were neither interested in nor capable of conducting influential ethnonationalist mobilizations. In the absence of mobilizing resources such as a developed infrastructure, external aid, political organizations, or communication networks, the only feasible way to manifest Kurdish nationalism was to rely on tribal groups, Sufi shaykhs, and their numerous tariqa orders. The predominance of tribal structures encouraged Kurdish chiefs to act according to their personal and tribal interests and not on behalf of a larger Kurdish nation. Instead of unifying against the Porte after the overthrow of Abdulhamid in 1908 and Sultan Mahmut II's centralization policies, Kurdish leaders conducted their own local revolts in the Mesopotamian Kurdish provinces. Kurdish nationalists such as Shaykh Ubaydullah of Nehri, who was against Mahmut's reforms, mobilized a local Kurdish league backed by the Porte, aligned with the Russians and Persians, and turned to the Nestorian patriarch, the Armenian ecclesiast, U.S. missionaries, and British officials.

Even if tribal chiefs had access to effective nationalist organizations, Kurdayetî is likely to have been relatively weak across society because the political space was too unevenly developed to have permitted a cohesive nationalist movement. Alongside traditional power structures, the Tanzimat reforms and Sultan Mahmut's centralization policies supported the rising commercial bourgeoisie, most of whom were located in western Anatolia. European influences spread new ideas, supported liberal associations, and created new cultural and political opportunities in urban centers. Ottoman cities became part of the liberalizing experiment, which helped politicize the Kurds. After the mid-1880s Kurdish notables, alongside Turks and Armenians, presented themselves in national and provincial assemblies.

These trends favored Christian and Turkish communities, but they also touched segments of Kurds living in city centers, giving rise to a Kurdish political renaissance. Kurdish nationalists took advantage of the open political space by creating Kurdish schools, Kurdish clubs, and local Kurdish cultural organizations. With a small printing press provided by the Chaldean patriarch some Kurds published their own journals in the Kurdish language. Kurdish intellectual communities from Diyarbakir and Istanbul formed Societies for the Progress of Kurdistan (Kurdistan Teali Cemiyeti), enabling them to make personal contacts, exchange information, and spread nationalist ideas. For instance, during a debate about Kurdish national rights at a meeting of the Kurdish society in Diyarbakir, one of the members, Hemdî Efendî, urged his colleagues to liberate Kurdistan from the gangrenous part of the Ottoman Empire, which he insisted "must be cut off and thrown away" (Soran 1996, 18).

Although Kurdayetî started to crystallize, it was not highly representative across Kurdish society, the majority of whose members were poor, tribal, and uneducated. In contrast to seventeenth-century Kurdish politics, whereby urban notables criticized the prince while apologizing for the shaykhs, late-nineteenth-century Kurdish intellectuals criticized tribal shaykhs while supporting their Ottoman patrons. Free to express their views in the open media, they argued that it was not the policies of the Porte but, rather, the presence of the shaykhly establishment that hindered the development of Kurdish culture and language. In one of the well-known political poems of the period, the Kurdish nationalist Hajî Qaderî Koyî (1817–1897) argued, "If a Kurd does not know the language of his father he must know that certainly his mother was an adulteress." Koyî went so far as to insult some Kurdish Sufi shaykhs for their false sense of nobility. He further wrote, "Oh sufi, tell your shaykh, the man who sells his wife for money, that he should not show himself to me like a noble" (Miran and Sharezahr 1986, 61, 146).[8]

Some Kurdish intellectuals identified as Islamists and affiliated with Sunni Turkish, Arab, and Albanian Muslim communities. To be sure, Said Nursî, known during this period as Mullah Said-i-Kurdî, urged the "Kurdish lions and courageous soldiers" to "wake up from their five hundred years of sleep and develop their national solidarity" (Alakom 1998b, 321, 326). Yet Nursî considered himself a mullah and not a Kurdish nationalist.

8. Koyî, a mullah by education, was obliged to leave his native town of Koysinjaq because it was dominated by shaykhs at the time and Koyî was not considered religious. He personally attacks the shaykhs in this poem, referring to them as pimps *(taress)*.

He presented the problem of Kurdish nationalism as one of general minority rights that should be resolved through Ottoman institutions and education, not as a Kurdish political struggle.

Others were more interested in promoting a liberal, secularized Ottoman identity of which Kurdish nationalism was a part than in saving the caliphate, supporting Kurdish tribal chiefs, or protecting landowning interests against Christian groups. Although some Kurdish shaykhs attempted to save Kurdistan from the Armenians, Abdel Qader affirmed at the 1909 Kurdo-Armenian Congress, "We must live like brothers with the Armenians . . . and strengthen our understanding and concord among Ottoman compatriots" (McDowall 1997, 97–99). Many chose Ottoman political institutions instead of, or alongside, Kurdish ones. Two of the four founders of the CUP, Abdullah Cevdet and Işak Sukuti, were Kurds. Kurdish notables such as Bedir Khan and Abdel Qader were honorary captain in the Ottoman Army and president of the Ottoman Council of State, respectively. The head of the Kurdish nationalist society Hiva-ye Kurd, Khalid Hassan Motki, was a member of the Ottoman Parliament. Şerif Paşa was a leading figure of Ottoman liberalism, Ismail Hakki became a leader of the CUP, and Ahmed Naim Babanzade was an important Islamist.

What emerged were two main nationalist groupings and sentiments, one among tribal shaykhs and another among urban intellectuals. Kurdish tribal leaders turned to tariqa orders and their personal militias to manifest their nationalist sentiment. Kurdish notables responded to Turkification policies by relying on the various political and cultural organizations tied to the opposition movement in Istanbul. After 1908, when a new "Turkified" CUP emerged, they turned to Ottoman opposition groups alongside Kurdish organizations such as the Society for the Progress of Kurdistan, Kurdish National Committee, Society for the Propagation of Kurdish Education, Committee for Kurdish Independence, and Friends of Kurdistan.

Even with legal outlets for nationalist expression Kurdayetî would not have been highly ethnicized because in the wartime context the Ottoman government was not Turkified enough to create boundaries of exclusion based on ethnicity. Although pan-Turkish nationalists started to close the political space for non-Turkish groups, they did not gain complete control of the government and could not transform the political system in a significant way. The Turkish nationalist current still needed to accommodate non-Turkish communities, particularly as World War I approached. Because Islam retained a key role in the Turkish nationalist identity, non-Turkish Sunni Muslim groups were welcomed. Russian Muslims and Turkish intellectuals merged into the Society Turk, which became an organ of the Islamic group Şirat-i Mustakim. Even Christian groups found a place in the Turkish nationalist movement. Some joined the Turkified CUP to escape the nationalizations in the Balkans. Others converted to Islam and called themselves Turks, which was one way to protect themselves from being Hellenized under the Orthodox patriarch (Karpat 1975, 285).

The ambiguity of the political space ensured certain opportunities for Kurdish groups. On the eve of World War I, while the Kurdish regions were under fire, the Kurds still had the legal right to speak their mother tongue, celebrate Kurdish traditions, and identify as a distinct ethnic community. Consequently, a constructive relationship between Kurdish leaders and the Porte continued alongside hostility and violence. Although he considered himself a Kurdish nationalist, Ismail Hakki Baban was a member of the CUP inner circles, representative in the Baghdad parliament, minister of education in the Ottoman government, and associate of the Turkish nationalist journal *Tannin* (Bakupov 1997, 103; Güzel 1975, 7–16).

The Qajar Empire: Shi'a Islamized Political Space

As in the Ottoman Empire, group identification in Qajar Persia was based on Islam, which elevated Muslims in the sociopolitical structure. The traditional social order and agrarian economy were also prevalent in Persia, favoring Kurdish landowners, tribesmen, and warriors. Yet Persia's Muslim identity was based on Shi'a Islam, which created different types of opportunity structures for the Kurds. Also, in contrast to the Ottoman Empire, the political space in Persia was more constant over time. Even as the imperial system crumbled and a modern Iranian identity started to emerge, the Qajar social order remained dominant. This continuity allowed traditional Kurdish groups greater space and time to enjoy their privileged positions.

Although there was an overlapping and changing relationship among the Persian language, nationality, and Islam, it was religion, not ethnicity, that defined Iranian identity. The early Safavis (r. 1501–1722) did not speak Persian, but they were the first rulers since the coming of Islam to promote Iran as a distinct nation, albeit one whose identity was closely tied to their own Shi'a and Sufi beliefs. Religion and politics also merged under their resurrection of the pre-Islamic title of *shah,* who was presented as the *padishah-e Islam* (king of Islam). A formal millet system did not exist; however, local populations were categorized by their religious identity. As in Ottoman society, this system favored Muslims over non-Muslims, who were referred to as *ahl-e dhimmat,* groups who had rights to practice their religious traditions.

Indeed, non-Muslim communities had economic and political opportunities in the empire. Qajar kings supported the Armenians by recognizing the Armenian religious hierarchy and referring to their leader as the caliphate of the Armenians (Bournoutian 1992, 174–76; Lambton 1987, 220–21; Issawi 1971, 31). Religious distinctions overlapped with ethnic affiliations, blurring the lines between Muslims and non-Muslims and Persians and non-Persian communities. Non-Muslim groups coexisted with various ethnically defined, Muslim family-run companies that formed the basis of Iran's merchant-capital commercial economy. In Kurdistan, for example, Sunni Kurdish *sarafs* formed trading houses that controlled the provincial retail network. In Saujbulagh (officially renamed Mahabad in the twentieth century by the successor Pahlavi dynasty), one firm controlled the distribution and pricing of wheat, which increased sixfold from 1895 to 1905. To the north of Kurdistan, in the agriculturally rich province of Azerbaijan, where Turkish-speaking Shi'a Muslims constituted the majority of the population, a Shi'a syndicate controlled the production of and trade in silk. Armenians became prominent in the wool trade, and the Zoroastrian Jamshidian family from Yazd became another big trading house (Lambton 1987, 95–100; Issawi 1971, 42–49).

As in the Ottoman Empire, in the agrarian-based Qajar society socioeconomic and political status was based on one's religious identity. The *tuyul* land-tenure system favored Muslim landowners *(tuyuldars)* over non-Muslims and peasant groups, even though landowners and peasants may have shared the same religious or ethnic affiliations or both. Although Armenian and Zoroastrian merchants could become landlords, crown lands *(khaliseh)* could be sold only to Muslims, giving their Muslim landlords even greater control over grain markets and peasants. Unequal opportunities reinforced religious and socioeconomic cleavages in Qajar society. Non-Muslims were considered impure and prohibited from working in the food industry. Jews were categorized as ritually unclean and could not open shops in the bazaar (Issawi 1971, 42–62). This restriction enabled Muslims to gain control over food production while encouraging non-Muslims to become active in nonfood commercial and banking sectors.

There were important differences, however, in the nature of the Shi'a Islamic political space that created a different repertoire of identities for Kurds in the Qajar Empire. Iran's Muslim identity was based on Ithna Ashura Twelver Shi'a Islam. The Safavi shahs had used Shi'a Islam as a way of distinguishing Iranians from Ottoman and Uzbek Sunnis, a distinction that continued into the twentieth century. However, in comparison to Ottoman Kurds, 90 percent of whom were part of the dominant Sunni Muslim community, about 30 percent of Iranian Kurds were Shi'a who could identify with the official state religion. Of the remaining Kurds in Iran, perhaps one-half were Sunni and one-half identified with Sufi and nonorthodox Shi'a Muslim sects.

In this political space Shi'a groups gained certain advantages over non-Shi'a groups. Even though the *ulema* claimed all Muslims were equal, Shi'a Islamic theology, the structure of the Shi'a religious establishment, and Qajar policies favored Shi'a Muslim communities. In contrast to Sunni Islam, the Shi'a Islamic tradition after 1501 maintained a special relationship between the clergy and the state. The presence of a formal clerical hierarchy enabled the Shi'a ulema to assume a more institutionalized role in Iranian society and politics than was the case in the Ottoman Empire (Abrahamian 1993, 18–19; Lambton 1987, 197; Martin 1989, 19). In each major city, influential ulema who had obtained the level of ayatollah (after 1800) supervised a clerical bureaucracy that included the *shaykh al-Islam, imam Jum'a, khatib,* and *pishnamaz.*

Clerical leaders also served as political intermediaries between the state and the people and as administers of justice in the religious courts. They influenced the educational system, which was under their exclusive control until the 1850s, when the government established the first state school to train young males for possible public service careers. Senior ayatollahs had student followers in the Shi'a seminary and shrine centers of Mashhad and Qom in Iran and An Najaf and Karbala in the Ottoman Empire. The Shi'a ulema were well funded, with many of them receiving government pensions and other benefits. Ulema were also administrators of *vaqf* lands. Tied to most segments of the population, including the merchants and artisans in the spacious bazaars, they were well empowered in the Iranian economy

(Milani 1988, 26; Algar 1969, 5, 53). The *bazaaris* relied on the clergy to educate their children and settle differences, whereas the ulema depended on them for financial support.

The existence of a clerical hierarchy offered Shi'a Kurds special incentives to integrate with other non-Kurdish Shi'a groups. Shi'a Kurdish notables from Kermanshah, for example, studied Shi'a theology in An Najaf and Karbala with renowned ulema from Pakistan, Afghanistan, India, and Africa. Some Kurds became leading ayatollahs alongside Persian-speaking Shi'a counterparts. The Kurdish Jelili family from the Ottoman Kurdish province of Mosul produced a line of respected ulema and intellectuals, including the celebrated shaykh Abdal Jelili bin Nader Kirkuki, Ayatollah Haji Shaykh Abdulrahim Jelili, and Ayatollah Haji Shaykh Muhammed-Hadi Jelili (Beglari 1997, 96–97).

Policies that favored Shi'a groups reinforced dichotomies among Muslim communities, including the Kurds. As in the Ottoman Empire, heterodox Muslim groups such as the Zoroastrians, Parsis, Ahl-e Haqq, and Baha'is had an inferior status as nonbelievers (Avery, Hambly, and Melville 1991, 182; Algar 1969, 107, 119). Even though they could go to the *diwankhana* in Tehran for judgments to avoid provincial prejudices, religious minorities had no legal rights in Muslim courts and were denied military and high government posts. Some political leaders and moderate ulema tolerated Sufi groups, many of whom were Kurds; however, orthodox ayatollahs vilified them, calling them "sons of burnt fathers and defiled mothers" (Meskoob 1992, 182; Avery, Hambly, and Melville 1991, 98, 170; Lambton 1987, 197). Even when certain Qajar shahs attempted to weaken clerical power they did not halt the discriminations against nonorthodox Muslim groups.

Yet in contrast to the Ottoman Empire, whereby certain non-Sunni groups took refuge in secluded mountain areas to escape discrimination, Sunni Muslim and Sufi minorities in Iran still had some cultural and political opportunities. Despite the Iranian-Ottoman rivalries and ideological differences between Sunnis and Shi'as, the two Muslim groups shared rights in the pilgrimage traffic to An Najaf and Karbala. They were also represented jointly in the courts during Qajar rule (Ruhani and Ruhani 1992, 509–12). Additionally, relations among the monarchy, Shi'a clergy, and nonorthodox Muslims were not naturally conflictual but depended on the politics of the ruling house, the shah's personal beliefs, and ulema influences. For instance, in contrast to the Safavi rulers, who claimed to descend from and to rule on behalf of the Twelve Imams, the Qajar shahs emphasized their tribal lineage as an inherent aspect of Iranian identity (Tapper 1983, 5; Beglari 1997, 4–12). Alongside Islam they consecrated stone carvings of Iranian kings in the monarchical tradition. The emphasis on the secular aspects of Persian identity created spaces for non-Shi'a groups and challenged the relations between the royal court and the clergy.

The ambiguous nature of the political space encouraged a more constructive relationship among the court, Sufi Kurds, and the religious establishment than that which existed between the Ottoman Empire and its Muslim minorities. Certain Qajar shahs were more tolerant of nonorthodox Shi'a groups than others. For example, although Fath 'Ali Shah (r. 1797–1834) gave orthodox ulema broad control over local affairs and allowed persecutions of nonorthodox Muslim groups, successor shahs acted more independently of the clergy in an attempt to increase governmental power. Muhammed Shah (r. 1834–1848) had Sufi leanings and allowed Sufi shaykhs to attain high posts in the court. Nasir al-Din Shah (r. 1848–1896) employed a Kurdish Sufi, Mirza Taqi Khan Amir Nezam, as his first chief minister (Lambton 1987, 198). Sympathies for Sufis increased tensions between the ulema and Qajar kings; however, they allowed a place for Sufi leaders in the political realm.

Additionally, in a society where traditional power structures were dominant, Kurdish Sunni groups accessed opportunities as part of the tribal community. Because the Qajar shahs did not develop a professional military as had the Ottomans, it was more necessary for them to rely on tribal groups for internal defense. To control tribal power the Qajars resettled tribes to distant regions, created new tribes where they did not exist, and arranged intermarriages between tribal groups and the Qajar family (Abrahamian 1982, 45; McDowall 1997, 68). In return for their services tribal chiefs were exempted from taxes, received free grazing rights or additional pasturelands, and were awarded government posts. Despite Nasir al-Din Shah's centralization efforts and the creation of a bureaucratic administration, tribal power remained prominent. Tribal chiefs were appointed to the 1858 consultative assembly *(mashlihat khaneh)* along with the council of ministers and the ulema. Furthermore, although Qajar rule was hereditary, government positions were not. Absence of an ethnic criterion in government appointments enabled non-Qajar, Sunni Kurdish tribal leaders and notables to purchase their offices and gain access to the political realm.

Consequently, as in the Ottoman Empire, landowners and tribal chiefs, including Sunni Kurds, benefited from the imperial system. Kurdish khans maintained their own militias, controlled their landed interests, and profited economically as tax collectors. Kurds also attained important political positions without having to deny their ethnic identity. In Azerbaijan, Mirza Muhammed Khan Zendeganeh, a Kurd, became governor, leader of the military forces, and envoy to Russia. Kurdish chiefs such as Latif Ali Khan and his son Hussein Ali Khan Gross became governors of Kerman and Mashhad. Gross also headed the government of Saujbulagh, the military regiments of Azerbaijan, and the administrations of Kurdistan and Kermanshah Provinces. Under the rule of Fath 'Ali Shah, various Kurds received high posts of military command, including Aziz Khan Serdar and Kurdish chiefs from Khorasan. More than a generation later, Kurds joined Nasir al-Din Shah's European delegations and had chances to pursue advanced studies abroad (Tavahodi 1980, 53; Busse 1972, 6; Lambton 1953, 158, 218; Ruhani and Ruhani 1992, 444–53).

Shifting but Stable Political Space

As in the Ottoman Empire, increasing external penetration, economic crises, and restlessness with arbitrary government rule challenged Qajar Iran's traditional socioeconomic and political order. Although foreign influence arrived thirty years later in Iran, it still impacted the financial, administrative, educational, and political affairs of the empire. Humiliating military defeats caused territorial losses and debt-repayment obligations to foreign powers. Like their Ottoman counterparts, Nasir al-Din Shah and Muzaffar al-Din Shah (r. 1896–1907) granted concessions to foreign governments, giving them control over the empire's finances and privileging foreigners over local nationals. Foreign powers supported missionary groups just as they did in the Ottoman Empire, which intensified conflicts between Muslims and Christians and between local communities and foreigners.

Still, the nature of foreign penetrations and Qajar policies differed from the ones in the Ottoman Empire, and these differences influenced the character of the political space for Kurdish groups. For instance, Iran did not develop economically the way the Ottoman Empire did during the nineteenth century. Whereas the Ottomans maintained strong commercial ties with Europe, Iran's geographical constraints and the inaccessibility of alternative commercial markets enabled the British and Russians to gain near monopoly power over the empire's resources (Bakhash 1978, 205). Great power rivalries and inefficient Qajar policies contributed to the division of Iran into zones of influence and hindered economic growth. By the late nineteenth century the total foreign investment in Egypt and the Ottoman Empire was $1 billion each, whereas in Iran it was less than $150 million. Even after the discovery of petroleum in 1908, Persia lacked an internal communications system, reliable electricity in the cities, and comprehensive transportation networks (Morsalvand 1995, 67; Issawi 1971, 239–40).

The limited nature of European economic penetration and the underdeveloped Persian economy protected the traditional Kurdish power structure. Unlike the Ottoman Empire, whereby European influences and centralization policies threatened the Kurdish traditional stratum, Kurds in Persia retained their economic and political status, even as external penetration increased in the late nineteenth century. Also, in contrast to the Ottoman Empire, which functioned within a bureaucratic administrative structure, the decentralized nature of Qajar rule, absence of secession laws, tradition of ombudsmen, and quasi-feudal tuyul system prevented the institutionalization of a bureaucracy that could have weakened traditional social structures over time (Avery, Hambly, and Melville 1991, 174). Although parts of Ottoman Kurdistan retribalized after the downfall of the Kurdish emirates, the tribal system maintained a greater role in Persia than it did in Ottoman society. The Ottoman elite centralized control of most localities, yet by the late nineteenth century Qajar officials continued to support the tribal tradition.

Furthermore, Qajar Persia's numerically small Christian population, the relatively weak links to external powers, and the decentralized political system limited the ethnic parochialism and separatism that became part of the Ottoman vilayet system. Instead, what emerged in Iran were rivalries between pro-British and pro-Russian groups and between local residents and foreigners. The growing resentment against foreign penetration and the increasingly active ulema often brought local communities together, despite their ideological, ethnic, and religious differences. During the protests against the tobacco monopoly (the Régie), for instance, the Armenian archbishop eventually joined Muslim protesters instead of turning to the British or other Christian communities (Lambton 1987, 236).[9]

Persia's nineteenth-century reform movement did not encourage the ethnic identification of the Qajar Empire's communities the way it did in the Ottoman lands. Although reformists became increasingly conscious of a Persian identity in relation to other nations, they did not develop a radical form of ethnic nationalism. There was no Young Persians' movement, no promotion of a nationwide Persian language program, and no equivalent of the Ottoman's CUP period in the Qajar historical trajectory. Local populations did not define Iranian identity *(Iraniyyat)* as being ethnically Persian. The political conflicts that emerged between the constitutionalists and monarchists in the early twentieth century and also within the ulema community were based not on Persian ethnicity, but on the role of Islam and foreign influence in the empire.

Indeed, orthodox ulema, monarchists, and tribal leaders wanted to protect the traditional power structures tied to the shah; they opposed the constitutionalists and were hostile to European influences (Chaqueri 1979, 53–62; Burrell 1997, 400; Martin 1989, 87).[10] The victory of the constitutionalists gave secular groups new political powers and encouraged the rise of modern Iranian nationalism. By 1906 Iran had a functioning national assembly (the Majlis) and a constitution based on the Belgian parliamentary model. Still, traditional sociopolitical structures remained, and discriminations against non-Muslims continued. Consequently, the relationship between Islam and modern Iranian identity remained unclear.

9. At this time, a petition was generated by the ulema in Tabriz stating that the Armenians would be exempt from attacks if they aligned themselves with the Muslims against the Tobacco Régie. The ulema later explained that their attacks against the Armenians were based on fear of an Armenian-British alliance, particularly those British residing in the Armenian quarter.

10. Taking *bast,* or sanctuary, was a form of refuge against the arbitrary legal system. It was also a political tool used by local populations and often encouraged by British and Turkish officials. Persian nationalists used foreign embassies and telegraph offices to make their demands for constitutional change. The Shi'a ulema also provided bast in their mosques, houses of *mujtahids* (individuals who apply Islamic law), and shrines to distressed people.

Segmented Dissidence and Tribal Resistance

Shifts in the political space encouraged some Kurds to revolt against the central government. Ismail Agha Simko, leader of the Kurdish Shakak tribe, conducted various revolts in Persia and called himself a Kurdish nationalist. Shaykh Ubaydullah of Nehri exported his Kurdish nationalist sentiment across the border to Persia, affirming that Kurdistan was a nation apart. Yet Kurdayetî did not become salient in Qajar Persia. Most Kurds continued to identify according to their tribal, local, and religious interests. Simko may have occasionally considered himself a nationalist, but his overriding demand was to protect his property rights and local power networks in the shifting early-twentieth-century political context.

One can argue that Kurdayetî was weaker in Qajar Persia because in contrast to the Ottoman Empire, whereby Turks and Arabs composed nearly 80 percent of the population by the early twentieth century, the population in Persia was more proportional on an ethnic basis. The Persian-speaking ethnic community constituted barely half of the population. The other half comprised Azeri Turks (20 percent), Kurds, Lurs, Afghans, Arabs, Armenians, Baluchis, and Turkomen. Ethnoheterogeneity created a greater sense of ethnic balance within Qajar society, which diminished the Kurds' sense of ethnic distinction in the empire. Kurds in Persia were also a relatively smaller community (less than 10 percent of the total population) and lacked political influence. In effect, they did not have the resources or organizational support to mobilize on a nationalist level. Still, even during the period of high external intervention and political instability, when the Kurds had the chance to turn to foreign and domestic opposition groups for support, Kurdish leaders did not make claims on behalf of a Kurdish nation. Why did the Kurds fail to take advantage of the political opportunities that could have advanced their group's national interests?

As in the Ottoman Empire, the political space privileged the traditional stratum, encouraging tribal and religious identities to become salient over nationalist ones. Decentralized and asymmetrical policies in the provinces reinforced the attachment to local identities. Although the Shi'a Kurdish region of Kermanshah grew into a key provincial center, the Sunni Kurdish province of Kurdistan lost its position in Persian political affairs, particularly after the fall of the Ardalan dynasty in the mid-nineteenth century (Clarke and Clarke 1969, 8; Lambton 1987, 49–50; Beglari 1997, 27; Avery,

Hambly, and Melville 1991, 66–67).[11] Different identities crystallized in the provinces. Most Kurds continued to think of themselves as Kermanshahis, Sanandajis, or Howremanis alongside their Muslim and tribal affiliations.

However, in contrast to the Ottoman Empire, whereby after 1909 the Kurdish tribal shaykhly establishment turned to influential Sufi orders to mobilize Kurdish communities, Kurdish Sufi brotherhoods in Persia did not have the governmental support or local networks to organize on a national or religious level. Whereas Ottoman Kurdish shaykhs had a devoted following in the rural areas, their counterparts in Persia could rely only on local tribal militias. Neither Simko nor Ubaydullah could secure sufficient organizational support to sustain a nationalist revolt. Further, Kurdish tribal chiefs in Persia did not confront the same types of challenges to their local political power as their Ottoman counterparts did in the late nineteenth century. Whereas the Porte's bureaucratic officials assumed responsibility of the Ottoman vilayets and imposed centralization policies after 1908, Qajar shahs allowed Kurds, Lurs, Bakhtiaris, and other groups to govern provincial and local affairs.

The Qajar leaders' greater attachment to traditional power structures protected the privileged position of tribal leaders and helped prevent the emergence of a Kurdish bourgeoisie to push forward nationalist ideas. Unlike the Ottoman elite, the Qajar shahs elevated tribal groups without developing city centers. Consequently, the Kurdish nationalist circles that emerged in the Ottoman cities in the late nineteenth century were absent in Iranian cities and towns. In Persia, there were no nationalist writers like Koyî or grand urban notable families such as the Bedir Khans to represent Kurdayetî in Isfahan, Tabriz, or Tehran. The privileges associated with the clerical establishment attracted most educated Kurds to the Shi'a schools of learning. Whether as notables or ulema, Shi'a Kurdish scholars were hardly the candidates to lead nationalist mobilizations in the urban centers.

---

11. Situated along the trade routes from East Asia through the Iranian plateau and representing one of the key agricultural producers in the empire, Kermanshah served as a commercial passageway for the caravans traveling between the Zagros plains, Baghdad, Basra, and India. Given its strategic position along the Ottoman-Iraqi border, Kermanshah also became an important defense against the Ottomans and marauding tribes. Even after territorial divisions were established in the May 1847 Treaty of Erzurum between Persian and Ottoman Iraq, Kermanshah continued to be used as a refuge for Kurds, political officials, and foreign powers moving between the two empires.

The absence of an urban bourgeoisie with modern nationalist ideas meant that urban tribal divisions that marked Kurdayetî in the Ottoman Empire would not be present in Qajar Iran.

Even if a budding urban bourgeoisie were present in Persia, it is unlikely that Kurdayetî would have become salient and ethnicized because the Qajar Empire was not ethnicized enough to stir the ethnic identification of Kurdish groups. Given the overlapping histories and shared cultural traditions of Kurds and Persians, the use of secular, monarchical, and tribal themes by Qajar leaders actually favored the Kurds over other ethnic communities. Some Sunni Kurdish leaders, such as the khan of Ardalan, capitalized on the shahs' pre-Islamic symbolic gestures by claiming to be related to the Qajar family.

In the absence of an ethnicized form of Iranian nationalism there was no reason for Kurdish groups to differentiate themselves ethnically from the political center. Although the Kurdish governor of Saujbulagh made demands for Kurdish autonomy in 1886, he did not discuss the notion of Kurdayetî. When Simko was engaged in local rivalries in the Urmiya region, other Kurds joined local Azeris and Armenians in the constitutional movement. Similarly, the head of the constitutionalist *anjoman* in Kurdistan, Qazi Fattah, called not for a Kurdish administration but for a representative government that would include all ethnic groups. The failure of Qajar elites to ethnicize or centralize the political system also explains why, even during the Constitutional Revolution period (1905–1911) or the chaotic World War I period, Kurdish groups did not take advantage of foreign support that could have advanced Kurdish nationalist claims. In fact, when a radical Majlis faction of anti-British and anti-Russian officials fled Tehran to Kermanshah in 1915 and established a provisional government, there were no Kurdish nationalists readily available or interested in demanding political autonomy (Lustig 1987, 3; Nasseri 1980).

Conclusions

In both the Ottoman and Qajar Empires the absence of an exclusive official nationalist project based on ethnicity prevented Kurdayetî from becoming salient or highly ethnicized. The political space supported traditional social structures, ensuring that tribal and religious identities remained dominant over nationalist ones. However, during the late nineteenth century the Kurdish historical trajectories started to follow different paths owing to variations in the political spaces. Exclusionary policies and modernization trends challenged the traditional power structures in the Ottoman Empire, while leaving the Qajar Empire essentially unchanged.

Consequently, Kurdish nationalism in the Ottoman Empire started to assume modern tendencies, such as the presence of a rising urban nationalist elite, organization of political parties, and nationalist publications. These forms of modern nationalism were absent in Persia, where Kurdish leaders and mobilizations were limited to the tribal milieu. Further, despite the rise of an ethnicizing tendency, the political space in the Ottoman Empire was not clearly or highly ethnicized, which resulted in an ambivalent relationship between Kurdish nationalists and the Ottoman elite based on hostility and compromise. In Persia, larger content and less variability in the political space encouraged a more consistent and constructive relationship between the Kurds and Qajar officials.

2

Iraq's Transition to a Colonial State

The consequences of World War I and the downfall of the imperial system structurally transformed the Ottoman provinces. Under the new mandate system Britain assumed control of Iraq, Palestine, and Transjordan while the French settled in Syria and Lebanon. The transition from empire to state also distributed the Ottoman Kurdish communities, territories, water resources, and petroleum deposits of the Fertile Crescent into geographically contiguous, sovereign territories. After the 1920 Treaty of Sèvres suggested Kurdish statehood and the ratification of the Lausanne Treaty in 1923, which rescinded the offer, the Ottoman Kurdish regions were legally subsumed into different administrative and political systems in Iraq, Turkey, and Syria. Kurdish communities no longer shared a common political center but became linked to separate governments as peripheral border populations.[1] Further, as British and Iraqi officials secularized, semimodernized, and partially ethnicized the state they reconfigured the political space for Kurds in Iraq. New relationships developed among the traditional Kurdish stratum, nontribal groups, and the central government, which in turn altered the expression of Kurdayetî across Kurdish society.

1. The largest portion of Kurdish territory is in Turkey (43 percent), followed by Iran (31 percent), Iraq (18 percent), and Syria (6 percent). Kurdish territories are also located in the former Soviet Union (2 percent).

Colonizing Iraq

Although the British government gained colonial rights over Iraq, it had not secured control of the political apparatus or strategically important territories. Key Arab communities, tribal groups, and regional states continued to destabilize the new government. In this insecure postwar transition period and with the fear of losing the oil-rich, Kurdish-populated Mosul Province, British officials made special efforts to pacify Kurdish communities (Olson 1992a; Danielson 1995). Majors E. B. Soane and E. M. Noel, colonial officers stationed in the Kurdish regions of Iraq and Turkey, gained the confidence of tribal chiefs and shaykhs by offering them political posts and financial incentives and promising to protect the caliphate. They also recognized the Kurds as a unique ethnic group and acknowledged their nationalist claims. During his travels with Kurdish notables, Major Noel ensured an independent Kurdistan with Alexandretta as the seaport. Major Soane spoke directly to the Kurds about their rights to self-determination.

The British even attempted to institutionalize Kurdish ethnic identity in the new state. The provisional 1921 Iraqi Constitution asserted that Iraq was composed of two ethnic groups—Arabs and Kurds—and that the Kurdish language had equal status with Arabic. Iraqi high commissioner Sir Percy Cox opposed the government's request to hoist the Iraqi flag in Kurdish provinces and refused to appoint an Arabized Kurd as governor of Sulaimaniya Province. Seeking Iraq's admission to the League of Nations, the British tried to ensure minority groups' rights in the new state. Cox welcomed outside intervention, inviting international commissions to Iraq that recognized the quasi autonomy of local groups.

By treating Mosul Province as a separate entity from Arab Iraq the British gave Kurdistan semilegitimate political status from the outset of the nation-state-building project. In contrast to the Ottoman elite they organized Arab and Kurdish regions into two zones referred to as al-Iraq al-Arab, or the southern and central Arab zone, including Baghdad and Basra Provinces, and al-Iraq al-Cadjmi (Irak-Perse), which comprised the northern Kurdish region of Mosul vilayet (Longrigg 1956, 92–98; Harik 1987, 35–36; Sluglett 1976; "The Iraq Government" 1927; *Iraq: Report* 1922; *Review of Civil Administration* 1920; *Report by High Commission* 1922). The high commissioner assumed direct responsibility for Mosul and treated Kurdistan as an autonomous, quasi-legal entity, evident in British accounting, fiscal, and administrative procedures. During the early 1920s, for instance, the accounting audits for Iraq divided British-controlled territories into "His Britannic Majesty's Government, the Government of India, and the Government of Sulaimaniya (Kurdistan)." A special edition of the British-edited *Al-Iraq Yearbook* listed the principal countries adjoining Iraq as Persia, Transjordan, Armenia, Syria, Lebanon, and Kurdistan, with the Kurdish shaykh Mahmoud Barzinji as the latter's leader (Edmonds 1936; *Iraq: Report* 1922; *Al-Iraq Yearbook* 1922–23, 39).

Yet the large political space was limited in time and content, which hindered the evolution of Kurdayeti in the legal sphere while heightening ethnic and socioeconomic dichotomies in Iraqi and Kurdish societies. As the British gained control of the government and settled their territorial claims, they employed new policies that favored secular communities, Arab nationalists, and tribal-landowning groups. Even though Islam became the official state religion and the sadah families retained their religious and political influence in the government, the British omitted the Şaria from the constitution as a way of separating religion and politics (Batatu 1978, 153–210).[2] Nor did they build upon traditional Islamic structures or employ pan-Islamism in their nation-state-building project. Instead, after 1925 the British tried to bring Iraqi populations together by constructing a secularized notion of Iraqi identity based on a sense of Iraqi unity *(al-wahda al-iraqiyya)*.

Rather than neutralizing ethnic and religious differences within the heterogeneous Iraqi society, which comprised Shi'a Arabs (51 percent), Sunni Arabs (20 percent), Sunni Kurds (18 percent), Shi'a Kurds, Shi'a Persians, Jews, Turkomen, and Christians (Chaldeo-Assyrians and Armenians (11 percent), the British reinforced them by elevating Sunni Arabs over other groups. After appointing the Arab nationalist Faysal I as the first king of Iraq, British officers assigned key posts such as minister of education, chief of staff, and minister of defense to Arabists Sati' al-Husri, Nuri Sa'id, and Jafar al-Askari, respectively. By Sunni Arabizing the government the British introduced a politics of ethnicity that antagonized minority groups and

2. The sadah families, also known as *ashraf*, claimed to be of the Prophet's blood. The real social status of the sadah families, however, was based on their wealth, tribal leadership, and political positions.

Shi'a populations. The Kurds were directly affected because they not only had lost their own bid to statehood but also were placed in a new context where their former Muslim counterparts were now their overlords.

To control unruly tribal groups and Faysal's power the British played off tribes against one another, instigating land disputes and encouraging internal hostilities. They arrested Kurds and expelled local Kurdish leaders. The Royal Air Force and Iraqi military bombed Kurdish villages indiscriminately, without compensation to civilian groups. Still, Kurdish chiefs and nationalist leaders continued to pledge their loyalty to the government. In fact, after 1925 some Kurds even developed a compromising relationship with the state elite.

Alongside coercion and control the British employed normative and utilitarian means of compliance that helped co-opt tribal and landowning groups. Although they courted Arab groups and repressed unruly nationalist leaders, the British gave tribal chiefs political and economic advantages over urban Kurdish communities. In contrast to Sultan Mahmut's late Ottoman reforms, which strengthened the towns at the expense of the tribes, British officials elevated tribal groups while urban centers expanded. Tribal leaders gained greater regional autonomy under the colonial administrative system. Instead of reviving the Ottoman reforms and institutions introduced by former Baghdad governor Midhat Paşa (1869–1872), the British devised a semidecentralized, cost-effective system based on indirect colonial rule *(Iraq: Report* 1922).

Despite Faysal's efforts to break tribal power with his conscription policy, the British vetoed the attempts as a way of ensuring tribal support. To administer the outlying Kurdish regions they appointed Kurdish chiefs from the leading landowning families as governors and gave them relative autonomy. Also, whereas the British retained direct control of the Royal Air Force and the Assyrian levies, they allowed tribal leaders to maintain their arms and personal militias. After 1921 the levies served as *shabanas,* irregular military forces under the service and pay of Britain, and increased considerably, from two thousand to seventy-five hundred, to include a Kurdish levy of Sulaimaniya *(Treaty of Alliance* 1925, 2; *Iraq: Report* 1922, 69).

Tribal groups further benefited as part of the landowning stratum. The British altered the traditional Ottoman land-tenure system so that tribal chiefs and shaykhs gained absolute possession of their lands, which were formerly the sole properties of the state and frequently redistributed among tribal family members. To end the migration to the cities and tie the peasants to the land the state elite passed laws favoring the landowning stratum, such as the law for the rights and duties of cultivators. Although Faysal added a bureaucratic layer to the government, he linked it to the privileged, landed stratum. These policies continued into the 1950s, ensuring that aghas and tribal communities enjoyed benefits over urban dwellers and nontribal rural groups. Certain tribes were excluded from the jurisdiction of national courts, were educated in separate schools, were "elected" to Parliament, and enjoyed special tax benefits. A special system of jurisdiction was created for tribes; however, no such comparable privileges were given to the nontribal urban dwellers. Section 40 of the Criminal Code stated, "Any undesirable townsman can be removed from tribal territories." Consequently, two policies emerged in Iraq, one for the tribes and one for the townsmen (Batatu 1978, 93).

Segmented Nationalism

During the early state transition period, when external penetration was high, when border regions were porous, and when the Paris Peace Conference was under way, the political space for Kurdish groups was large in size and content. The Kurds could safely recognize themselves as an ethnic group and speak their language relatively freely in the political arena. Opportunities for Kurds were available because the political system was not highly ethnicized, militarized, or under the control of a dominant political faction. During the war the British replaced the Ottoman Sharifian officers (army officers from the Sunni sect in Baghdad and northern regions of Iraq representing the middle and lower classes) with British and Indian officials so that by 1920 Arab groups composed less that 4 percent of the administration. Even though the British required Iraqi officials to allocate not less than 25 percent of their total revenues toward the defense and security of the new state and King Faysal regarded the military as the spinal column for nation building, the Iraqi military remained relatively weak.

Influenced by President Wilson's Fourteen Points and other groups demanding self-determination, some Kurds took advantage of their open political space by emphasizing Kurdish national identity. During one of his many breaks with Britain Barzinji declared himself king of Kurdistan, issued his own Kurdish stamps, hoisted a Kurdish flag, and demanded an in-

1. Shaykh Mahmoud Barzinji with Major Noel and British officers, ca. 1925. Photograph courtesy of Rafiq Studio.

dependent Kurdish state. Some Kurds in Sulaimaniya called for independence under the trusteeship of the British government while "recognizing nobody as their leader *(hukemdar)* except Shaykh Mahmoud [Barzinji]." Rashid Zekî, referred to as a delegate of Sulaimaniya Southern Kurdistan, petitioned the French for an independent Kurdistan under the sovereignty of Barzinji. Abdel Qader promised French merchants they would have sole access to Kurdistan ("Lettre de Sheikh Abdul Qader"; Zekî 1919). Spiritual leaders such as Shaykh Nuri al-Brifkani and Baha ud-Din Bamarni sent petitions to the Iraqi government, demanding Kurdish rights. Kurdish intellectuals, such as Faik Abdullah Bêkas (1905–1948), wrote political poems about the Kurdish nation *(qawmiyya Kurd)* (Kerîm 1986, 53).[3]

Yet Kurdish nationalists could not market their political claims at the time. Kurdayetî became salient; however, it was not highly representative across Iraqi Kurdistan. Early-twentieth-century rural Kurdish society was stratified and heterogeneous. Socioeconomic and political status was based on distinctions between tribal and nontribal communities, Muslims and

3. The editor created a section of the book called "Kurdayetî" in which he placed Bêkas's poems about Kurdish national identity.

non-Muslims, warriors and tillers of the land, landowners, peasants, and urban groups (Batatu 1978, 58–61; van Bruinessen 1992, 40–41). In the traditional power structure, tribal leaders, aghas, and shaykhs, and not urban notables, were most influential in Kurdish politics and society.

The political space that favored the traditional stratum encouraged fragmentation, not unification, of Kurdish communities. Rather than affiliating with Barzinji's administration in Sulaimaniya, some Kurds reacted to Armenian territorial acquisitions by joining Turkish Muslims against European-Christian influences. Pro-Turkish Kurds called for a Kurdistan separated from the Kurdish regions in Turkey under the protectorate of Persia, Russia, or Iraq (Hewrami 1969a, 62; Hewrami 1969b, 96–110; "Trouble in Kurdistan" 1919). The Kurdish tribal chief Haidari advocated Kurdish self-determination in Iraq, but later accepted the idea of incorporating Iraqi Kurdistan into Turkey or forming a Kurdish Soviet republic. Others turned to Atatürk's agent, Sayid Ahmed Senusi, the grand sharif of Tripoli, who traveled throughout the Kurdish regions promoting pan-Islamic and anti-British views ("Télégramme de Monsieur Gouraud" 1921; "Le Mouvement Kurde" 1927).

Britain's blatant policies that co-opted the aghas and tribal chiefs further stifled Kurdish nationalist potential. They reinforced the economic relationship between rural areas of Kurdistan and Baghdad. For instance, to spur the production of tobacco *(tutin* and *tumbak),* the main cash crop of Iraq, the Iraqi state revenue department issued more than 2,700 new tobacco licenses to merchants in Baghdad and the Kurdish regions. Of the total 3,419,834 kilos of tobacco *(tutin)* received in 1922 in Iraq, the bulk was from the Kurdish cities of Sulaimaniya (66.8 percent), Mosul (19.8 percent), and Kirkuk (13.2 percent). By 1945 about 14,000 of the 16,000 pounds of tobacco produced in Iraq annually was supplied by the Kurdish North. The British also cancelled Ottoman customs taxes that had increased as much as 15 percent during the war. Kurdish aghas became some of the wealthiest landowners in Iraq (Ross 1959, 84; Marr 1985, 65; Lenczowski 1962, 264; Batatu 1978, 56–61, 90–93; "The Iraq Government" 1927).

Consequently, it was more advantageous and politically safer for Kurdish aghas to protect their landed interests than to mobilize against the state on behalf of Kurdish nationalism. Many developed a conciliatory relationship with the central government. Kurdish nationalist tribal chiefs such as

Ahmed Muhktar Begî Jaf (1897–1935) and Mullah Mustafa Barzani became the monarchy's strongest supporters. In their correspondence with state officials some tribal leaders asked to "let bygones be bygones, as long as [Britain] would continue to pay salaries and treat them with the same honor and favor as before the trouble." Nontribal Kurdish leaders also turned to the British at this time. After learning about the new language law, Kurds from Sulaimaniya, including the governor, sent telegrams of gratitude to the Iraqi government ("Confidential Letter" 1930). The relatively large and ambiguous nature of the political space led Kurdish nationalists to believe that they had the unanimous support of one of the great powers of the day.

Also, in a political space where communications and transportation systems were undeveloped and local populations were geographically isolated, attachments to the former Ottoman vilayet system remained salient. Some Kurdish regions such as Sulaimaniya were still tied commercially and culturally to Persian communities, whereas others, such as Mosul Province, were more integrated with Arab and Turkoman groups. The state elite reinforced these demographic, geographic, cultural, and political realities by treating the Kurdish regions differently from one another. At no point during the colonial period did British officials make any effort to unify Kurdish populations or their regions. Instead of trying to bring the various Kurdish factions together under one political umbrella, the British organized different Kurdish administrations within separate jurisdictions that were governed by rival Kurdish leaders: the Bedir Khan family in Istanbul, Shaykh Mahmoud Barzinji in Sulaimaniya, Ahmed Muhktar Begî Jaf in Halabja, and Shaykh Seyid Taha in Rowanduz along the Iranian-Iraqi border.

Administrative policies were equally divisive. The Kurdish provinces were not only differentiated from Arab Iraq on a territorial and ethnic basis but also governed separately from one another until 1945. Sulaimaniya was tied directly to British control, although it enjoyed political autonomy until 1925 (Edmonds 1937; Hakim 1992, 125–26).[4] Language laws were also unevenly implemented. Kurds in Sulaimaniya were permitted to speak and teach Kurdish, but Kurds in Arbil (Hawlêr) used Kurdish and Arabic. Oth-

4. The internal divisions of Kurdistan in Iraq correspond to the early Kurdish principalities: Badinan (Mosul Liwa), Soran (Arbil Liwa), and Baban (Sulaimaniya and part of Kirkuk Liwa).

ers in Mosul Province relied on Arabic for communication and administration purposes. The absence of standardized Kurdish language instruction or Kurdish schools encouraged the use of local dialects rather than a unified Kurdish language that could have built nationalist sentiment.

Thus, during the early state-formation period Iraqi Kurds were still a nonimagined community. Although a certain map image of a greater Kurdistan may have existed in the minds of many Kurds, the notion of Kurdayetî was weak, localized, and fractured across Kurdish society. During the elections for King Faysal, instead of supporting a Sulaimaniya-based Kurdish government, most Kurds in the Mosul plains aligned with Arabs, Turkish Muslim tribes, or foreign powers. Kurds from Kirkuk also refused to be placed under Barzinji's government in Sulaimaniya *(Iraq: Report* 1922, 12–15).

Ambiguous Political Space

Although the character of the political space was relatively large, it was ambiguous and variable over time. This ambiguity was linked to the absence of a dominant, exclusionary notion of Iraqi citizenship. Even after Iraq entered the League of Nations and gained nominal independence in its internal affairs, in 1932, Britain's refusal to let go of the country, the deaths of Faysal and his son Ghazi, and the creation of another weak government under Faysal II and his regent prevented any one political tendency from controlling the government. Political power waxed and waned among the monarchists, *taba'i* (official or imperially dependent) nationalists, those individuals seeking full Iraqi independence, Communists, and Arab nationalist factions. As the political elite progressed with its nation-state-building project, local populations started questioning what type of political entity Iraq should become: a protectorate of Britain or a truly independent state. Should this state be guided by leftist ideology or Arab nationalist principles? What implications would these choices have on the manifestation of Kurdish national identity?

Until the early 1940s the idea of an official taba'i Iraqi nationalism, or one dependent on the British Crown, was popular among tribal groups, former Sharifian officers, the bureaucratic elite, the Hashemite family, the sadah families, and the old social classes who wanted to ensure their landowning privileges. Taba'i nationalism appealed to Kurdish tribal chiefs because it tolerated Kurdish nationalism as part of an Iraqi-first identity and offered the Kurds some protection against Arab nationalist tendencies. Until his expulsion from Iraq, Mullah Mustafa Barzani demanded "Kurdistan for the Kurds under British protection." Kurdish ministers without portfolio Majid Mustafa and Daus al-Haidari called for Kurdish autonomy that cooperated with Baghdad. Although he wrote about the "moaning of his heart for the sadness of Kurdistan," Jaf remained loyal to the British, who ensured his generous salary and political influence as a nationalist leader (Jaf 1969, 134–36).

A different type of Iraqi-first identity emerged alongside the leftist movement. Communist and socialist influences emerged in the 1930s after the world depression, economic changes that marginalized peasant and urban communities, hostility to British rule, the rise of fascism, and the creation of regional leftist groups, including the Iraqi Communist Party (ICP) (Laqueur 1957, 175; Ismael 1979; Batatu 1978, 389–439, 659–99). The emergence of leftist tendencies encouraged new collective identities to become salient among economically disfranchised, urban Kurdish communities that coexisted or became prominent over their Kurdish identity. One of the leaders of the 1936 military coup, General Bakr Sidqi, a Kurd, identified as a socialist and not a Kurdish nationalist. Left-leaning Kurds also identified with the ICP, working classes, and anti-imperialist movement.

A third ideological current was Arab nationalism, which represented the core beliefs of most military officers and the al-'Ahd society (a secret organization formed in 1913 by pan-Arab officers in the Ottoman Army involved in the movement for Arab autonomy) within the government. Arab nationalists had distinct ideas about the past, present, and future Iraqi identity based on pan-Arab nationalism *(qawmiyya)* and Iraqi patriotism *(wataniyya)*. Unlike other ideological currents, qawmiyya nationalism was ethnicized; it emphasized the revival of the Arab nation, of which Iraq was considered an integral part (Devlin 1979, 4; Jaber 1966, 23; Raouf 1984; Bassam 1990; Batatu 1978, 172, 197).[5] Most members of the Iraq Renaissance Socialist Party (Ba'thists) were qawmiyya nationalists, although not all Arab nationalists were Ba'thists. Qawmiyya nationalists employed particular myths that denied Kurdish ethnicity. In Ba'thist ideology the Kurds were

5. In November 1952 Michael Aflaq's Arab Ba'th Party merged with Akram al-Howrani's Arab Socialist Party to form the Arab Ba'th Socialist Party.

considered of Arab origin, separated from their true motherland because of colonialism. Ba'thists even claimed that Salahaddin, the famous Kurdish warrior, was an Arab (Hakim 1992, 139–40).

The highly ethnicized qawmiyya nationalism restricted the political space for Kurds. Ba'thist ideology attempted to include all ethnic groups in an Arab state, where Islam would play a moderating role and act as a regulator between ethnic communities. One of the leading pan-Arabists, Sati' al-Husri, a Syrian-born educator whom the British and King Faysal put in charge of Iraqi education, envisioned a secularized, ethnicized, Arab Iraqi identity as necessary to protect Arab culture from imperialism and Zionism. His pan-Arabism was influenced by Herderian linguistic nationalism: "The nation is nothing but a group of people speaking the same language . . . so that every Arabic-speaking people is an Arab people" (al-Husri 1959, 218–19; Yousif 1991, 173; Nuseibeh 1956, 40–41; al-Jundi 1968, 42–46; Cleveland 1991, 91–93; Bassam 1990, 116–23). As minister and director general of education, al-Husri and Sami Shawkat introduced Arab nationalist themes to school curricula and Arabized language and history instruction. After the creation of the State of Israel in 1948, qawmiyya nationalism was outwardly expressed in harsh anti-Israeli and anti-Western rhetoric. What emerged was a radical form of nationalism committed to fundamental social change for Arab freedom and unity.

Yet qawmiyya nationalism did not become a single dominant ideology among Arab groups. It coexisted with a territorial strain of Arab nationalism based on the notion of patriotism to the fatherland *(watan),* as well as linguistic and cultural ties between groups living in the same geographical area. Wataniyya nationalists supported the idea of an independent Iraq that could exist within a federation of Arab states, but not as part of an Arab union. Their myths about Iraqi identity claimed that Iraqis are the direct twentieth-century descendants of the Mesopotamian and Babylonian civilizations. Recognizing the local identities of non-Arab ethnic groups, wataniyya nationalists viewed the Kurds as partners in Iraq with their own distinct language, culture, and territory (Bensaid 1987, 151).[6] Consequently, this strain of Arab nationalism offered greater cultural and political space to non-Arab groups and even gained the support of some secular Kurdish

6. The terms *watan* and *wataniyya* have undergone changes in the Arab states in which they are used.

communities. Wataniyya nationalism also strengthened owing to the secular nationalism of Christian Arabs and European policies that supported regional development and Arab local identities.

Limited Ethnonationalism

Just as Arabs attempted to protect their Arabness against European encroachments, some Iraqi Kurds reacted against growing Arab hegemony. After more than two decades of British and Hashemite rule a gap remained between the regime's discourse and policies toward the Kurds. Although the British recognized Kurdish ethnic identity and promised Kurds cultural freedoms, the Anglo-Iraqi treaty of 1930 made no mention of the Kurds or minority rights in Iraq. Political, educational, and economic opportunities were unequal between Kurdish and Arab provinces. From 1920 to 1936, only four Kurds held posts among fifty-seven cabinet positions (Hassanpour 1992, 114). Iraqi Kurds were also influenced by Kurdish mobilizations in Syria, Turkey, and Iran. In the late 1930s the Kurdish Khoybun Society, based in Damascus, organized Kurdish revolts in Kurdistan in Turkey while Iranian Kurds created a temporary Kurdish government in Mahabad in 1945.

In this ethnicizing political climate a Kurdish ethnonationalist current also emerged. In his correspondence to the British high commissioner of Iraq in September 1930, Shaykh Barzinji criticized the Arab government's "atrocities against Kurds in Sulaimaniya," which, he argued, "had no precedent in Kurdistan." Affirming that it was impossible for Kurds and Arabs to live together, Barzinji requested, "in the name of the Aryan nation," that "the Kurds be liberated from the Arabs and remain under British protection" ("Letter from Barzinji" 1930). Other Kurds took advantage of cross-border support networks and created their own nationalist parties, including the Kurdistan Democratic Party (KDP), led by Mullah Mustafa Barzani.

The organization of semilegal political parties urbanized the Kurdish movement and spread nationalist ideas. Government printing presses and an underground publishing network ensured the use of Sorani Kurdish as a political language and reinforced the sense of a distinct Kurdish ethnic identity. During this period the writings of Kurdish nationalists such as Muhammad Amin Zekî (1881–1948), Ahmed Muhktar Begî Jaf, Faik Abdullah Bêkas, Piramêrd (Tawfik Mahmud Agha [1867–1950]) and Goran (Abdullah Sulayman [1904–1962]) became popularized in the Kurdish political discourse. Zekî tried to develop a political consciousness about the distinct Kurdish ethnic identity by asking, "What race are the Kurdish people and from where did they come?" (Zekî 1931, 1).[7] Bêkas responded to central government repression against Kurds by urging the Kurdish youth to become strong and nationalistic: "Oh fatherland . . . at the moment of prison and captivity where I have chains on my legs I have not forgotten to think of you. Do not believe that the prison, torture and the humiliation has made me forget you. . . . [N]ever has the flame extinguished nor has it broken" (Kerîm 1986, 55–56). Goran also reacted to the ethnicizing and restrictive political space by encouraging Kurdish nationalism. Arguing that the "time had come for action" he demanded the Kurds "attack, make a stronger effort . . . and not to economize the life of Kurdayetî" (Goran 1943, 402–3).

Still, Kurdish nationalism was relatively weak and fractured. Zekî's curiosity about Kurdish ethnic origins, Bêkas's idea of a Kurdish fatherland, and Goran's call for Kurdish uprising generated attention to the Kurdish problem; however, their nationalist sentiment did not penetrate across Kurdish society. As in the Ottoman and transition periods, the underdeveloped nature of the political space favored traditional and local power structures, which stifled the growth of Kurdish nationalist sentiment in the countryside. Socioeconomic status was still tied to the land, the size of one's personal militia, and the influence of tribal chiefs in Baghdad. The Iraqi government's tribal-support policies allowed tribal leaders to administer their regions, collect taxes, settle land disputes, and regulate commercial affairs in their localities. Kurdish tribal chiefs, not urban intellectuals, were most representative and influential in Kurdish society.

If the nature of Kurdish nationalism is tied to traditional social structures, why then did Kurdayetî fracture along socioeconomic and provincial lines and not according to religious affiliations? Kurdish society, like other Muslim communities at the time, was defined by its loyalties to Islam and the orders and sects to which it belonged: Naqshbandiyya, Qadiriyya,

---

7. Zekî was influenced by the Young Turk movement and became tied to the Kurdish nationalist circles in Istanbul. He started to write this book in Istanbul; however, his notes were destroyed in a fire in 1906.

Kaka'i (Ahl-e Haqq), and Yezidi. Until his expulsion from Iraq, Mustafa Barzani and his brother Ahmed relied on their Naqshbandiyya affiliations to settle local disputes. Kurdish nationalists in the Soran region turned to Qadiriyya orders to ensure their local powers. Rival Kurdish groups could have emphasized their religious identities as Naqshbandiyya or Qadiriyya shaykhs, particularly since the shaykhly establishment retained a significant role in Kurdish society. Yet the notion of an Islamic-Kurdish nationalism or a religious autonomy tied to the Kurdish tariqa brotherhoods did not become a salient part of Kurdayetî. Why did the Kurdish leaders choose not to emphasize their Muslim identities, particularly when they had fought so hard to protect the caliphate just twenty years earlier?

Barzani, Barzinji, and urban notables may have considered themselves Muslims, but they did not emphasize Islam or their particular Sufi orders because by the 1940s pan-Islamism was no longer a salient feature of the political space. Islam retained an important role in the private sphere; however, it no longer defined the boundaries of inclusion or exclusion in the official political realm. Indeed, the British elite took corrective measures against Communist influences by trying to strengthen their support among religious communities. After World War II they started visiting Sunni and Shi'a groups in the hope of awakening key spiritual leaders, such as Shaykh Muhammed al-Husain Kashif ul-Ghata in An Najaf. Iraqi officials elevated religious families in Baghdad, but by the late 1950s the sadah families and their ulema functions diminished in value.

Islam also gradually lost its role in the Arab nationalist movement, particularly as secular Arab nationalism promoted by al-Husri and Ba'thist ideology became salient. Even though qawmiyya Arab nationalists viewed Islam as an inherent part of Iraqi identity, the dominant trend was based on a secularized notion of Arab nationalism. Thus, it was not by identifying as Muslims, Naqshbandiyyas, or Qadiriyyas that Kurds could have ensured their national interests but by aligning themselves with the colonial structures that gave Kurdayetî its new meaning. Even though they considered themselves nationalists and Muslims, most Kurds chose to identify as a Jaf, a Barzani, a Barzinji, a Sorani, or a Badinani.

The political space that favored the tribal establishment, however, was ambiguous and variable, creating erratic relationships between the nationalist elite and central government. For instance, in the attempt to weaken communism after World War II, and in response to complaints from the

Iraqi regent about the dual policy for Arabs and Kurds, British officers replaced their pro-Kurdish staff with Arabist officials. This change strengthened the government's Arabizing tendency, broke ties with Kurdish elite, and antagonized relations with certain tribal leaders ("The British Embassy" 1945; "Kurdish Situation" 1945b, 1945a).

Also, Kurdish tribal communities were treated differently from one another, which exacerbated the dichotomous nature of Kurdish politics and society. Some tribes were placed under greater centralized government control, whereas others retained their administrative autonomy. For example, to limit Barzani's power the state elite refused to implement a wartime agreement that promised to provide grain and relief work to local populations in the Barzan Valley. They resettled Assyrian refugees in Barzani's territory but not in other regions. The British also offered economic concessions unequally across Kurdistan. During World War II, when tobacco prices fell by 15 percent while the cost of food commodities imported into Kurdistan increased tenfold, the government raised prices for transporting and grading tobacco. Tobacco farmers in Sulaimaniya Province continued to benefit at the former prices, but other Kurds in distant northern regions such as the Barzan Valley had to reduce their prices and sell their crops to wealthy merchants who could pay for the transportation costs.

Consequently, different relationships developed between the central government and Kurdish tribal chiefs and between Kurdish groups. In contrast to the late Ottoman period, when diverse tribal leaders revolted against Sultan Mahmut's centralizing and secularizing tendencies, the revolts during the early colonial period were limited to the Barzan region. Rival Herchi, Serchi, and Zibari tribes were more interested in preventing the growth of Barzani's power than in mobilizing as an ethnic community against the central government. Nor were other Kurdish nationalists willing to jeopardize their economic and political interests for Barzani's land problems. In fact, when Barzani revolted in 1945, some members of the KDP complained that he had become involved in an uprising "before other Kurds were ready." Instead, they sent petitions to the central government demanding a change in policy regarding the set purchase price of tobacco and the method of classification of the leaf (Jawad 1979, 171; Farouk-Sluglett and Sluglett 1990, 12; "Kurdish Situation: Notes" 1945; "The Kurdish Problem" 1946).

New types of factionalization also emerged among the budding urban classes. Although the early Kurdish revolts were defined by the segmented nature of Kurdish society, the mobilizations of the 1940s and 1950s were more complex, reflecting the political space that emerged from the state's uneven modernization and industrialization processes. The development of petroleum reserves after World War I added a new wealth to Iraqi society. From 1938 to 1959 oil revenues increased from 26 to 61 percent of total government spending. Overnight, Iraqi revenues more than tripled (Whittleton 1989, 64–66; Sader 1982; Marr 1985, 130). Agreements with the Iraqi Petroleum Company and the reconstruction of new pipelines to Haifa and Tripoli during the 1950s allowed Iraq to realize 50 percent of its own oil profits.

The resources available to state officials increased, enabling the government to implement industrialization programs that mobilized an urban elite and improved the lot of some unemployed masses. New commercial networks and national roads expanded local markets and helped integrate the Kurds into the Iraqi political economy. Educational opportunities also improved, expanding the intellectual class and adding to the secularization trends under way. Yet the state elite did not make any real effort to alter the socioeconomic structure of the country. Although the first push of modernized industry occurred in the late 1920s with Kurdish tobacco and textile refineries, industrialization efforts did not commence until after World War II, as part of the U.S.-British postwar reconstruction programs. Even then, the modernization in Iraq largely failed. Iraq's ties to the British sterling and British policies created a certain type of development that thwarted the creation of state-supported industrialization. By 1951 industry was still undeveloped, constituting only 8 percent of the gross national product (Rondot 1958).

Rather than transform political power by developing industry, state officials depended upon supportive agricultural policies to ensure power based on land. Even though the agricultural sector received only 20 percent of state investment, grain production increased 50 percent over pre-World War II levels. Similarly, although Britain's development program was targeted at peasant populations, landowners and the old social classes profited. By 1958 1 percent of landowners controlled 55 percent of all cultivable land. The remaining 45 percent of the land was divided among 64 percent of all landowners (Kingston 1996, 98–99; *National Development Plan* 1971, 114, 131). Agrarian-support policies ensured a key role for traditional elites in Kurdish politics and society. Also, although state wealth created a new urban elite and improved the lot of the unemployed masses, it did not rectify the overall situation of the urban poor. Upper classes gained access to education opportunities; however, the majority of the Iraqis were illiterate. Disastrous floods and poor harvests in the rural areas brought a fourfold increase in the Baghdad population, creating new socioeconomic crises in the country.

Dichotomous policies polarized socioeconomic groups, encouraging divisions rather than cooperation between the Kurdish town and country. The simultaneous strengthening of urban and tribal power centers reinforced fragmentations between the rising urban classes and shaykhly leaders. One of the underlying themes of Kurdish nationalist sentiment was the negative role of feudalism in the Kurdish movement. The Kurdish leftist Komala Party referred to Kurdish tribalism as the "source of all misery and bitter outcomes" (Hassanpour 1992, 114). Jaf, a tribal leader who gained from the colonial system, criticized the presence of feudalistic tendencies in Kurdish national consciousness. In his well-known call to Kurdish nationalism Jaf urged Kurds to wake up from the hands of ignorance:

> O Kurds, wake up, it is late. The sleep is detrimental to you. The history of the world gives witness to your virtue and your talent. Go, struggle, oh honorable people, alone and oppressed. Walk in haste along the road before you. Study, because the studies can defend you. . . . Since a long time this country is captive in the hands of ignorance. Today, thanks to science, the time has come for your awakening. (1969, 23)

Jaf reacted to the government's discrimination against the Kurds. He was aware of his Kurdish ethnic identity and acknowledged his sense of Kurdish nationalism. Yet his nationalist sentiment was based on the backwardness of Kurdish society and not the state's Arabizing tendencies.

Similarly, Faik Bêkas belittled Kurdish shaykhs and landowners for being "impassioned by money, placing no importance on industry, science, and knowledge . . . and having an idea of honor based on wearing the biggest turban (jamadani) to demonstrate their megalomania" (Kerîm 1986, 66). Bêkas noted that although servitude to the foreigner prevented Kurds from realizing their goal, Kurdish internal fracturing explained why they did not have a state. Qani' (Shaykh Muhammad Abdul Qader

[1899–1965]), a mullah-turned-revolutionary nationalist, criticized the traditional stratum for the undeveloped nature of Kurdish nationalism. The ultraleftist nationalist Kurdish group Komeley Azadî Jiyanawey Yekitî Kurd (KAJYK), an association for liberty, life, and Kurdish unity created by Jemal Nebez, used religion antagonistically toward the traditional Kurdish stratum.[8]

Certainly, even if the political space were more evenly developed, personal jealousies, historical cleavages, and ideological differences between rival Kurdish groups would likely have continued anyway. What is less certain, however, is whether these rivalries would have been manifested inside Kurdish nationalist organizations. That is, by recognizing tribal chiefs as the official representatives of Kurdistan instead of the urban-educated leftist leaders and permitting only one large Kurdish party (the KDP) to develop instead of diverse political organizations within a multiparty system, the state elite allowed the urban-tribal dichotomy to crystallize within a single Kurdish nationalist organization. By the late 1940s the KDP was split between traditional groups loyal to Barzani and urban, educated leftists influenced by Ibrahim Ahmed, a Baghdad-educated lawyer. With no real political alternative in Iraq, leading Kurdish leftists turned to Iranian Kurdish leftist groups rather than affiliate within the tribally dominated KDP.

Collective Identities

With Barzani evicted from the country and his influence weakened in the KDP politburo, it would seem that the Kurdish urban leftists would have used this period to mobilize on behalf of Kurdayetî. By 1955 most Shi'a Communists were imprisoned, the ICP became Arabized, relations with the Communists cooled, and the KDP was not invited to join the United National Front. Instead, Ibrahim Ahmed, who became the KDP's acting leader, moved the party ideology leftward and further away from the Kurdish nationalist traditional stratum. Rather than pronouncing racial dif-

8. Nebez was a math professor in Sulaimaniya who was influenced by Germany's National Socialist ideas. KAJYK was an extremist group and the only Kurdish party to demand the creation of a Kurdish state including four parts of Kurdistan. After the 1975 Barzani Revolution, it changed its name and orientation to the Kurdish Socialist Party, known as KSP or PASOK.

ferences with Arabs or demanding territorial separation, Kurdish leftists allied with Arab leftist nationalist groups. Most chose to be Iraqis first and
emphasize Kurdish nationalism within a democratic Iraq. Why did nontribal Kurds who considered themselves nationalists choose not to ethnicize their Kurdish national identity at this time?

By the early 1950s the political space had created neither an available
Kurdish nationalist leader, legal Kurdish political party, nor a developed
Kurdish region that had the economic resources with which to mobilize
Kurdish groups. Nuri Sa'id's imposition of martial law, Communist witch-
hunts, the destruction of Kurdish villages, and the banning of political parties, including the KDP, suppressed any nationalist programs that may have
been organized during this period. Local populations did not have the legal
political channels to express themselves, neither in the form of democratic
institutions, a civil society, permanent trade unions, nor free elections. Although the Iraqi government was based on the British parliamentary system with an elected bicameral legislature, the political apparatus remained
repressive and closed. Kurdish nationalists had little choice but to turn to
other groups that either legitimated their activities or encouraged violence.

Because Kurdish nationalist parties were banned, nontribal Kurds
turned to the ICP because it was the only political organization that recognized Kurdish ethnic identity while promoting socioeconomic reform. The
growing influence of the leftist movement, the highly organized nature of
the ICP, and the collective identities that formed between the socioeconomic classes allowed a Kurdish nationalist-Communist alliance to blos-
som. With most of the Arab cadres in prison from 1949 to 1955, the Kurds
gained prominence in the Communist Party (Batatu 1978, 650–94). In fact,
for one year, 1949–1950, the ICP was directed from Kurdistan, not Baghdad. The presence of leftist organizations also gave Kurdish groups new
channels to mobilize and encouraged the leftward shift of Kurdish nationalist sentiment. Urban and landless peasants who migrated to the cities responded to the ICP's discourse toward minority groups and the
economically oppressed. Kurdish workers in the petroleum refineries demanded workers' compensation and trade union rights. Some Kurdish
peasants even turned to the local Communist chapter and revolted against
their landowners (Batatu 1978, 533–45).

Even if Kurdish nationalist parties were legalized, it is unlikely that
urban Kurdish leftists would have pronounced an ethnicized form of Kur-

dayetî because Iraqi politics was not highly ethnicized in the colonial period. The coexistence of competing political currents, the undeveloped nature of pan-Arabism, and the rise of anti-imperialist opposition forces prevented the centralization of Arab nationalist power. Also, World War II marked a breaking point in the relations between local populations and the Hashemite-British ruling house. As the British lost their support base, particularly after their reoccupation of Iraq during World War II, the idea of taba'i nationalism came under increasing criticism by local populations. Changes in Britain's Iraqi policies and the estrangement of military officers in the government heightened tensions among local populations, the monarchy, and its Iraqi circles. Monarchists broke with the Hashemites and turned to leftist, Arab, and Kurdish nationalist ideologies.

As the anticolonial movement gained force, group loyalties shifted, bringing together Communists, Arab nationalists, and Kurds in a larger opposition movement under the banner of Iraqi independence. Although the Arab nationalist movement promoted a radical form of ethnic nationalism after 1948, its political framework focused on the anti-imperialist struggle and Palestinian liberation. Arab nationalists considered themselves anti-Communists and were hostile to Moscow's support for the United Nations' plan for Israel; however, they temporarily supported the Soviet Union and backed liberation and nonalignment movements in the developing world. The arms trade and regional defense programs established among the superpowers and their Middle Eastern clients, the 1952 Egyptian revolution, and the 1956 Suez crisis increased anti-imperialist sentiments among Iraqis, including leftist Kurds (Rondot 1958, 1959; Gallman 1964). Ba'thists, Arab workers' parties, and Communists also shared similar views on labor issues and affiliated with a left-leaning workers' association, the Federation of World Syndicates.

Shared spaces for Arabs and Kurds within the anti-imperialist movement encouraged the Kurds' collective identity as Iraqis to become salient alongside their sense of Kurdish ethnonationalism. In contrast to the Ottoman period, wherein Kurdish notables mimicked the shaykhs while supporting the Porte, by the mid-1940s Kurdish intellectuals blamed Iraq's colonial rulers alongside the tribal shaykhs as the cause of their malediction. Indeed, when making their political claims after World War II the executive committee of the Rizgari Party (a short-lived organization formed in 1945 by Kurdish Communist and leftist students in Baghdad with representatives in Kurdistan) presented a map of a greater Kurdistan similar to the one presented by Şerif Paşa at the Paris Peace Conference some twenty-five years earlier, comprising Kurdish territories in Iraq, Turkey, Syria, and Iran. Still, the Rizgari elite issued a memorandum demanding Kurdish national rights within a democratic Iraq ("Memorandum Presented" 1946; Pacha 1919).[9]

Instead of demanding Kurdish statehood during meetings with Major C. J. Edmonds, the British adviser to the Iraqi Ministry of the Interior, in 1945, Faik Bêkas wrote about the oppression of colonial rule, which after twenty-seven years had left the Kurds "captive and desperate." He asked when the old colonial regime would end and placed his sense of Kurdayetî within the larger struggle for Iraqi independence. Ensuring the relationship between Arab and Kurds in the dear Iraqi state, he wrote: "This dear Iraq, a land of flowers that has become bloody, as long as she has not obtained her rights, she will not abandon the idea of vengeance of her blood. . . . [T]he [snow] ball is rolling, the idea of colonialism is outdated, no one dances anymore with the flute and the tambourine of colonialism, the old friendship of Kurds and Arabs, of which history is a witness; let the enemies die of jealousy (of Kurdish-Arab friendship)" (Kerîm 1986, 82–83). The leftist publishers of the popular Kurdish review *Gelawêj* (1949–1956) also failed to ethnicize their nationalist writings. They could have differentiated Kurds from Arabs by focusing on genealogies and popular etymologies of Kurdish ethnic identity. Instead, most articles pronounced a cultural form of Kurdish nationalism in the form of biographies of Kurdish leaders, analyses of the Kurdish language, and leftist, liberal ideology as espoused by Jean-Jacques Rousseau, John Stuart Mill, and Mao Tse-tung (see *Gelawêj* 2 (1940): 1–7; 5 (1947): 1).

The attachment to the Iraqi-first identity was a function of the colonial context. Although the state elite failed to draw Kurds into the center, it did not ethnicize or colonize Kurdistan enough to encourage Kurdish ethnonationalism. The traditional stratum retained its role in Kurdish and state politics, urban groups were mobilized, and local populations had space to express Kurdish ethnic identity. The anti-imperialist current that became prominent emphasized wataniyya nationalism and had an inclusive element

9. The claims also underlined the plight of the Kurdish people in Turkey being "exterminated by the fascist Turkish government."

for Kurds and Arabs alike. Consequently, on the eve of the Iraqi revolution the parameters of inclusion and exclusion in the state were not clearly, ethnically defined but were based on the boundaries between the rulers and the ruled. Some nontribal Kurds joined Arab nationalists and Communists in an anti-imperialist opposition group, whereas some tribes remained loyal to the British.

Conclusions

The duration of the colonial presence and the policies that elevated the tribal and landowning establishment ensured the continuation of traditional structures in Iraqi Kurdistan. Even after Iraq gained quasi independence in 1932, landowning groups enjoyed privileged positions in socioeconomic and political affairs. Consequently, it was not the urban intellectuals but the Kurdish tribal leaders who played a leading role in Kurdish nationalist politics. Additionally, the nature of the political space did not produce a coherent modernizing Kurdish elite or the political institutions needed to support a unified Kurdish nationalist organization. The uneven development of the Iraqi state reinforced competing power centers and antagonized relations between the town and country. These strategies created two main identities in opposition in the Kurdish periphery—one among the tribes and another among nontribal groups.

3

Iraq's Transition to an
Independent Republican State

Iraq's transition from a colonial to an independent state led to new nation-state-building strategies that altered the nature of the political
space. One important change in the postrevolutionary context was in the
opportunities for Kurds to manifest their ethnic identity. With the British
gone and the monarchists out of power, taba'i nationalism lost its position
on the political agenda. Additionally, the rise of the Iraqi Ba'th Party,
Nasserism, and the United Arab Republic project supported Arab nationalist groups, which pronounced pan-Arabism as an integral aspect of Iraqi
identity. As this current gained prominence in the government the boundaries of inclusion and exclusion in the state became increasingly ethnicized,
which encouraged the ethnicization of Kurdish nationalism.

Arab-Kurdish Republic

After expelling the British from Iraq and massacring their local parti-
sans, the July 1958 revolutionaries, led by the new Iraqi president, Brigadier
General 'Abd al-Karim Qasim, and vice president, Colonel 'Abd al-Salam
Arif, started their republican experiment. An essential part of this nation-
state-building project was to consolidate power, particularly since the alliances created between opposition groups dissipated after the revolution
and tensions continued among the various Arab nationalist factions in the
government. New challenges also arose from the communist movement,
which became salient in the Arab world. Uprisings in Lebanon, the

1958 Ba'thist military coup in Syria, and Iraq's ties to communist-bloc countries gave leftist groups a key role in regional politics. What emerged were competing political projects sponsored by Arab nationalists, communists, and military and civilian cliques in the Iraqi government over the notion of *wahda,* or Arab unity. Whereas Qasim and his leftist supporters promoted an Iraqi-first identity tied to wataniyya nationalism, Arif espoused an anticommunist agenda based on qawmiyya Arab nationalism (de Sainte Marie 1960; Monterserat 1959, 24; Dann 1969, 7; Laqueur 1969; Delistre 1959, 14).

The chaotic postrevolutionary period, Arif's expulsion from Iraq, and the predominance of communist and leftist factions in the government checked the ethnicizing tendencies of qawmiyya Arab nationalists. A big part of Qasim's official state discourse and propaganda tried to create a sense of Iraqiness based on Kurdish-Arab fraternity. In their plan to liberate Arab nationalism, for example, Arab leftists wrote that "Iraq is not only an Arab state, but an Arabo-Kurdish state. . . . [T]he recognition of Kurdish nationalism by Arabs proves clearly that we are associated in the country, that we are Irakians first, and Arabs and Kurds later" (Rondot 1959).[1] The ICP circulated reprints of its manifesto dedicated to the Kurdish question, which talked about Kurdish statehood as one step toward realizing the larger goal of world socialism.

Additionally, although the Free Officers, the secret cells of army engineers in the Iraqi Army that espoused pan-Arabism, were uninterested in Kurdish equality, Qasim attempted to institutionalize the idea of Kurdish autonomy. He established a provisional constitution that recognized Iraq's binational character, which stated that the Kurd-Arab relationship was a partnership despite the larger Arab union in which Iraq was situated. Qasim also made symbolic gestures such as placing the Kurdish sun on the Iraqi national flag, adding the Kurdish dagger crossed with an Arab sword on the republic's constitution and coat of arms, welcoming Mustafa Barzani to Iraq after twelve years of exile, legalizing the KDP, and releasing Kurdish political prisoners from jail (Jawad 1979, 173–74; Farouk-Sluglett and Sluglett 1990, 80; Kimball 1972, 214; Khadduri 1951).

---

1. The complete original version was written in a 1959 ninety-two-page *Baghdad Review* brochure, *Editions of the New Culture,* called "The Kurds and the Kurdish Question," by Dr. Shabur Khobak.

2. Mullah Mustafa Barzani with Iraqi president 'Abd al-Karim Qasim, 1958. Photograph courtesy of Rafiq Studio.

Inclusionary discourses and policies gave the Kurdish nationalist leaders and organizations semilegitimacy and influence in Iraqi and Kurdish politics. They also encouraged a constructive relationship between the Kurdish nationalists and the state elite. Barzani, whose living expenses were being paid by the government, supported Qasim. Kurdish leftists turned toward Iraqi leftist parties, blurring the lines between Kurdish nationalism and Iraqi patriotism just as they had during the late colonial period.

Indeed, Kurdish nationalists thought of themselves as Kurds in Iraq and made claims for Kurdish rights. One of the unintended consequences of the state's liberal management policies was that some Kurds took advantage of their political and cultural opportunities, perhaps even more so than the Iraqi government expected. Kurds started using their media privileges to criticize the government's policies and emphasize their ethnic identity. In early 1959 numerous articles on Kurdish ethnic and linguistic unity appeared in the Kurdish press, attempting to prove that Kurds were the descendants of Aryans, Medes, or the Sassanids, and not of Arab or Persian stock. Others focused on differentiating the Kurdish language from Arabic and Persian and devising measures to preserve its distinction *(Hetaw,* no. 134–38 [1958]: 1).[2]

Still, Kurdish nationalist sentiment focused on ethnocultural rights: the official recognition of Nowruz, the Kurdish new year; inclusion of Shi'a Kurds, or Failis, within the definition of Iraqi citizenship; and language equality. Territorial separation was not part of Kurdish claims because most Kurds did not see themselves as a separate political entity from Iraq. Instead of talking about a Kurdish state or differentiating themselves as an autonomous ethnic group, the KDP, still dominated by a leftist politburo, congratulated Qasim for "bringing freedom to Kurds and Arabs in the new democratic Iraq" and for his struggle against imperialism, "a goal of Kurds and Arabs alike" *(Hetaw,* no. 127 [1959]: 1; no. 147–48 [1959]: 1–3; no. 166 [1959]: 1). With the socialist international, KDP leaders pledged to maintain international peace in line with the resolutions made at the Bandung Conference and with the Afro-Asian bloc.

Ethnicized and Militarized Political Space

Although the political space was relatively large, it was not constant over time. Alongside rising Kurdish nationalist sentiment, the reddening of Iraq worried the U.S.-led noncommunist bloc, pan-Arab military factions, and regional Arab states. During this period of cold war jostling, Arab nationalists gained support from the United States and Moscow, neither of which wanted to jeopardize its relationship with Gamal Nasser. Power struggles in the Iraqi government, fanned by regional politics and superpower rivalries, weakened the ICP, caused tensions between the Soviets and the ICP, and gave Arab nationalists a free hand against leftists. In late 1959 Arab nationalist Free Officers became active in plotting anticommunist schemes such as the abortive Mosul, or Shawaf, revolt and affiliated uprisings in Kirkuk among Turkomen, Kurds, and communists.[3]

2. The author argues that Kurds are the offspring of the Sassanids and attempts to prove their historical roots by referring to variants of the name *Kurd,* such as *Mard, Karduqh, Kermanj,* and *Scythie.*

3. The Mosul revolt, or Shawaf uprising, was conducted by Colonel Shawaf and the Free Officers and supported by Nasser as an attempt to remove Qasim and communist in-

To protect his nation-state-building project Qasim strategically withdrew from his left-leaning, pro-Kurdish agenda. Pressured by Arab nationalist and military factions he employed new strategies of assimilation and control. After 1959 Qasim imposed martial law, Arabized the names of Kurdish localities, closed down Kurdish organizations (including the KDP), arrested leading Kurdish nationalists and communists, and started bombing rural areas. He eased press restrictions on pan-Arabists and appointed the anticommunist, pro-Arab militiaman Ismail al-Arif as acting minister of guidance and minister of education. Further, Qasim started employing a qawmiyya nationalist discourse that negated Kurdish ethnic identity. After annulling the Kurdish teachers' conference in 1961 Qasim gave a speech claiming that *Kurdu* was actually a title bestowed by ancient kings of Persia upon valiant warriors whose descendants were part of the conquering Muslim army. His references to Iraq as "one nation rather than a collection of peoples" outraged Kurdish leaders (Dann 1969, 333). What followed was a series of media wars in March 1961 between the Arab-nationalist paper *Al-Thawra* and the KDP newspaper *Khebat* over the issue of ethnic minorities in Iraq (Hassanpour 1992, 119).

Arab nationalist influences restricted the political space for Kurdish groups. Although the Ba'thist military coups in Syria and Iraq fractured Arab unity and challenged the Nasserist currents, they elevated military officers and secular Arab nationalist ideology in the government. After the overthrow of Qasim and assumption of power by 'Abd al-Salam Arif on November 19, 1963, the qawmiyya Arab nationalist current strengthened, hindering any real opportunity to draw the Kurds into the state as Iraqis first. To be sure, in the attempt to consolidate his power base Arif initially reached out to Kurdish groups. Like Qasim, he recognized Kurdish ethnic identity and reaffirmed the partnership between Kurds and Arabs in Iraq as "genuine and basic facts" (Entessar 1992, 117).

Although he talked about Kurdish-Arab brotherhood, Arif stressed qawmiyya nationalism as the basis of Iraqi identity. In contrast to the 1958 constitution, which recognized a Kurdish-Arab partnership, Arif created a new provisional constitution stating that "the Iraqi people are part of the Arab people, whose aim is total Arab unity" *(Hizb al-Ba'th* 1970–1971,

---

fluences in Iraq. Some Kurdish tribes in the Turkish and Iranian border regions also supported Shawaf.

48–97). He also revived the racist ideologies of Sati' al-Husri and pan-Arabist historians at the University of Baghdad, all of whom attempted to prove the Arab origins of the Kurds (Raouf 1984, 6–8). Managing the Kurds also involved a combination of eliminationist and control strategies, including torture and internal expulsions from Kirkuk and other sensitive border regions. Regional politics influenced and was influenced by these trends. In 1963 Syrian officials implemented their Arab Belt plan to save Arabism in the Jazireh, or Syrian Kurdistan. They also sent armed forces to Iraqi Kurdistan to assist Baghdad in its war against the Kurds.

The Arabization of Iraqi identity continued under the rule of Abdul Rahman Arif, who assumed the presidency in 1966 after the unexpected death of his brother. Like his predecessors, Rahman Arif initially tried to appease the Kurds by recognizing the binational character of Iraq, promising Kurdish autonomy, and negotiating with the nationalist elite. He also appointed a civilian premier, Rahman al-Bazzaz, to settle the Kurdish question. Al-Bazzaz devised a plan that promised to create six government-chosen Kurdish governorates that would control their own areas of education, municipal affairs, social welfare, transportation, taxation, and financial administration. Al-Bazzaz's decentralization project went further than any previous effort and even gained the support of Kurdish leaders (Khadduri 1969, 268–71; Ghareeb 1981, 64). Barzani called a cease-fire and was willing to negotiate with the government.

Yet in a political space controlled by Arab nationalist factions, these efforts could not be sustained. Conservative Arab military groups pulled back the overassertive civilian premier, just as they did with Qasim in 1959. Rahman Arif retreated from authentic Kurdish autonomy, annulled the decentralization plan, and removed al-Bazzaz from office (Hewrami 1966a, 1966b). He reinforced the state's restrictive and ethnicizing political boundaries by arresting Kurdish nationalists, militarizing Kurdish regions, and prohibiting Kurdish nationalist organizations.

Fluctuating Kurdish Ethnonationalism

Inconsistent Kurdish management policies created a relationship between the Kurdish nationalist elite and central government that fluctuated between compromise and hostility. Even as the political space became increasingly restrictive and ethnicized, state officials sporadically attempted to negotiate with the Kurdish leadership. They recognized Barzani as the official Kurdish leader and the KDP as a quasi-legal Kurdish party, giving the nationalist elite and organizations semilegitimacy in Iraq and Kurdistan. Yet Baghdad's divide-and-rule tactics left large gaps between the discourse and the practice and weakened the credibility of governmental policies. In one of his initial memoranda to Rahman Arif, Barzani acknowledged that the al-Bazzaz plan did not reflect the national rights of the Kurds, but was willing to compromise with Baghdad. Several months later, however, he wrote that it was when some government officials changed the strategies by "narrowing the Kurdish issue down to the reconstruction of the north" that the policies became unacceptable ("Memorandum from Barzani" 1966). Negotiation turned to hostility once again, just as it did under the Qasim regime.

There was a difference, however, in the nature of the political space in early republican Iraq, which influenced the manifestation of Kurdayetî. As the boundaries of inclusion and exclusion became ethnicized and militarized, Kurdish nationalists started to express a highly ethnicized and violent form of Kurdish nationalism. The Kurds were able to do so because by the 1960s they had gained access to necessary mobilizing structures: a semilegitimate nationalist leader, an organized umbrella political party, clandestine networks, external support, and financial resources, all of which increased the influence and significance of their nationalist mobilizations. During this period Kurdish *peshmerga,* or militias, started blowing up pipelines and transportation routes to impede the flow of petroleum from Kirkuk ("Kurds and Syrian Arab Socialism" 1968).

Other Kurds turned to the pen and ethnicized the nationalist sentiment. Kurdish nationalism appeared in a distinctly ethnicized form in a political poem called "Kurdayetî" written by Kemal Gir, who was affiliated with Nebez's extreme Kurdish nationalist group KAJYK. In contrast to earlier writings about Kurdayetî, Gir used the idea of Kurdish nationalism as a response to the communists, establishing it as an ideology that could not be separated from humanism. The distinction was based on the belief that Kurds were ethnically different from Arabs and more nationalistic than the communists. The ethnicized notion of Kurdayetî also became popular with the left-leaning Kurdish elite. During the 1960s Jelal Talabani gave a series of lectures to Kurdish military cadres and published them under the title of

Kurdayetî. The writings of Kurdish nationalists such as Hêmin, Bekhûd, Piramêrd, and Goran were also reprinted and disseminated at this time.

In contrast to the colonial period, whereby Kurdish intellectuals criticized the backward Kurdish society and repressive colonialist regime, in the ethnicizing Iraqi state anti-Arab themes became prominent in Kurdish nationalist literature. In his well-known political poem of the period "Bukî Azadî," Qani' explained why his nation committed revolutionary acts to achieve liberty, which was "desirable like a woman with the red henna for the hands and feet":

> Although the enemy thinks that by putting me in prison I will become mute, the corner of the prison is a school for me. My thoughts on liberty in prison have increased a lot. . . . The arrests and torture and assassinations are the factor of liberty. The cannon and machine guns and handcuffs around me are like a myth; they do not exist. I am waiting for a revolution that will liberate everyone. (1979, 229)

What is significant is that the idea of liberty has changed. The stranger is no longer the imperialist but the Arab, whom Qani' blames for creating the Kurdish malediction through arrests, torture, and assassinations. The idea of the fatherland is no longer Iraq but Kurdistan. Kurdish nationalists also claimed that the Iraqi identity was formed of two parts, a Kurdish and an Arab part, and that only the Arab part formed part of the greater Arab nation.

Still, most Kurds did not seek territorial secession from the state. Even during the Kurdish war years Barzani and the KDP continued to emphasize Kurdayetî as compatible with the Iraqi identity. In his letter to the United Nations dated January 1, 1966, Barzani complained about the racist and oppressive policies of the Iraqi government against the Kurds. Instead of calling for a Kurdish state, however, he demanded the right to preserve the Kurdish language, cultural heritage, national personality, and autonomy within the boundaries of Iraq. Autonomy for Kurdistan did not mean separation or a step toward it, but having a distinct local identity within the Iraqi state (Şivan 1997, 312–13; Jawad 1981, 93).

Even though Kurdish nationalism became salient, ethnicized, and influential, it was not unified in the Kurdish periphery. Personal jealousies and the segmented Kurdish social structure kept the nationalist grouping fragmented, just as they did during the imperial and early state periods. Instead of softening or bridging these differences, Iraqi and foreign governments reinforced them by favoring particular Kurdish groups over others. For instance, the Iraqi government's socioeconomic programs gained the support of Kurdish leftist, urban, and nontribal communities seeking to modernize Kurdish society. However, the reform policies, which aimed to break the power of tribal landowners by decreasing the size of plots and their distribution within families and creating state-owned entitlements, antagonized Barzani and the Kurdish traditional stratum (Stork 1979, 42; Marr 1985, 171). From 1958 to 1971 the percentage of land owned by the top 1 percent of landowners decreased from more than 55 percent to 22 percent, further weakening the influence of the Kurdish aghas.

Foreign military support was equally divisive. During the Kurdish wars of the 1960s foreign governments channeled military aid to the Barzani faction and not the Talabani leftists. Urban leftist-nationalists then turned to the anti-imperialist and nonalignment movement, and even Baghdad, against Barzani and the KDP, at least until revolutionary Arab nationalist ideology emerged after 1967 (Adamson 1965, 208–15; O'Ballance 1973). Consequently, the Kurdish nationalist elite and organizations fragmented according to the two oppositional identities that had emerged since the early state period.

The Arab Police State

As the Kurds were feuding among themselves and against the state, new political transformations were under way. By July 1968 the Ba'thist military faction gained power over the Nasserists and civilian elites. This coup d'état, however, was more than just a regime change. Ba'thist ideology and politics fundamentally altered the political, economic, and social structure of Iraq. Ahmad Hassan al-Bakr assumed the roles of president, prime minister, and nominal head of all branches of the government and its national forces, the Revolutionary Command Council, and the regional command of the Ba'th Party. Saddam Hussein became vice president. To ward off internal challenges al-Bakr and Hussein crippled the leftists by conducting more communist purges. For the first time in Iraqi history a single party had gained majority representation in the government.

Yet Baʿthist leaders needed to strengthen their political base, particularly since power struggles continued between socialist and conservative groups. The central government was also ostracized by Iran, the Arab Gulf states, and Egypt; challenged by the unsettled Shatt al-Arab border issue; and confronted with Shiʿa uprisings in the South. The Kurdish wars, which cost $270 million annually from 1961 to 1968, were draining the state economy. Iran, Israel, and the United States recommenced their aid to the KDP, further threatening the stability of the political system *(L'Irak revolutionnaire* 1974, 107).[4] Thus, it became politically and economically expedient to seek Kurdish support.

Like previous leaders, the Baʿthists tried to appease Kurdish groups. Hussein employed a wataniyya discourse, telling Iraqis "not to consider himself as a Kurd only or an Arab only but as an Iraqi with Kurdish nationality, or an Iraqi with Arab nationality" (Hussein 1977, 15, 23). Al-Bakr created a constitutional amendment stating that the Iraqi people consist of two main nationalities: Arabs and Kurds. High-ranking Baʿthist officials such as Brigadier General Saʿdun Ghaydun started taking symbolic tours of Kurdish provinces, promising to implement development programs for their Kurdish brothers. They also continued to negotiate with the Kurdish elite, ensuring its semilegitimacy at the local and national levels. In the attempt to resolve the Kurdish problem, or give the appearance of doing so, Hussein promoted the March 11, 1970, Manifesto, or Autonomy Agreement (Hussein 1973, 9–18; Ghareeb 1981, 87–91; *La Solution* 1970). Drawn from the twelve-point al-Bazzaz plan, the agreement promised limited political self-rule and cultural expression within the given territorial boundaries of Iraq. Iraqi officials implemented parts of the plan, creating a Kurdish administration in the North and another Kurdish province called Dihuk.

As a result of these political overtures, for nearly two years relations between the Kurdish nationalists and the central government were relatively conciliatory. Yet Hussein's Kurdish management policies, like the strategies of his predecessors, were not real attempts to open the political space, but

4. After the 1968 coup the United States ended its support for the new anti-American Iraqi government. In return for fourteen million dollars, Barzani was supposed to help overthrow the Baʿthists, refrain from harming Iran or supporting the Iranian KDP, and have no relations with the communists.

rather time-gaining tactics to help consolidate political power. When it was no longer necessary to appease the Kurds, particularly after Iraq had reaffirmed relations with the ICP, the Soviet Union, and conservative Arab states, Hussein stopped implementing key parts of the Autonomy Agreement. He further restricted the political space by centralizing, Sunni Arabizing, Ba'thicizing, and militarizing the state.

Transformations in the political economy, particularly the "petrolization" of Iraq, gave the central government a new type of power never before realized in Iraqi history. After the 1971 OPEC accords, the full nationalization of Iraqi oil in 1972, and the 1973 oil crisis, Iraqi oil revenues quadrupled, giving the government windfall profits, greater internal sovereignty, and unrestrained power over local populations. These developments altered the notion of Iraqi identity, the nature of the state's incentive structures, and the strategies for managing Kurdish groups. Government power was transformed into state repression. The Ba'thist military forces, which became an ideological army (Jaysh al-'Aqa'idi), created an environment of fear throughout the country (Abbas 1989, 217; Farouk-Sluglett and Sluglett 1987; al-Khalil 1989). They destroyed Kurdish villages and forced Kurdish families to resettle in alternative governorates, southern desert areas or collective towns *(mujamma'ât)*, where they had greater control of their daily lives. Iraqi leaders also violently quelled Shi'a uprisings in the South, commenced a scorched-earth policy in Kurdistan, and conducted more communist witch-hunts.

As the Iraqi state petrolized, the political elite started to ethnicize essential oil-rich Kurdish territories. Iraqi officials constructed a series of homes called the Arab Circle around the Kurdish quarters in Kirkuk, deported Kurds from their homes, granted land deeds only to Arabs, and gave Kurdish localities Arabic names (Raouf 1984, 143; Hakim 1992, 140).[5] Shifts in international politics also encouraged the militarization of the Iraqi state. During this period the Iraqi Army grew from nearly 200,000 to more than 1 million, giving the Iraqi elite new means to control the Kurds with the use of force. In 1987 and 1988 Hassan al-Majid orchestrated the Anfal campaign, which chemically attacked and destroyed more than 4,000 Kurdish

5. Interview with the representative of New Kirkuk governorate in Sulaimaniya, Iraqi Kurdistan, Jan. 7, 1997.

villages, killing about 150,000 people and leaving more than 180,000 missing (Karabell 1995; al-Hafeed 1993; Middle East Watch 1993).

Certainly, the repressive Arab state elite tried to give the impression of political tolerance. While al-Majid was gassing the Kurds in the towns and countryside the directorate of the Iraqi Ministry of Culture and Information was promoting Kurdish culture in the cities. In 1988 it sponsored a two-day seminar on the famous Kurdish poet Mewlewî, in Sulaimaniya, and then published the papers in a book called *Mihrecanî Mewlewî* (Mewlewî's festival) (Kerîm 1998, 67). The Iraqi Ministry of Education published journals, books, and texts in the Kurdish language, including one used for the Kurds' mandated courses in the modern history of the Arab world, *Mêjûy nwê w hawçerkhî niştîmânî 'Ereb*.

Yet these efforts did not alter the exclusionary and ethnicized notion of Iraqi identity. In fact, they reinforced it. The gap between the discourse and reality had become so large that government efforts to create a sense of Iraqiness had lost all meaning and credibility. Al-Bakr and Hussein talked about Kurd-Arab unity; however, the Ba'thists claimed they would "assimilate Kurds into a crucible of the Arab nation and if necessary, by force" (Hakim 1992, 140). Government-printed Kurdish-language texts talked about Arab history, yet they neglected the distinct Kurdish identity in the Iraqi state. By the late 1970s the political space had changed so fundamentally that to be an Iraqi citizen was to be a Ba'th Party member. Hussein introduced new texts and curricula into schools and universities based on a Ba'thist interpretation of Iraqi identity, including the standard texts required for graduation, *Fikr al-qa'id fi al-tarikh* (The thought of the leader on history) and *Al-Minhaj al-thaqafi al-markazi* (The methodology of the central culture).[6]

Even the use of Iraqi-first discourse had changed its meaning so that to be wataniyya was to be qawmiyya. For example, Hussein's multibillion-dollar rewriting of history project *(mashru' i'adat kitabat al-tarikh)* and the Mosul spring festivals highlighted the Mesopotamian role in Iraqi history and called for ethnic minorities to view themselves as Iraqis first. However,

---

6. For students of political science, there was the *al-thiqafa al-qawmiyya* (The nationalist culture). Secondary school students used the modified version, *al-Tarikh al-thaqafi* (History of the culture).

by using Arab metaphors they Arabized Mesopotamian culture and negated the Kurds' Median ancestry as an integral part of Iraqi local identity (Davis 1991, 1–35; Baram 1991, 1983b, 1983a, 429). The Ba'thists also popularized a new myth claiming that the Kurdish new year, Nowruz, was attributable not to the Kurdish hero Kawa, but to an Arab called Jaber Enscira, a compatriot of the Prophet.

Suppressed Ethnonationalism and Economic Opportunism

Contradictory, racist, and militant policies turned the relatively compromising relationship between Kurdish nationalists and the state in the period 1970–1972 into hostility once again. Although the Kurds initially accepted the March 11, 1970, Autonomy Agreement, they mocked the government's efforts to increase Kurdish political representation as a "bizarre action that displayed a few characters whose great great grandparents may have been Kurdish ministers . . . but who are not even remotely connected with the Kurdish movement" ("Two Years After" 1968). The Kurdish elite ultimately did not respond to Hussein's appeals because the gap between the discourse and practice had become too large and the political space too variable to appear real. Government policies had become so unbelievable that although Hussein referred to the Autonomy Agreement as the most important accord for Iraqi-Kurd relations and created the first Kurdish legislative assembly in Iraqi Kurdistan, both Barzani and Talabani refused to participate in the state's United Popular Front (al-Jabha al-Wataniyya), the political grouping directed by the Ba'th Party in which other Iraqi parties participated.[7]

As the state elite centralized the political system and Arabized Kurdish lands, the threshold of Kurdish nationalism changed. Kurdayetî was no longer just about cultural and political rights, but was now centered on the authentic ethnic origins of Kirkuk. Petroleum played a key role in this debate. Although Hussein demanded Arab oil for Arabs, Kurds were claiming Kurdish crude for Kurdistan. Despite their personal differences Barzani and Talabani refused to negotiate over Kirkuk and essential Kurdish lands. The Kurdish elite's refusal to compromise with the central government is

---

7. Hussein declared the Autonomy Law of Iraqi Kurdistan on Mar. 11, 1974, and created the Legislative Council for the Autonomous Region.

noteworthy because it highlights the sense of resistance that had become a central element in Kurdish nationalist sentiment. The Kurdish peshmerga, a symbol of this resistance, was now an integral part of Kurdayetî in the cities and countryside, among tribal and urban educated populations. Yet the highly ethnicized, salient, and violent sense of Kurdayetî did not remain that way. In fact, after the collapse of the Barzani revolution in 1975 the Kurdish nationalist movement seems to have stopped. What explains the fifteen-year period of quiet in Kurdish nationalism, particularly after the political space had become so highly ethnicized and militarized? Why did some Kurds turn toward Baghdad even when militant Iraqi Ba'thism peaked after 1975?

The restrictive political space closed all legal opportunities for Kurds to organize as a nationalist group. Opposition groups were banned and basic freedoms denied. The exodus of more than 250,000 Kurds to Iran after the 1975 revolt created a political void in Iraqi Kurdistan. Nor did the Kurds have alternative political parties to mobilize as a nationalist group. The purging of the remaining communist cadres in the late 1970s, the weakening of cold war politics, and the friction that developed between the Kurds and communists removed the ICP as a viable political alternative for Kurdish nationalists. In 1980 the KDP tried to regroup with the ICP and other Iraqi Kurdish parties under the National Iraqi Democratic Front; however, the front had neither the influence nor the representation across Kurdish society to play a viable role in Kurdish nationalist politics. Without regional backing and open organizational support it was difficult, if not impossible, to resume Kurdish mobilizations inside Iraq. Consequently, Kurdish politics went underground in the border mountain areas or outside the country, where more than ten small political parties formed and fractured.

Although the political space became militarily and ethnically repressive, it did not close completely in all parts of the Kurdish North. Alongside coercion and control the Iraqi elite implemented normative and utilitarian means of compliance toward certain Kurdish populations. It protected residual tribal chiefs and assured aghas of their landowning privileges in Kurdistan, stifling Kurdish nationalist potential in the countryside. As part of their wartime strategies the Ba'thists offered special salaries and incentives to certain tribes and created a network of various *jash* (that is, traitors) among the Kurds, who found favor in the political center. Nor did the Iraqi elite make any serious attempt to modernize Kurdistan. Although the

Ba'thists secularized and semi-industrialized the state, their reforms favored the central and southern Sunni Arab regions. Except for a few factories, mining, and dam projects, Iraqi Kurdistan remained nonindustrialized and tied to traditional socioeconomic and political structures. Pockets of tribal chiefs and aghas remained partially influential, challenging the influential nationalist elite and its agenda across Kurdish society.

Moreover, as the state elite petrolized the economy it turned to expenditure mechanisms that made its policies more politically palatable to local populations (Beblawi and Luciani 1987, 51–52; Whittleton 1989; Eftekhari 1987; Gause 1994). It placated Kurds by providing them with free monthly food rations, health care, and educational programs. In some regions Hussein distributed color-television sets to Kurdish civil servants, casino owners, and Ba'th Party members (Zimmerman 1994).[8] The expansion of commercial opportunities allowed merchants, contractors, trading companies, and local businesses to prosper. With oil rents and Western assistance the Iraqi social welfare state devised five-year plans that included radical agrarian reform, housing construction, and industrialization. Under a five-year program aimed at explosive development, state investment increased from approximately 72 million Iraqi dinars in 1968–1969 to 1.2 billion dinars in 1975–1976 *(National Development Plan* 1971). Many Kurds integrated into Iraqi society, taking advantage of the educational, commercial, and cultural opportunities that were tied to the country's new oil wealth.

Ba'thist policies altered Kurdish society and the economy and helped reshape Kurdish political identities. Given the particular nature of its capital-intensive chemical industries, Iraq provided high value-added intermediate goods that depended on imported machinery and multinational labor forces for work, rather than local populations. Instead of relying on local Kurdish agricultural production to meet increasing consumption patterns, the state elite turned to food imports, which they paid for with their petro-

8. In 1979 the Iraqi state elite gave some thirty thousand television sets to Iraqi Kurdish refugees from Iran. The populations resettled after the 1988 Anfal campaign received no such state assistance. According to my Kurdish informants, the central government's monthly food allocations accounted for nearly 75 percent of a family's monthly living expenses.

leum rents.[9] Iraq's industrialization strategy, alongside declining investment in the agricultural sector, added more cadres to the urban unemployed (Amara 1987; Stork 1979, 30). Disfranchised rural communities and war-effected populations migrated to or were forcibly resettled in cities, which increased urbanization trends. Rural areas were vacated, whereas Kurdish cities quadrupled in population (Sherzad 1991).

The displacement of Kurds from their lands broke a key sector of the Kurdish economy, destroyed traditional living patterns, and increased the Kurds' dependence on the state. Rather than integrate into the industrial sector, increase their agricultural production, or become Ba'th Party members, most Kurds in the towns and cities lived off the government. What emerged was a rent-seeking mentality among Kurdish communities. That is to say, income generation in Iraqi Kurdistan was not viewed as part of a process integrated in a chain, but rather as an isolated activity that brought windfalls quickly. By not having to pay taxes or participate in political affairs Iraqi Kurds became their own class of rentiers because they simply collected profits from the state's oil rents (Abdel-Fadil 1987). Nowhere was the rent-seeking mentality more evident than in Iraqi Kurdistan, where the big-daddy syndrome became salient. Dependent on the state's social welfare handouts, Iraqi Kurds changed from a society of producers to one of consumers.

Given the highly fluid context of the political space, it was often economically necessary or politically advantageous to accept the state's handouts. In Iraqi Kurdistan there was an absence of systematic patterns of economic development and political stability. Towns that grew were destroyed. Families that were displaced were resettled elsewhere. Villages that were depopulated were reconstructed, destroyed, and reconstructed again. Refugee groups that were once resettled became internally displaced or part of the growing diasporic communities. The very turbulence of Iraqi Kurdish politics and society, the underdeveloped nature of the Kurdish economy, and the transience of Kurdish populations prevented any type of political institutionalization from evolving in the North. Although Kurds may have been conscious of their ethnonationalist identity, they turned to

9. Rentier states are based on outside sources of revenue and differ from nonrentier states whose income depends on domestic taxation.

the central government as a way of seeking stability and economic opportunities, and not necessarily because they viewed themselves as Iraqis first.

The Autonomous North: Expanding Political Spaces

Having failed to create a sense of Iraqiness among the Kurds, the state elite turned to more creative efforts to draw Kurdish communities into the political center. After the 1991 Gulf War Hussein moved away from secular Ba'thist ideology and tried to Islamize the Iraqi identity. In his propaganda campaign he portrayed himself as a devout Muslim, placed the phrase "Allahu Akbar" (God is great) on the Iraqi flag, and reframed the Kurdish-Arab partnership as a Muslim fellowship necessary to combat U.S. and Zionist forces. Yet these appeals, as well as Hussein's calls to his "dear Kurdistan," lost all credibility as the government continued to bomb Kurdish regions, burn Kurdish farmlands, attack and assassinate relief workers, cut off electricity to Kurdish regions, impose blockades between northern and southern Iraq, and sponsor radical Islamic groups to destabilize the North.

Iraqi Kurds had other reasons to avoid Saddam. After the Gulf War they gained access to new types of opportunity structures, such as an autonomous safe haven protected by coalition forces and the democratically elected Kurdish Regional Government (KRG), which reinforced the distinct Kurdish ethnonational identity apart from the rest of Iraq. In their protected northern enclave the Kurds developed new forms of political organization within an emergent civil society. Nongovernmental associations, women's organizations, and youth groups started to voice their opinions freely in the media. Local political powers developed in municipalities, each with its own layer of civil servants, student unions, and private-sector entrepreneurs. Political boundaries in the autonomous North also became more inclusive of multiethnic and religious groupings, which created a more tolerant form of Kurdayetî, at least at the institutional level. After passing laws requiring the provision of education for minorities in their own language, in March 1993 the KRG created the Directorate of Syriac Education responsible for translating and printing school textbooks in the Syriac language. By the time the fourth ministerial cabinet took power in 2000, its representation included members of the region's diverse ethnic and religious communities: Turkoman, Yezidi, Assyrio-Chaldeans, and the moderate Islamic Movement.

The expanding political space diversified Kurdish nationalist organizations by giving local populations greater alternatives to express their national sentiment outside the two main Kurdish nationalist parties. Various leftist parties, including the Kurdish Communist Party and the Toilers of Kurdistan, joined the KDP and PUK in a budding multiparty political system. Further, although Iraqi Kurds turned away from Hussein's Islamic appeals, after 1990 some started expressing Kurdayetî as an integral part of their Sunni Muslim identity. Islamic parties such as the Islamic Movement of Kurdistan, Komal Islam, and the United Islamic Party became part of Kurdish nationalist politics, calling for an Islamic Kurdistan. Kurdish Islamic groups gained influence at the local level, sponsoring new mosques, Islamic radio and television stations, and Islamic clothing stores in Kurdish cities and towns. Supported by regional networks, some enticed physicians in outlying border regions to leave their low-paid positions in KRG clinics by offering them up to two thousand dollars monthly to work in Islamic-affiliated hospitals.

Political and cultural opportunities for Kurds opened further after the April 2003 Anglo-American intervention and overthrow of Saddam Hussein and the Ba'thist regime. For the first time in the history of the Iraqi republic the Kurds could mobilize as an ethnic group throughout the country without fear of repression from Baghdad. In fact, they were encouraged to do so. As in previous postregime change periods, the transitional ruling elite tried to consolidate power by making overtures toward the Kurds. U.S. officials from the Coalition Provisional Authority and Iraqi representatives of the Governing Council recognized the distinct Kurdish ethnic identity, offered Kurds high-level positions in the provisional government, and promised to institutionalize Kurdish autonomy in a federal Iraq.

Large political space encouraged cooperation between Kurdish nationalists and the state elite, just like it did in the early colonial period. Instead of configuring their nationalist agenda in opposition to Baghdad, Kurdish officials compromised their nationalist goals by engaging in Iraqi state-building politics in the South. Some left their positions in the KRG and assumed new roles as representatives in the Iraqi provisional government, dividing allegiances between the KRG in Arbil (Hawlêr) and Sulaimaniya and the Governing Council in Baghdad. Former KRG minister of reconstruction and development Nesreen Berweri became minister of public works in Baghdad. Hoshyr Zibari, a high-ranking member of the KDP politburo, became the Iraqi foreign minister. Jelal Talabani, leader of the Kurdish national party, the PUK, became the first Kurdish president of the Iraqi government. The Kurdish nationalist elite also made temporary concessions on Kirkuk while gaining regional autonomy in the Transitional Administrative Law (TAL) for the State of Iraq, signed on March 8, 2004.

This accommodating form of Kurdish nationalism, however, may be limited in time. Although Kurdish leaders attempt to negotiate Kurdayetî inside Iraq, the political space after 1992 has encouraged differentiation, not unification, between Kurds and Arabs. Third-party interventions may have emphasized the territorial integrity of Iraq, yet the U.S.-led effort to prevent the "Saddamization" of Kurdistan has reinforced the notion of an Iraqi Kurdish identity separate from Baghdad. Additionally, in contrast to the colonial period, whereby the presence of an occupying power brought Kurds and Arabs together in an anti-imperialist alliance, in post-Saddam Iraq it has exacerbated ethnic and religious cleavages. Kurds remain U.S. allies while other Iraqi populations, mainly in the Sunni Arab triangle and parts of the South, revolt violently against foreign presence on Iraqi territory. Further, even though the post-Saddam context has provided Kurds with new options to express their ethnonational identity, the ethnicized political boundaries in Iraq have not fundamentally changed. The coexistence of different political systems, economies, security contexts, ethnicities, and languages has reinforced the sense of a distinct Kurdish national identity separate from Baghdad. Since 1991 Iraqi Kurdistan has assumed a territorial identity apart from central and southern Iraq.

Indeed, the Iraqi Governing Council and its successor interim government are attempting to "de-Ba'thicize" Iraq and create an Iraqi identity based on an ethnically inclusive notion of Iraqiness inside a federal state. School texts and Iraqi histories are being rewritten to include the histories of Kurds and other ethnic minorities in the state. Still, after more than eighty years of Arabization and Ba'thist repression, Iraqi Kurds are not so willing or able to forget their past. Historical memories and political realities remain highly salient in Iraqi Kurdistan. Since 1992 local populations have come to depend upon the KRG as a viable government representing Kurdish interests, and not the government in Baghdad. Moreover, the liberation of Kirkuk has encouraged thousands of Kurdish families to return to their original lands, which has led to new territorial claims among Kurdish, Arab, and Turkoman populations and the reinforcement of the Kurdish ethnic claims to the city and its oil revenues. Differences over the nature of the Iraqi constitution and Kurdish political autonomy and the strengthening of radical Shi'a influences in the South have further diminished the chances of accommodating Kurdayetî in a future Iraqi state.

The highly salient sense of Kurdayetî also has important challenges ahead. Regional pressures continue to constrain Kurdish nationalism in the autonomous region. Radical nationalist cross-border groups, including the Kurdish Worker's Party (Partiya Karkarên Kurdistanê [PKK], renamed Kongra-gel in December 2003), radical Islamic parties, and Iranian Kurdish opposition groups use Iraqi Kurdistan as a staging ground for their own political projects, stirring rivalries between Kurdish parties. The Turkish government, which until April 2003 controlled the sole legal border of entry for humanitarian relief and commercial goods into Iraqi Kurdistan, sporadically closes the border to relief supplies and bombs Iraqi Kurdish villages in search of members of Kongra-gel. It also impedes journalists, relief workers, researchers, and civilians from entering and exiting Iraqi Kurdistan.

Nor do Iraqi Kurds have unconditional backing from the United States, the United Nations, or the central government in Baghdad. The TAL may have given the Kurdish regions veto power over federal laws and established the groundwork for real political autonomy, but it was not included in UN Resolution 1574, adopted in June 2004, to establish an interim Iraqi constitution. Iraqi Kurdistan has been accorded political autonomy, yet Kurds have no assurance that the future Iraqi government will respect the principles of federalism at a national level. Until the KRG receives de jure status, most international political, economic, and security programs will be negotiated through an Iraqi government in Baghdad, not the KRG in Arbil (Hawlêr). Additionally, the failure of the transitional Iraqi governments and U.S. officials to significantly change the political space in Baghdad, despite the overthrow of Saddam Hussein, makes the federalist solution fragile and uncertain. If federalism fails and right-wing Arab nationalist or Islamic extremist factions gain power, accommodating Kurdish nationalism is likely to turn antagonistic again.

The future of Kurdayetî is further challenged within the Kurdish regions. The political and economic development of Kurdistan has not been accompanied by social restructuring at the local levels. In fact, the very nature of the political space in the autonomous North has reinforced the two oppositional identities that have evolved since the state-formation period, which limits the extent to which Kurdish nationalism can flourish within an open, multiparty political system. For instance, Kurdish election laws and the 1992 power-sharing arrangements created a strong two-party government favoring the KDP and the PUK (Natali 1999; Stansfield 2003, 201).[10] Even though the Kurdish elite attempted to remove tribal chiefs from the government, they eventually offered them posts on an ad hoc basis, resulting in a new form of client state among the KDP, PUK, and certain powerful tribes.[11] Also, although the KRG was designed as a decentralized system, final decision making remains highly centralized between the two main parties, reinforcing Barzani's and Talabani's positions as joint nationalist elites. The bipartisan nature of Kurdish nationalism was further reinforced in 1994, when the KRG dissipated into two separate administrations run by the KDP and PUK in Arbil (Hawlêr) and Sulaimaniya, respectively. The Kurdish parties may have unified under a single Kurdish ticket for the January 2005 Iraqi elections and give overwhelming support to Talabani as Iraqi president, but underlying power-sharing and leadership issues remain.

Even Islamic tendencies have failed to seriously weaken the influence of the traditional power structure in Kurdistan. Although they have co-opted some conservative Kurdish communities, Islamic parties did not attain seats in the 1992 parliamentary elections. In the 2001 municipality elections in Dihuk and Arbil (Hawlêr), the first in more than sixty years, the Islamic Union came in second place with less than 20 percent of the vote. However, Barzani's KDP gained an overwhelming 81 percent and 75.6 percent of the total votes, respectively. Islamic influences have had even less success in the Sulaimaniya municipality elections, where the PUK gained the overwhelming majority, leaving the Islamic Party with less than 5 percent of the vote. In fact, in trying to protect the secular nature of Kurdayeti, most urban educated Kurdish nationalists in the Sulaimaniya region expressed

---

10. Interview with Dr. Nuri Talabani, London, Mar. 13, 1995. Independent candidates and more than forty parties participated in the 1992 elections; however, they did not obtain more than 5 percent of the total vote.

11. Interview with Adil Beg, leader of the Barwari region, at his home in Barwari, Iraqi Kurdistan, July 31, 1992. After the elections tribal leaders also wanted to form a tribal advisory committee similar to the British House of Lords, but the KRG rejected the idea. Tribal groups then created the Kurdistan Tribal Union, located in Shaqlawa.

outright hostility to Islam in Kurdish nationalist politics. Some local populations went so far as to criticize Talabani during his attempts to make concessions with local Islamic leaders as a way of diminishing tensions with Iran.

Conclusions

During the 1960s the political space became more clearly ethnicized, centralized, and militant, which led to a more ethnicized and violent nationalist sentiment across Kurdish society. State-building strategies in republican Iraq, like those practices in the colonial period, created a particular type of political space that was highly variable over time and supported traditional power structures in Kurdish society alongside the rising urban nationalist elite. What resulted was an organized, fractured, ethnicized nationalist movement that fluctuated between compromise and violence. Despite the demise of Saddam Hussein, creation of the autonomous Kurdish Regional Government, and a new government in Baghdad, the character of Kurdish nationalism is still largely shaped by the two identities in opposition and their political organizations that have crystallized since the state-formation period.

4

Turkey's Transition to an
Independent Republican State

Although Iraq transitioned to a colonial state, the Turkish provinces of the Ottoman Empire attained independence as early as 1923. The absence of colonial rule enabled the Turkish elite to engage directly in their nation-state-building project from the outset, allowing Turkish nationalist institutions to take root. Like British and Iraqi officials, Turkish leaders altered the traditional Ottoman system by secularizing the notion of citizenship and modernizing the state. Yet early republican Turkey's centralized, secularized, and highly ethnicized political boundaries made it clear that Kurds would have no opportunities to express themselves as an ethnic community. Whereas the political space in Iraq was relatively large for Kurds, for Kurds in Turkey it became virtually nonexistent.

Transition Period

Like British colonial officers, the new Turkish elite inherited a territory marked by postwar havoc and political uncertainty. The economy was devastated, refugee populations were swelling, the Mosul issue was unsettled, Kurdish tribes were destabilizing the border region, and the French were conducting pro-Armenian campaigns in Cilicia (Zürcher 1991, 13–15; Mardin 1973, 181; Kerr 1973, 252; Özok 1990, 67–68; "Lettre de Seyid Ahmed" 1919, 7; "Telegramme Confidentielle" 1919, no. 1317; "La Question" 1921, 17–22). Tensions lingered between Christians and Muslims, particularly after the Armenian genocide in 1915. Further, despite backing of key military officers, Mustafa Kemal, leader of the Turkish independence movement, lacked support from local populations and external powers. The Entente powers' antiunionist measures had weakened clandestine wartime networks such as the Karakol (the Guard), whose aim was to protect the Muslim community against the Entente powers and Christian threats.

In this unstable context Kemal made special efforts to appease the Kurds. They now represented about 20 percent of the population, while Kurdish territories made up 30 percent of the country's total land mass and 32 percent of agricultural lands, with the greatest concentration in Diyarbakir Province. To gain support of strategically important Kurdish regions and communities tied to Ottoman structures, Kemal promoted Sunni Islam as a key identity marker in the future Turkish state. To be sure, during the early debates in the national assembly about the official Turkish identity, the Turkish elite talked about Hanafi Turkish-speaking Muslims as being real Turkish citizens, despite the fact that the overwhelming majority of Kurds were (and still are) Shafi Muslims who did not speak Turkish (Kirkisci and Winrow 1998, 96). Instead of emphasizing these distinctions, Kemal advanced the idea of a unified Sunni Muslim community in which the Kurds and Turks were both a part. Promising to protect traditional Ottoman structures, Kemal stated, "[A]s a co-religionist, I pray you must not heed the strife stirred amongst us and which has separated us. . . . [W]e want to save the country and Islamism from the hands of the enemies who think that our country is a digestible mouthful" (Şimşir 1973, 215).

To make his claims appear credible Kemal dressed in religious attire alongside key ulema leaders and sent the photographs to Kurdish tribal chiefs. He offered gifts to Kurds and wrote letters promising to save the caliphate from the West (Sayan 1987, 10; Silopi 1969, 51; Beşikçi 1979, 270). Relying on the former Ottoman Hamidiyan forces, Kemal created an Islamic militia of some Kurdish and Arab tribes, called the Kuvay-i Islamiye, which he paid to fight British forces. He also ensured the traditional religious stratum a leading role in political affairs. Among the fifty-six delegates at the Erzurum and Sivas congresses held from July to October 1919, twenty-one were affiliated with the medreses. Twenty-five percent of the membership of the first national assembly represented the Islamic establishment.

In contrast to Ottoman officials, Kemal also appealed to Muslim minorities, including Alevi communities. In his discourses he addressed Alevis as the true sons of the Anatolian land, leading many to believe they would have a special place in a secular Turkish state. When visiting Alevi villages with the prominent Bektaşi leader Cemalettin Çelebi Efendi, Kemal did not talk about the caliphate but rather an Alevi Bektaşi doctrine as Turkey's official religion (Şener 1994, 11–16, 35–53; Poujol 1999, 55). Kemal appointed a small number of Alevis to the first national assembly, gave them local political positions, and employed their leaders to garner Alevi support in the Kurdish regions. In response to the Koçgiri rebellion, which was led by Alevi tribes and Kurdish nationalists, Kemal appointed the Alevi Kurdish leader Alişan Beg as governor of the Dersim Koçgiri region.[1] He then sent various officials to the region, attempting to buy off Koçgiri tribes with presents and financial incentives (Şener 1994, 11–16).

Additionally, the political space in the transitioning Turkish state was relatively large for Kurds as an ethnic group, just as it was in the late imperial period and early Iraq. As part of the Anatolian independence campaign Kemal talked about the legitimacy of Turkish-Kurdish sisterhood and a federation of Kurdish states backed by Turkey. Instead of using Turanian histories he pronounced myths about the Ottoman heritage that defined the Kurds as an integral part of the modern Turkish state. To make his discourses appear real Kemal brought two Kurdish boys dressed as Kurdish soldiers with him during his tours of the Kurdish regions (Sayan 1987, 51). The idea that Kurdistan and the Kurds were integral to Turkey was reaffirmed at the Turkish-Kurdish congress in Diyarbakir, which promised Kurdish autonomy in return for the Kurds' military support. Similarly, at the Lausanne conference (November 1922 to July 1923, organized to decide a peaceful settlement of former Ottoman territories), İsmet İnönü may have told Lord George Nathaniel Curzon, the British delegate, that the Kurds were of Turanian origins; however, he affirmed a place for the Kurds in the future Turkish state. Arguing that Turks and Kurds have al-

1. After 1914 Alevi leaders Alişer and Seyit Reza abolished the Turkish administration and established a Kurdish government in Dersim. Although the government was short-lived, Dersim remained relatively autonomous from the central government since that period. Dersim-state relations became antagonistic when Atatürk incorporated Dersim into the Turkish bureaucracy in 1920. The state assumed greater control over Dersim in January 1936 by disconnecting it administratively from Erzurum and Elaziz (Beşikçi 1990, 14–17).

ways lived together, he promised, "[T]he government of the grand national assembly of Turkey is the government of the Kurds as much as it is that of the Turks because the true and legitimate representative of the Kurds sits at the national assembly" (McDowall 1997, 190).

Kemal even attempted to institutionalize Turkish-Kurdish equality in the new state, just like the British did in early Iraq. He created the first provisional constitution of the national assembly on April 23, 1920, that claimed the Turkish republic consisted of two groups, Turks and Kurds. Article 8 affirmed the cultural sense of Turkish nationalism: the people of Turkey, regardless of their religion or race, were, in terms of citizenship, to be Turkish (Kirkisci and Winrow 1998, 90–94; Olson 1989, 166–68). On February 10, 1922, the Grand National Assembly created a draft law for proposed autonomy in Kurdistan. Referring to the Kurds as a nation, the law offered the Kurds the right to establish an autonomous administration that recognized Kurdish national customs.[2]

Indeed, provisions for Kurdish autonomy were limited. After 1919 Kemal started to emphasize Turkish identity as a key element in the future state, arrested Kurdish nationalists, and closed Kurdish clubs in Diyarbakir. Although he promised Kurdish language instruction, Kemal required Kurds to speak Turkish in official political and administrative affairs. At the Izmir Economic Conference (held February 17 to March 4, 1923, to define the economic orientations of the new Turkish state), he made no mention of the Kurds (Ali 1981, 107). Still, the political space during the transition period gave the Kurds some rights to participate in the political realm. Twenty-nine Kurdish deputies were representatives in the national assembly from 1908 to 1920, including Shaykh Abdel Qader, who was an appointed senator (Kutlay 2004, 1–3).

Segmented Nationalism

As in the late imperial and Iraqi transition periods, the political space in the transitioning Turkish state was relatively large. Kurdish communities could express their ethnic identity, participate in political affairs, speak their language, and assemble as a national group. Former political associations

2. The proposal limited the boundaries of Kurdistan to the provinces of Van, Bitlis, Diyarbakir, and Dersim.

were still functioning in Istanbul, including the reinvigorated Friends of the British society and the Committee for the Independence of Kurdistan. These organizations, as well as Wilsonian ideas of self-determination, gave Kurds resources and support to manifest their national identity. Major Noel was also active in Kurdistan in Turkey, promising the Kurds political autonomy under British protection.

Like their Iraqi Kurdish counterparts, some Kurds took advantage of the large political space by emphasizing Kurdish nationalism. They created organizations in the cities, including Azadi (Freedom) and the Kurdish Society of Diyarbakir, calling for different forms of autonomy, Kurdish rights, or independence ("Comitey Estiqlali Kurdistan" 1966). Nationalist organizations and access to high-level foreign officials gave the Kurdish elite semilegitimacy and increased the significance of Kurdayetî, just as it did in the new Iraqi state. Bedir Khan, a representative in the Ottoman Parliament and secretary of the Committee for the Independence of Kurdistan, traveled with British officials throughout Kurdistan, making nationalist claims as part of Britain's anti-Turk campaign. Emphasizing his distinct Kurdish identity, he argued, "[W]e have nothing in common with the Turks. . . . [T]hey are of the Turanian race, we are of the Aryan race. Our language is different. The Turks speak a language composed of Chagatay, Arab, and Persian, while Kurds speak their own language with its origins from Pahlavi" ("Lettre de Bedr Khan" 1920). Others, such as Ekrem Cemilpaşa, a member of one of the prominent nationalist families of Diyarbakir, also traveled and negotiated with foreign officials throughout the Kurdish regions, calling for an independent Kurdistan.

Despite its significance, the emergent sense of Kurdayetî was not highly representative or influential across Kurdish society. As in Iraqi Kurdistan, early-twentieth-century Kurdistan in Turkey was still a stratified, heterogenous, rural society whereby status was based on distinctions between tribal and nontribal communities and Muslims and non-Muslims. Even with the void left in the Kurdish economy after the Armenian genocide, the Kurds did not become prominent in the commercial sector. Most were landowners or tillers of the land. Tribal chiefs, aghas, and shaykhs were most influential in Kurdish politics and society, not urbanized intellectuals in the cities.

Instead of bridging internal dichotomies the Turkish elite allowed them to continue, hindering Kurdish nationalist potential. Like British officials,

Mustafa Kemal made no effort to alter the traditional system of local administration or to develop transportation or communication networks that could have weakened the saliency of provincial identities. Although external boundaries altered after 1918 and refugee movements brought demographic transformations, internal borders based on the Ottoman vilayet system remained relatively intact. Kurdish Alevi communities from Maraş and Sivas, for instance, maintained closer ties with secular Turkish and Armenian communities than they did with Sunni Kurds from the southeastern towns of Diyarbakir or Batman. Kurds from Mardin, Siirt, Cizre, and Nusaybin were commercially and often politically closer to Arabs and Kurds in the Badinan region of Iraq than to Kurds in the northeastern regions of Ağri and Van.

The saliency of socioeconomic, tribal, and localist identities prevented a unified sense of Kurdayetî from emerging across Kurdistan. Most Kurds were more interested in protecting their personal, religious, and tribal interests than in turning to Kurdish organizations to advance nationalist claims. Instead of joining Bedir Khan's intellectual nationalist circles in Istanbul, the anti-British procaliphate Kurdish Clubs in the Kurdish cities, or the Azadi Party in the outlying provinces, many Kurdish aghas supported the Kemalists to protect their Ottoman landownership, which became integrally tied to the Armenian problem. After learning that the Sèvres Treaty offered Armenian statehood they protested, refusing to accept an Armenian entity that would reduce their individual property rights. Some allied with Turkish nationalists in the Committee for the Defense of the Rights of the Vilayets in the East, which promised to prevent the transformation of Kurdistan into Armenia. The presence of foreign troops and land reappropriations to Christians stirred tensions in Kurdistan. Kurdish chiefs joined Turkish groups against the Christian (Armenian) threat. Others summoned Assyrians and Chaldeans in neighboring villages to their cause.

In the political space that favored Islam and traditional social structures Kurds identified according to their particular Muslim identities and not Kurdish nationalism, just like they did in the transitioning Iraqi state. Some Sunni Kurdish shaykhs and intellectuals responded to Kemal's pan-Islamic discourses that promised to preserve the sanctity of the caliphate in a Turkish Muslim empire. Naqshbandiyya Kurds, including Shaykh Said of Piran, were among the leading supporters of the Turkish independence movement, garnering financial support for the military, spreading the goals of

Mustafa Kemal, and discrediting the Istanbul government. Other Kurdish shaykhs, such as Abdulhakim Arvasî and Muhammed Rashid, identified as Muslims first and gained followings among Turks, Arabs, and Kurds in the region (Zarcone 1998, 110–13).[3] Said Nursî criticized the idea of nationalism and ethnicity as a poison, arguing:

> I refuse one hundred million times to sacrifice 350 million brothers among whom are the absolute majority of Kurds, who have a certain fraternity and who assist me with their prayers . . . to the idea of a negative ethnicity and nationalism. I refuse one hundred million times to abandon these numerous sacred brothers, to win over those small impious numbers who have entered a profession without confession and who carry the name of Kurds. (Bozarslan 1992, 22)

The Kurdish Islamist Naim Babanzade also continued to emphasize his Muslim identity instead of Kurdish ethnonationalism. Like Nursî, he referred to nationalism as a European sickness and praised his Kurdish brothers "for not having yet been contaminated by the disease" (Bozarslan 1992, 14–15).

Alevi groups reacted to Kemal's juxtaposed narratives by emphasizing their distinct Alevi identity alongside or instead of Kurdish nationalism. Indeed, some Kurdish Alevi chiefs, particularly from Dersim and Sivas, supported Kurdish nationalist revolts and called for an independent Kurdistan. One of the first meetings between the leaders of the Koçgiri movement and various tribes took place in the *tekke* of Hussein Abdal in Kangal/Sivas (Yellice). The Kurdish Alevis decided to "take arms . . . until the end . . . in realizing the formation of an independent Kurdistan" (Kieser 1993, 3). Yet after the government installed martial law in Koçgiri the leaders sent telegrams to Ankara and changed their demands from independence to autonomy. Others turned to the Turkish Alevi community and the Turkish independence movement, referring to Mustafa Kemal as the imam and grandson of Haçi Bektaşi Veli (Kieser 1993, 13; van Bruinessen 2001,

3. Abdulhakim Arvasî, originally from Van, migrated to Istanbul at the turn of the 1900s to pursue his religious studies. He became a shaykh in the Naqshbandiyya tekke in Istanbul and was later imprisoned. Since 1990 his tekke and followers have developed a politic of publications that focuses on religious themes.

17–18). Populations from Dersim may have shown no enthusiasm for the Kemalists; however, they too, supported Kemal in his war of independence.

Even if Kurdish society was detribalized and homogenous it is unlikely that Kurdayetî would have become salient and ethnicized because Turkish politics was not highly ethnicized during the transition period. As in the early Iraqi state period, the boundaries of inclusion and exclusion were based not on ethnicity but on the lines between the rulers and the ruled, which included religion. Kemal's discourses emphasized Turkish nationalism; however, they were grounded in a sense of Turkish liberation and anti-imperialism, which had a partially inclusive place for Kurds. By emphasizing Islamic fraternity Kemal brought Sunni Kurds and Turks together in a common front against those people seeking to destroy the caliphate, especially Greeks and Armenians. Consequently, despite rising Turkish nationalism after 1919, the relationship between most Kurds and the political center fluctuated between accommodation and hostility.

Indeed, some Kurds were uncompromising nationalists. In 1922 the Azadi Committee, organized from the Erzurum movement, called for Kurdish independence. Still, most placed Kurdayetî within the Turkish independence movement or the declining Ottoman context. At the June 1919 national congress of the Kurdish movement in Erzurum the Kurds declared their support for Mustafa Kemal and Turkish liberation, as long as it recognized Kurdish autonomy. Other Kurds from Sivas, Diyarbakir, Harput, Van, and Bitlis refused separation from the Ottoman community. Kurdish chiefs in the Erzincan region protested against Şerif Paşa, arguing that the Kurds were the "legitimate brothers of the Turks" and demanding not to be separated from their compatriots ("Monsieur de France" 1920). Shaykh Abdel Qader, a Kurdish notable and member of the Ottoman Council of State, criticized Kurds who demanded independence, claiming it was indignant to Kurdish honor (Algar 1996, 54; Dersimi 1990, 120). Like Bedir Khan, Abdel Qader refused to support Şerif Paşa's map of Kurdistan presented at the Paris Peace Conference.

Independent Turkish Republican State

Although Mustafa Kemal (later, in November 1934, called Atatürk) won independence and proclaimed a new Turkish republican state on October 29, 1923, he still had not consolidated political power. After the war, new struggles commenced between opposition groups within the government. The economy was devastated, political institutions were weak, and the country's diverse communities lacked any cohesive sense of national identity. However, rather than encouraging political pluralism, building local consensuses, or establishing committees in the eastern Kurdish regions like he did in the transitioning period, Atatürk purged political rivals from the government, including former unionists and leftist factions (Zürcher 1991, 45–58). He then centralized political power by becoming president, leader of the Turkish military forces, and head of the Republican People's Party (Cumhuriyet Halk Fırkası [CHF]).[4]

Like early British officials, Atatürk attempted to bring the country's diverse populations together by creating a unified, secular, and modern official state nationalism. Yet the concentration of Turkish nationalist power in a highly centralized political system created a fundamentally different type of political space than that which developed in colonial Iraq. Whereas the British elite gave Kurds limited rights as an ethnic group, Turkish nationalist officials denied Kurdish ethnic identity in the new state. Instead of using Ottoman myths or talking about the people of Turkey as he did during the transition period, Atatürk drew upon Turkish nationalist histories that elevated the ancient peoples of Anatolia, such as the Hittites and Sumerians, and called them Turks. Kemalists constructed new myths claiming that Kurds were really Turkish Akhuns, descendants of Hungarians, Göktürks (true Turks), and a clan linked to the Oğuz and Bugduz tribes with Turanian racial origins (Özok 1990, 17–22; Arvasi 1986).[5]

Whereas Iraqi identity remained relatively ambiguous in colonial Iraq, the Kemalist republican state created clear, exclusionary political boundaries based on ethnicity. Kurdish territories in Iraq were acknowledged as distinctly Kurdish; however, in Turkey they lost their Kurdish names and meanings (Akin 1995, 79–82, 195–200).[6] Ten years after talking about a

4. The CHF changed its name at its fourth congress in 1935 to Cumhuri yet Halk Partisi (CHP).

5. The name Göktürk refers to an ancient Turkish nation that lived in central Asia. Arvasî claimed that the Kurds of Maraş, Elbistan, Malatya, and Harput were not really Kurds but Turkoman tribes.

6. Turkish scholars established various neologisms linking the word *Kurd* to *Karluk,* or "those who live in the snow," *Eskimo, avalanche,* and *heavy sleet.*

federation of Kurdish states and a Kurdish-Turkish partnership, Atatürk negated the existence of essential Kurdish lands. In a public speech in Diyarbakir in 1932 he declared, "I come to a heroic corner of the Turkish land. It is a shame they call it the land of Bekir when originally it was the land of Turks. It came to be called Bekir only later, but we know what our original land is. Our original land is the land of the Oğuz Turks" (Feyzioğlu 1982, 177). In fact, all aspects of life became Turkified. Pan-Turkish symbols reemerged on stamps, national currencies, and university hats, reinforcing the Turkishness of official state citizenship. After 1924, the sense of Turkish nationalism changed from a cultural to a racial one.

Kemalist state nationalism was also based on modernizing and secularizing the state, just as it was in colonial Iraq. However, the nature and timing of Turkey's modernization processes differed from the Iraqi case, creating a less tolerant form of political space for the traditional stratum tied to tribal structures and Islam. Whereas the British gave Kurdish nationalist chieftains semilegitimacy and autonomy in their regions, Atatürk considered the Kurds bandits and treated them as such. After 1924 Turkish officials arrested, deported, and killed Kurdish nationalist leaders. They hanged Shaykh Said and deported his extended family and friends to western Turkey or outside the country. Dersim was razed, its name was changed to Tunceli, and its Kurdish notables, including Seyit Reza, were executed.

Further, although Atatürk tried to separate the army from the state, after 1924 he put the army in its service to safeguard the republic. With a ten million lira credit granted by the Turkish Grand National Assembly, secret funds for the army, and a supplementary credit of one hundred million francs from France, the state elite became increasingly reliant on force as a means of managing the Kurds. Atatürk centralized and militarized Kurdish regions; arrested Kurdish activists; deported Kurdish, Armenian, and Laz families to the West; and transferred Turkish families to Kurdish towns. He also replaced most Kurdish deputies in the national assembly with Turkish representatives, many of whom had no contact with Kurdistan. State-appointed inspector generals tied to the military establishment became the supreme chiefs of the Kurdish provinces. After 1935 they created or reorganized Hakkâri, Bitlis, Bingöl, and Tunceli (Dersim) and gave them budgets for the police that represented 50 percent of state spending ("Le Mouvement Kurde" 1927; Bozarslan 1996b, 24).

The drastic manner in which Atatürk secularized Turkey, as opposed to

3. Front page of Turkish newspaper *Cumhuriyet,* during Kurdish revolts in Kemalist period, 1930. The headline reads: "The Bandits Are Being Surrounded: The Measures Taken Are Complete and Perfect." From Rohat Alakom, "Di medya tirkî de karkîkaturîzekirina serhildana (1930î)," *Çira,* no. 14 (1998): 18–92.

the gradual process in Iraq, disfranchised the traditional stratum tied to the Ottoman system. No longer tolerating Islamic and Kurdish shaykhly communities, in 1925 Atatürk stated: "Gentlemen and those of the nation: all of you should know that the Turkish nation cannot become a nation of shaykhs, dervishes, religious fanatics, and charlatans. The most correct and truest path to the nation is the path of contemporary civilization" *(12 September* 1982, 313). Whereas British and Iraqi elites secularized the state but tolerated influential Islamic communities, the Turkish elite created a more hostile political space toward Islam. It replaced the Şaria with parts of the Swiss, German, and Italian civil and penal codes; abolished the institution of the caliphate; closed dervish brotherhoods and medreses; prohibited public prayers and the practice of Islamic traditions; and banned the *hejab* (wearing of the veil) from public places. The Unity of Education Act secularized curricula and placed academic institutions under government control. Atatürk's secularization policy also included using Islam to create tourist attractions by making museums out of the dervish monasteries, including the Sancta Sophia mosque in Istanbul (Houston 2001, 13; Landau 1984; Ramsdan 1989; Pope and Pope 1997; S. Ayata 1993, 60).

Certainly, Atatürk's reforms took place within an Islamic framework, which did not necessarily disappear after 1923. He initially made allowances for Islam by referring to the Turkish citizenry as Muslims and making a connection between the Turkish nation and religion. However, Atatürk reconfigured the relationship between the state and Islamic institutions by putting Islam under state control. Secularization policies that elevated urban classes while weakening the traditional stratum removed most opportunities that Kurdish shaykhly groups enjoyed during the late imperial and early transition periods. Whereas the sadah families and shaykhs retained their status in Iraq until the early 1950s, their counterparts in Turkey were disempowered in the early 1920s. In the second Grand National Assembly of 1923 the percentage of deputies with a religious occupation decreased from 20 percent to 7 percent and then to 1 percent in the seventh assembly, in 1943 (Toprak 1981, 71).

Further, in contrast to colonial Iraq's gradual and partial modernization, Atatürk's strategies, informed by the ideology of Abdullah Cevdet and Ziya Gökalp, emphasized civilization by synthesizing Turkish nationalism and Western capitalism (Sayan 1987, 15). Whereas Britain's economic policies and Iraq's ties to the British sterling created a certain type of development that thwarted state-supported industrialization, Kemal's commitment to economic development encouraged the rapid accumulation of financial capital and private industry. Atatürk opened the Izmir Economic Conference in February 1923, which among other objectives served as a framework for modernizing the state's administration and finances based on the capitalist path and private-sector development. He promised to "develop the national commerce, open the factories, exploit the riches under the ground, and assist the commercial classes of Anatolia so that they become rich" (Ali 1981, 112). By 1924 foreign investors controlled ninety-four societies, representing about 50 percent of large enterprises. The 1927 Law for the Encouragement of Industry further elevated the industrial bourgeoisie over landed, commercial groups (Ökçün 1968, 251–53; Ramazanoğlu 1985, 58–59; Galip 1989, 66–74). What emerged in Turkey and was absent in Iraq was early industrial growth linked to foreign capital.

Atatürk's state-controlled economic development and industrialization programs influenced the Kurdish nationalist trajectory because they created asymmetrical opportunity structures that heightened socioeconomic and ethnic cleavages in Turkish and Kurdish societies. Given the structure of the Turkish political economy, industrialization mainly benefited the Aegean and western coastal regions whose geographical proximity to Europe and open ports and exposure to liberal ideas were already geared toward Western capitalist markets (Margulies and Yıldızoğlu 1987, 273). By 1920 Turkish commercial classes had assumed control of industries, chambers of commerce, insurance companies, and financial institutions. Also, even though Turkey lost most of its Christian populations before and during World War I, there still existed a Turkish commercial bourgeoisie tied to European markets. It was this group, as well as army officials and bureaucratic elite, that profited from Western-financed industrialization programs, not landless Kurdish peasants in remote regions of eastern and southeastern Anatolia.

Ethnoreligious Nationalism

In contrast to the relatively large political space in the Iraqi colonial and Turkish transition periods, in republican Turkey it was nonexistent. The Turkish elite prohibited the Kurdish language, militarized Kurdish territories, outlawed Kurdish parties, and banned Kurdish cultural activities. The shift in the official discourse from the people of Turkey to the Turkish people differentiated the Kurds from the political center on an ethnic basis. Although the Kurds were the second largest ethnic community in the country, they were discriminated against as an ethnic minority. They were now part of the Other because they were not Turkish ethnically and could not identify as Kurds in the public sphere.

As the political space became highly ethnicized and hostile, so too did Kurdayetî. For fifteen years, from 1923 to 1938, Kurdish nationalism was manifested by ethnocultural claims for the Kurdish language and violent rebellions against the Turkish government (Ilhan 1991; Paşa 1986; Olson 1989). In 1937 the Kurdish intellectual Nuri Dersimi wrote a letter to the secretary-general of the United Nations in the name of the tribes of Tunceli (Dersim), warning about the "Turkification of one part of the Kurdish nation and extermination of the other" (Dersimi 1990, 299–303). Bedir Khan attempted to create a Kurdish government in Ararat that would liberate all of Kurdistan. He also published a Kurdish review in exile, emphasizing the distinct Kurdish language and ethnic identity (see *Hawar*, no. 1 [1932]: 5–6; no. 2 [1932]: 5–6; no. 5 [1932]: 1–2).

The violent and highly ethnicized nature of Kurdayetî destabilized the political system and increased the significance of Kurdish nationalism in Turkey, just as it did in early colonial Iraq. Yet Kurdayetî also assumed a different character than its Iraqi counterpart. Atatürk's draconian secularization and centralization policies, in contrast to the gradual de-Islamization of the Iraqi space, created a sense of Otherness based on religion as well as ethnicity. Although the Kurds may have been juridically unable to dissociate from the Turkish nation because they were Muslims, they were socially and politically disfranchised because of their allegiance to Islam.

Consequently, some Kurdish shaykhs reacted to the rupture in their tacit contract with the central government by emphasizing their Islamic identity, alongside or instead of an ethnicized sense of nationalism. They complained that "the Turks have, moreover, themselves destroyed the last bond which remained between the Kurds and themselves, that of religion. Since the Khalifate has been cast off like a cracked water-pipe, all that remains is the feeling of Turkish oppression" ("Kurds and Turks" 1925). The Kurdish Naqshbandiyya shaykh Said of Piran called for a struggle against the Turkish infidels and demanded the creation of an Islamic state, or a Kurdish state based on the Şaria. Shaykh Said wrote letters to Kurdish ulema and tribes, bemoaning the Turkish betrayal of Islam. He even issued a fatwa criticizing Atatürk for being hostile to Qur'anic orders and demanding Muslims to overthrow his illegitimate regime (Bozarslan 2003, 180; Toprak 1981, 64–65; Olson 1989). Other Kurdish shaykhs joined Sunni Turks to protest European dress codes that prohibited the wearing of tribal caps and Islamic attire. Sunni Kurds allied with Turkish Muslims in the group the Protection of Religion and Association for Advancing Islam or local organizations that promoted pan-Islamism, none of which was ethnicized.

Even though Kurdish ethnoreligious nationalism was salient and significant across Kurdistan, it did not remain that way. In fact, after the late 1930s, and for about twenty years, Kurdish nationalists stopped manifesting in the public sphere. What explains this gap in the nationalist trajectory, particularly as the political space became clearly ethnicized and centralized?

Kemalist republican Turkey's ethnicized and restrictive political space prevented the emergence of an influential nationalist elite and organizations. Whereas the ambiguous political space in colonial Iraq tolerated traditional Kurdish nationalist leaders and gave them semilegitimate status, at least until Barzani's expulsion in 1945, the Kemalist republican state delegitimated them. Kurdish nationalist chieftains and shaykhs, having been killed, arrested, or deported from their regions, lost any potential role they could have played as nationalist leaders. Nor did Atatürk replace the traditional Kurdish stratum with a modernizing nationalist elite. Urban notables such as Bedir Khan and his small intellectual circle remained unrepresentated among the largely tribalized and segmented Kurdish society.

The political space in early republican Turkey also failed to provide the institutional basis from which nationalist organizations could have evolved. Whereas Kurdayetî in colonial Iraq developed within a quasi-legal, nationalist organization, and later the leftist opposition movement, it ceased inside early republican Turkey. Political associations from the late Ottoman and early state transition period were banned, which removed the support base for urban nationalists. Indeed, Atatürk responded to popular discontent and demands for political pluralism by accepting the creation of an alternative group, Serbest Cumhuriyet Fırkası (SCF) or Serbest Firka, in August 1930. However, in the highly centralized Kemalist political space, this overture was short-lived. The SCF lasted only four months before it was closed.[7]

Atatürk's secularization policies also placed prohibitions on tekkes and Sufi brotherhoods, which after 1924 weakened, and in many regions eliminated the traditional stratum's legal political-religious networks. Some brotherhoods continued to function clandestinely in the countryside; however, the majority were closed in the urban centers. Tariqa orders and medreses that so effectively assisted the shaykhs in mobilizing Kurds during the imperial and transition periods were confined to the private sphere. Nor did Kurds in Kemalist republican Turkey have access to foreign government advisers or external support that could have helped legitimate their nationalist claims like their counterparts did in Iraqi Kurdistan. Indeed, with the backing of the Armenian revolutionary federation (Tashnaksoutioun) and Bedir Khan's Khoybun League in Damascus, Kurdish nationalists accessed resources to create a temporary government and national army in Ararat. Yet regional powers worried about uprisings from their own Kurdish communities, including the French in Syria, obstructed transnational support networks. Consequently, whereas Kurdayetî developed on an organizational level in colonial Iraq, in Kemalist Turkey it ceased, went underground, or was exported outside the country.

The denial of Kurdish ethnic identity, harsh secularization policies, prohibition of opposition groups, and militarization of the Kurdish regions prevented the continued evolution and open manifestation of nationalist sentiment. Checked by the powerful state military establishment and prohibited from publishing or speaking the Kurdish language, Kurds in Turkey did not have the same opportunities to express their ethnic identity as

7. Atatürk agreed to the creation of the SCF as a means of keeping popular discontent within the new regime's borders. The founders were carefully chosen and included at least two of Atatürk's closest friends, Fethi Okyar and Nuri Conker, as well as fifteen deputies of the CHF. According to its program and political tendencies, the SCF was a liberal party defending private enterprise and foreign investment. However, it soon gained large support from poor and working masses who believed they had found a channel for expressing their grievances against repression and heavy taxes. The meeting in Izmir (Sept. 5, 1930) had been a huge success regarding mass participation, although it resulted in clashes with the police. In the local elections the SCF gained support in some cities; however, Atatürk called for its dissolution on Nov. 16, 1930.

Kurds did in early colonial Iraq (until the mid-1940s). Iraqi Kurds could learn and use their language alongside Arabic; however, Kurds in Turkey could not speak Kurdish in public. Iraqi Kurds acknowledged their distinct Kurdish identity and territories, yet Kurds in Turkey had to deny their existence as Kurds. In school they had to repeat every day: "I am a Turk, I am honest, I am hard working. My law is to protect the children, to respect the elderly and to love my country and my nation more than my own being. My ideal is to elevate myself and to advance. May my existence be sacrificed to the Turkish existence."[8]

One can argue that even if Kurds in Kemalist republican Turkey had access to large political space Kurdayetî would have been weak and fractured anyway. As in the late Ottoman and Iraqi colonial periods, dichotomies existed within and between Kurdish communities, hindering the emergence of a unified sense of Kurdish nationalism. Personal rivalries in the segmented Kurdish power structure continued among Kurdish leaders, separating nontribal from tribal communities, just as they did in Iraqi Kurdistan. Even after Shaykh Said's execution and the removal of tribal chiefs from Kurdish nationalist politics, Bedir Khan could not attract Sunni Kurdish tribes to his nationalist movement in Ararat.

Still, instead of trying to bridge Kurdish dichotomies, Kemalist policies enhanced them. At no point did the Turkish elite attempt to unify the Kurds as an ethnic community within the Turkish republic. Instead, it employed divide-and-rule policies that kept Kurds apart from one another, just like British and Iraqi elites did in colonial Iraq. For instance, during the Shaykh Said and Ararat revolts, the central government tried to prevent the tribes in southwest Tunceli (Dersim) from lending support to fellow Kurds. State inspectors sponsored meetings with Kurdish delegations from Tunceli, swearing that Atatürk was an Alevi and promising school and road construction and cultivation of plots for the landless (Ilhan 1991, 42). Also, although the Turkish elite removed tribal chiefs from the Kurdish nationalist leadership, it supported certain tribes in Kurdistan. Turkish army generals made deals with some chiefs, allowing them to purchase pardons by handing over Kurdish nationalists to the government. The state's inspector generals armed certain tribes and paid them to act as informants, civil servants, and army regulars.

8. I thank Ali Ayverdi for this passage.

Atatürk killed, arrested, and deported tribal nationalist leaders and suppressed Kurdish ethnonationalism; however, he made a tacit alliance with the Kurdish aghas. State-appointed governors, gendarmeries, tax centers, and schools controlled life in the towns and cities. Yet the aghas retained their important role as conflict negotiators in the villages, in cooperation with the prefect and some tribal chiefs. Although medreses were officially closed in urban centers, the government allowed Kurdish aghas to control the schools in certain outlying regions. Continuation of medrese education, even in clandestine form, elevated the status of the Kurdish agha, while protecting Kurdish Islamic identities in the private realm (Zarcone 1998, 111–12).

Atatürk's economic and agricultural policies reinforced the status of large landowners and further stifled Kurdish nationalist potential in the countryside. As in colonial Iraq, Kemalist policies weakened Ottoman power structures but did not encourage social restructuring at the rural level. Even though Atatürk promised to improve the peasants' lot and said that the villager was the master of the nation, his policies did little to change peasant income and status in Kurdistan. The government abolished the Ottoman land tithe in 1924, distributed fields to villagers with twenty years of credit, and provided small-interest loans to assist poor landless peasants; however, by the late 1940s feudalist land relations continued (Schick and Tonak 1987, 41).[9] Atatürk's failure to restructure the rural level through land reform privileged the traditional landowning stratum. Kurdish aghas retained their landowning privileges, control over village communities, and influence in local power networks. The shift from laissez-faire to statist economic policies in the late 1920s also created new incentive structures for large landowners. Atatürk initiated land reclamations, imported tractors, created the Ministry of Agriculture, and assisted farmers with state subsidies. From 1923 to 1929 total agricultural output increased by 115 percent (Issawi 1980, 368; Georgeon 1986, 138). Not surprisingly, many Kurdish aghas maintained an accommodating relationship with the central government.

9. The removal of the Ottoman land tithe allowed poor middle peasants and farmers with sufficient land to keep and sell 10 percent of the nontaxed output. It had greater effect on regions in central and western Turkey, where peasants were able to keep the surplus, than in Kurdistan, where sharecroppers were controlled by aghas.

Indeed, agricultural policies continued to favor Turkish commercial classes and landowners in western and central Anatolia. However, because statist programs partially switched from export-oriented to cereal-producing sectors, they benefited certain Kurdish regions as well. To lower transportation costs and raise productivity and profits the state elite built transportation systems in cereal-producing regions, including the Sivas-Samsun Railroad, one of eight new railroad lines built in Kurdistan from 1927 to 1939. Overall, the real value of agricultural produce in Kurdistan rose by 20 percent (Margulies and Yıldızoğlu 1987, 273; Galip 1989, 112–13; Ali 1981, 143).[10] Kurdish landowners and family-owned businesses profited from the rise in cultivation and increase in land prices, particularly in the grain-producing Kurdish provinces of Diyarbakir and Erzurum.

Agricultural support programs strengthened the culture of wheat that came to define some Kurdish regions, just as they did in Iraqi Kurdistan during the colonial period. Not only did big Kurdish landowners gain economically, but they also became integrated into the government's political-economic network at the local and regional levels. Client-state links heightened the central government's dependence on local Kurdish notables while reinforcing dichotomous relations between Kurdish landowners and peasants and between the rural masses and the state bureaucracy. Some Kurdish communities may have considered themselves Kurds ethnically; however, they took advantage of the new opportunity structures and supported the central government, despite the existence of the ethnicized political space.

For instance, with the switch to a wartime economy during the late 1930s the growth of rural-based merchant capital halted, wheat production nearly halved, prices dropped, and transportation costs increased. Kurdish peasants, small farmers, and laborers saw their real incomes decline and were forced to sell their land. Large landowners profited from increased food demands. Also, although the state elite militarized some Kurdish regions and prohibited brigandage, it arranged various accords with Western powers that ensured transportation lines in the eastern provinces. These

10. Wheat and barley production increased approximately 205 percent from 1929 to 1938. During the 1930s cereals increased from 78,000 to 372,000 tons in Erzurum and from 67,000 to 264,000 tons in Kars.

agreements allowed commercial trade to continue, particularly in strategic Kurdish border areas (Harris 1974, 25; Lenczowski 1962, 134–40). Alongside wartime industrialists, Kurdish landowners, speculators, smugglers, and tax profiteers benefited. The war also terminated any attempt at land reform, further strengthening the position of the Kurdish agha.

One Constantly Ethnicized Turkish Identity: Hostile Kurdish-State Relations

Whereas the official state national identity in colonial Iraq was relatively ambiguous, it remained clearly and continuously ethnicized in Kemalist republican Turkey. New debates emerged among the various political groupings during the 1930s and 1940s over the nature of the Turkish state: whether Turkey should be a single-party state or liberalize its political system and the nature of the economy and Turkey's alliance with the West. Still, in contrast to the Iraqi colonial period, whereby Iraqi-first tendencies and competing notions of Arab nationalism challenged the Arab qawmiyya nationalist current, the official notion of Turkish national identity remained unchanged. Most serious debates within the government about Turkish identity were between different strains of Turkish nationalists.

In fact, although Atatürk limited his notion of Turkish nationalism to the territorial borders of Anatolia and emphasized the *vatan* (fatherland) instead of Turan, his racial overtones encouraged pan-Turkish nationalism. Ethnicized political boundaries continued under the rule of İsmet İnönü, who assumed the presidency and became leader of the Republican People's Party after Atatürk's death in 1938. İnönü insisted that Turanism and Turkish nationalism were unrelated and arrested a group of fourteen pro-German Turanians, among them Alparslan Türkeş, who later became leader of the fascist movement in Turkey. However, his government allowed the radical, pro-German Turkish nationalist current to retain influence in political life (Landau 1981, 72–81; Georgeon 1986, 128; Ağaoğulları 1987, 188). Ongoing diplomatic relations between the Turkish elite and Franz von Papen, the German ambassador in Ankara, gave pan-Turanian and Nazi groups opportunities to spread anticommunist propaganda.

In contrast to the fluctuating Kurdish trajectory in colonial and early republican Iraq, the uncompromisingly ethnicized political space encouraged a continuously hostile relationship between Kurdish nationalists and the state elite. Whereas Arab socialist leaders in Iraq tied their nationalist agenda to liberation movements and appealed to Kurdish leftist-nationalists, at least during the pre-Ba'thist years, Turkey's NATO membership, alliance with the West, and intolerant attitude toward Kurdish ethnicity reinforced antagonisms between Kurdish leftists and the central government. The unchanging, restrictive political space also preempted the evolution of legal Kurdish nationalist organizations in the public sphere. To be sure, during the late 1940s, after the termination of the one-party state and creation of the Democratic Party (Demokrat Parti [DP]) in 1946, the Kurdish nationalist current resurfaced, particularly as news of Barzani's revolt and his expulsion from Iraq reached Kurdistan in Turkey. Some Kurdish intellectuals in Diyarbakir and other Kurdish cities organized clandestine meetings, hoping to spread their nationalist views. Semilegal Kurdish journals appeared, such as *Dicle Kaynağı,* calling Kurdish youth to engage in the eastern question (Akin 1996, 114). As in Iraqi Kurdistan, Kurdish nationalist sentiment emphasized the distinct Kurdish ethnic identity apart from Turks, Arabs, and Persians and the need to protect the Kurdish culture and language.

Yet whereas the Iraqi elite repressed Kurdish nationalists but also tried to negotiate with them, the Turkish elite closed Kurdish meetings, arrested Kurdish organizers, and banned Kurdish journals, leaving no possibility for political institutionalization of Kurdish nationalism. Nor could Kurds in Turkey turn to alternative political parties to advance their nationalist claims. Despite the institution of universal suffrage and the multiparty elections of 1946, the Cumhuriyet Halk Partisi (CHP) still controlled the political system and prevented the open political expression of Kurdayetî on an ideological or organizational level.[11] In this closed political context the only feasible manner for Kurdish nationalists to mobilize was to relocate outside Turkey's borders. In Syria, Bedir Khan and his supporters continued to publish Kurdish journals, including *Ronahî* and *Roja Nû,* which helped spread nationalist ideas *(Roja Nû,* no. 36 [1944]: 1; no. 40–42 [1944]: 1–2; no. 61 [1945]: 1–3). Still, the small intellectual elite linked to Western circles outside the country was hardly representative of the larger Kurdish society,

11. The first multiparty elections were held on July 21, 1946. Although the Democratic Party obtained 66 of 465 seats in the Grand National Assembly, the CHP continued to dominate the political apparatus (Ahmad and Ahmad 1976, 21).

the majority of which was illiterate, poor, and tied to traditional social structures.

Conclusions

In contrast to colonial Iraq, the highly ethnicized, centralized, and exclusionary political space in early republican Turkey removed all opportunities for the Kurds as an ethnic group, giving rise to a more ethnicized and violent form of Kurdayetî. It also prevented the evolution of Kurdish nationalism on an ideological or organizational level. Whereas a large semilegal nationalist party directed by two oppositional identities emerged in Iraqi Kurdistan, the small handful of urban Kurdish nationalists from Turkey had to take their activities outside the country. Further, although a changing political space encouraged both compromise and hostility between the Kurdish nationalists and the state elite in Iraq, the absence of variation in Turkey after 1924 resulted in a continuously hostile relationship between the Kurdish nationalists and the state elite.

5

Turkey's Transition to a Quasi-Democracy

Complex Political Space

Throughout the Kemalist republican period the political space was ethnically restrictive and dangerous for Kurdish nationalists. The Kurds could not speak their language, celebrate national holidays, or mobilize as an ethnic group. However, after 1950, when Turkey turned toward the West and engaged in democratization processes, a more expansive political space emerged. In February 1950 the Grand National Assembly ratified laws that called for secret ballot elections, political party representation, and an independent judicial system. Interest groups became active, giving rise to a Turkish civil society. Increasing complex space created greater diversity in the manifestation of Kurdish political identities, including nationalism. Although Kurds were still restricted from mobilizing as an ethnic group, they had legal channels to manifest as Turkish citizens or part of leftist, conservative, and Islamic tendencies.

An Ethnicized and Liberalizing Turkish State

Whereas Arab nationalist and communist factions struggled over the character of Iraqi identity in the early independent Iraqi republican state, the official state nationalism in Turkey remained clear and constant. Instead of trying to create a sense of Kurdish-Turkish partnership, Prime Ministers Adnan Menderes (1950–1960), leader of the Democratic Party, and Süleyman Demirel (1965–1971), head of the Justice Party (Adalet Partisi [AP]), made no changes in the official ideology of Turkish citizenship. Anticommunist rhetoric generated by the United States and supported by the Turkish government encouraged right-wing groups harboring Turkish nationalist and anti-Russian views. After being acquitted in a second trial and making a career in the army, Alparslan Türkeş recommenced his radical Turkish nationalist activities and later became president of the Nationalist Action Party (Milliyetçi Hareket Partisi [MHP]) in 1969. The MHP was a minority group, but it had support from conservative factions in the army and government. Through the fascist youth organization Hearths of Idealism it promoted the notion of *soyculuk,* or lineage, promising to cleanse Turkey of its minorities. Emphasizing the sense of Turkish greatness in the "Citizen, Speak Turkish!" campaign, right-wing factions trained Turkish nationalist youths to fight subversive ideologies such as communism, which they now linked to Kurdish nationalism. Turkeş also organized youth associations and fascist paramilitary forces and gave commando education in camps, all with the secret assistance and open indifference of the state police (Ahmad and Ahmad 1976, 349; Ağaoğulları 1987, 194–97).

While denying Kurdish ethnicity, government officials appealed to the traditional stratum as part of its favored conservative constituencies, including right-of-center groups from the rising middle and commercial classes, just like Atatürk did. Following Atatürk's commitment to industrialization Menderes promised to create a millionaire in each neighborhood and make Turkey a small United States (Aydin 1993, 114–16; Akçay 1988, 20–21; Cigerli 1991, 17; Issawi 1980, 369). However, he also responded to pressures by industrialists, landowners, and Western lending institutions by replacing Kemalist statist policies with liberalization programs based on free enterprise and import-substitution industrialization (ISI). The shift toward a liberal economy continued under Demirel's rule, aided by foreign loans and state-planning organizations, which encouraged industrialization and rural development.

Economic privatization programs impacted the Kurdish trajectory because they strengthened rural structures and reinforced the government's political base in the countryside (Toprak 1981, 88). One of the objectives of the ISI program was to use rural areas as large internal markets so that the agricultural sector would be the major foreign-currency earner. A key component was agricultural reform. In contrast to the Iraqi programs, the Turkish elite did not attempt to weaken the landowning stratum by transforming land-tenure relations or altering the size of landholdings. It tried to redistribute state-owned lands; however, the major push was based on mechanizing the means of production. From 1948 to 1953 the number of tractors distributed by the government to farmers increased from 1,750 to 30,000 (Ceyhun 1989, 55–56; Galip 1989, 139–40).

As the government's role in economic management expanded, the state elite had new means to appease conservative constituencies. It became increasingly attentive to developing rural areas and supporting efficient agricultural production. The central government provided credit extensions, implemented pilot projects, and created research institutes in Kurdistan, including agricultural universities in Erzurum and Diyarbakir. In cooperation with the U.S. Agency for International Development it introduced several high-yielding wheat projects throughout the Turkish countryside and parts of Kurdistan, including Sivas, Urfa, Erzurum, and Diyarbakir. Although the credit extensions were limited, agriculture as a percentage of the gross national product declined from 45 percent to 26 percent from 1948 to 1971, and the programs were only partially successful, agricultural output increased by 75 percent (Aresvik 1975, 1966; McDowall 1997, 299; Akçay 1988, 11).[1]

The political space also expanded for Sunni Muslim groups. Menderes remained committed to laicization; however, he moved away from the rigid, secularist policies of the Atatürk-İnönü period and permitted the politicization of Islam in the public sphere. Promising that Istanbul would become a second Kaaba, he created new secondary schools that offered religious instruction, established religious seminaries, permitted Qur'anic radio broadcasts and Islamic publications, and authorized Sunni Muslim holidays. The Menderes government constructed fifteen thousand new mosques throughout Turkey and the Kurdish regions (Zarcone 1998, 113; Thomas 1952, 22; Toprak 1981, 75–82). Instead of emphasizing differences between the Kurdish Shafi and Turkish Hanafi schools, it adopted doctrinal elements of the Kurdish Naqshbandiyya brotherhood in Istanbul, attempting to bring together Turkish and Kurdish Sunni Muslims.

Opposition groups even found a limited place in the political system,

1. One of the reasons for the projects' limited success was the nature of the land and the price ratio between cotton and wheat in the coastal regions.

which after the 1960 military coup and reinstallation of a civilian government opened further. Presidents Cemal Gürsel (October 1960-March 1966) and Cevdet Sunay (March 1966-March 1973) ensured military control of political institutions and militarized Kurdish regions. However, the political space became more representative of various political groupings. In the new 1961 constitution, new laws and amendments limited presidential power; placed political parties under constitutional safeguards; established a system of checks and balances among the executive, legislative, and judicial systems; and created a bicameral legislature (Harris 1965, 172–73; 1974, 51–52). The central government also passed a series of civil rights legislation permitting labor unions and workers to strike. Consequently, the state elite had a more complex society and political system to manage. Democratization supported associational life by creating a framework in which civil society could take form. Leftist groups were legalized, new political parties became active, and interest group activities expanded. From 1950 to the mid-1970s the number of officially registered voluntary associations grew from about two thousand to thirty-eight thousand, while the percentage of nonagricultural workers in labor unions rose from 6 percent to 50 percent (Kalaycioğlu 2002, 253; Bianchi 1984, 110–14). What emerged in Turkey and was absent in Iraq was a complex civil society in which diverse associations and opposition groups could mobilize openly in the political space.

Urbanized, Secular, Leftist Ethnonationalism

Although the government implemented the most liberal legislation in Turkish history, it continued to deny the existence of ethnic particularities. Uneven economic development programs heightened ethnic distinctions between the Kurdish regions and Turkish Anatolia. Mustafa Barzani's return to Iraq, Qasim's concessions to Kurds, Iraqi Kurdish revolts, publication of a Kurdish newspaper in Tehran, and Turkey's removal of the Iraqi cultural attaché, the well-known Kurdish historian Rafik Hilmi, from his post further sensitized the Kurds in Turkey to their political situation.

In this ethnically defined political space Kurdayetî became salient and ethnicized in the public sphere. Prior to his death in Urfa in 1960, Said Nursî, who identified as a Sunni Muslim, stated: "I have a friendly and brotherly relation with the true Turks. . . . Yet, you take the identity from millions of Kurds who are real Turkish citizens, brothers in combat in the holy war of the Turks. You make them forget their identity and their ancient language. . . . This is a barbaric procedure. This submission cannot be imposed on me and we will not submit" (Alakom 1998b, 330). Other Kurds took advantage of the liberalizing climate and started emphasizing Kurdish ethnonationalism. In contrast to the ethnoreligious sentiment of the early Kemalist period, however, urbanized, secular Kurdish nationalists such as Mehdi Zana and Musa Anter published journals in the Kurdish (Kurmanji) and Turkish languages, making claims for Kurdish ethnic identity and language and not Islam. Similarly, Faik Bucak from Urfa and Said Elçi from the Bingol region, encouraged by Fehmi Bilal, former secretary of Shaykh Said, and their supporters created the Kurdistan Democratic Party of Turkey in 1965. The organization emphasized the distinct Kurdish identity and economic development in Kurdistan, not religion (Kutschera 1997, 230).

Still, in comparison to pre-Ba'thist Iraq, the nature of the political space in post-1950 Turkey checked Kurdish ethnonationalist potential. Whereas Qasim semilegalized the nationalist elite and supported an umbrella nationalist organization, at least temporarily, Turkish state officials prohibited Kurdish nationalist leaders and associations. The Iraqi KDP became quasi-legalized; however, the KDP Turkey was clandestine from the outset. For open activities, the KDP Turkey supported the Yeni Türkiye Partisi, a small right-wing party. Nor did Kurds have continued access to external support networks that could have increased the significance of their nationalist claims. Whereas Iraqi Kurds received U.S., Israeli, and Iranian government backing as part of their anti-Arab and anticommunist programs, Kurdish nationalists in Turkey, many of whom were affiliated with the communist and socialist movements, were targeted for their leftist political ideology.

The political space also prevented the legal, open manifestation of Kurdish ethnonational sentiment. By 1960 the Kurds still could not legally use the term *Kurd* in public or speak their language without the risk of repression. State officials arrested Musa Anter for publishing a poem in the Kurdish language, alongside forty-nine other Kurdish nationalists.[2] They

2. After the massacres of Turkoman communities in Kirkuk, Turkish deputy Asim Eren asserted that Turkey would "avenge the Kurds" (McDowall 1997, 403). The government then arrested forty-nine Kurdish nationalists who led the protests against the government's policies.

considered Kurdish publications subversive and shut them down. In fact, after the May 27, 1960, military coup d'état, the political space remained as dangerous and restrictive for Kurdish nationalists as it was during the Kemalist period. The state elite deployed commando units in Kurdish villages, terrorizing local populations and institutionalizing the military's role in the Turkish political apparatus. Alongside threats to Kurds as a whole, Turkish nationalists warned that the red Kurds (that is, the Alevis) would be massacred like the Armenians. The Demirel government arrested twenty-one Kurdish communists for leftist and separatist activities (Malmîsanij and Lewendî 1993, 146–49; Landau 1974).

One can argue that even if the political space tolerated Kurdish ethnic identity, the heterogeneous Kurdish society is likely to have weakened the influence of Kurdayetî anyway. Although Kurdistan in Turkey lost some segmented structures, by the late 1960s local populations identified according to socioeconomic roles in the stratified village communities. Kurdish tribes in the Hakkâri region retained influential ties with the central government, just as they did during the Kemalist period. Others referred to themselves by their regional identities: *khalke* (people) Maraş, khalke Diyarbakir, and khalke Mardin. Kurds in Erzurum identified by their local identity as Dadaş, which was tied to their geographical position and culture as a frontier community (Yalçin-Heckmann 1989, 301; Yavuz 1999, 122). Dichotomies also remained between the traditional stratum and urban leftists and between Alevi and Sunni Kurds. The KDP Turkey was fragmented between supporters of Said Elçi and Dr. Şivan (Sait Kırmızıtoprak), a Kurd from Dersim who advanced revolutionary leftist ideology in the ranks of KDP Turkey. Alliances between the KDP Turkey and the Iraqi KDP terminated with internal conflicts, weakening the KDP's potential as a representative nationalist party, even in clandestine form.

Instead of trying to bridge or weaken these dichotomies the Turkish elite reinforced them. Despite new transportation and communication systems Turkish officials failed to educate and modernize Kurdistan, which limited the nationalist potential of the Kurdish masses. According to the 1960 census, an average of 85 percent of the populations in fifteen Kurdish provinces was illiterate (Beşikçi 1992, 104). The militarization of Kurdistan also hindered contact between regions and further constrained the development of a standardized national language for Kurdish communities.

Yet if the dichotomous and underdeveloped nature of Kurdish society accounts for Kurdish nationalism or its absence, then how can we explain differences in the nature of Kurdayetî in Iraq and Turkey, despite the fact that Kurdish society in both states was heterogeneous and undeveloped? During the mid-1960s Kurdayetî in Iraq was highly ethnicized and manifested by two main groupings within one mass influential, semilegitimate Kurdish nationalist party; however, in Turkey it radicalized and splintered within the leftist youth movement. Whereas the traditional Kurdish stratum in Iraq manifested an ethnicized nationalism, their counterparts in Turkey supported the central government and even integrated into Turkish society. Why did the traditional Kurdish stratum in Turkey refrain from manifesting their sense of Kurdayetî, particularly when they were active leaders in the Kurdish revolts just thirty years earlier?

Kurdayetî in the liberalizing Turkish state was more complex than the tribal-urban dichotomy that defined Iraqi Kurdish nationalism or the segmented mobilizations that marked the late imperial and early republican periods. Industrialization processes, economic restructuring programs, and the growth of capitalism in Turkey transformed the nature of Kurdish society and politics by diversifying the workforce into various occupational groups. Demographic transformations heightened economic polarizations. From 1950 to 1975 agriculture as a percentage of the gross domestic product decreased from 49 percent to 26 percent while industry increased from 13 percent to 25 percent. By the mid-1970s only 1.7 percent of rural populations worked as agricultural laborers whose incomes were derived exclusively from wage employment (Keyder 1986, 91–92). As the traditional Kurdish economy dissipated, peasant groups were forced either to sell their land or to rent it out, which meant leaving their villages to seek employment elsewhere.

Demographic and socioeconomic changes urbanized Kurdish communities and encouraged new collective identities to become salient. Whereas Iraqi Kurds were forced into isolated collective towns in Kurdistan and became further dependent upon state handouts, Kurdish migrant populations in Turkey were displaced throughout cities in Kurdistan and central and western Anatolia, and into alternative workplaces such as automobile factories and construction sectors, without state assistance. Many became wage laborers in manufacturing plants owned by multinational corporations, seasonal workers, or unemployed squatter populations in *gecekondus,* or city slum dwellings. Others left their mountain enclaves to work as Gastarbeiters in Germany (Peker 1996, 8–9; Bianchi 1984, 36–44; Akçay 1988, 16). Displaced populations may have been conscious of Kurdish national-ism; however, within the diversified workforce they also became part of working-class and leftist movements, and they identified as such in the pub-lic sphere.

Increasing socioecononomic diversification, the uneven industrializa-tion of the state, the rise of a Kurdish proletariat, and the availability of legal leftist organizations encouraged the leftward shift of Kurdayetî. From the early 1960s, the legalization of socialism, foundation of the Turkish Worker's Party (TİP), and its attainment of parliamentary seats in 1965 of-fered Kurdish nationalists a safer, open channel of expression in the Turk-ish political arena. The TİP did not initially support Kurdish nationalism; however, it became the sole legal proponent of Kurdish rights, albeit in terms of the "eastern question," that is, inequality, exploitation, poverty, and feudal backwardness, just like the ICP did for Iraqi Kurdish leftists dur-ing the late colonial and early Qasim periods (Güzel 1975, 424–552; Kutschera 1997, 232–34). Individuals with leftist tendencies within the Kurdish Democratic Party of Turkey, particularly among the younger gen-eration, participated in open activities in the TİP. In the second half of the 1960s, they began to discuss more outspokenly the "eastern question" and the nation's right to self-determination.[3]

However, in contrast to the leftward shift of Kurdayetî in Iraq, leftist Kurdish nationalism in Turkey was part of a more complex political space, which created greater diversity in the nationalist organization. Turkey's pro-portional representation and multiparty system, as opposed to the closed-party system in Iraq, encouraged the growth of small parties and a splintering and radicalization of Turkish and Kurdish politics (Landau 1974, 42, 248).[4] Whereas Iraqi Kurdish leftists shifted between the ICP and KDP, at least until the late 1970s, their counterparts in Turkey had greater

3. At their fourth party congress in October 1970 the TİP adopted a resolution that ad-dressed the Kurdish problem. Now focusing on "human freedom," the TİP recognized the Kurdish people's existence in the East, condemned the Turkish oppression against the Kurds, and criticized the underdevelopment of the Kurdish regions.

4. In the Turkish "National Remainder System," in every electoral district seats in the national assembly are allocated to the party that obtains the necessary number of votes. All remaining votes are divided by seats among the winners proportionately and at the local level.

alternatives among various leftist associations, political parties, the youth movement, working classes, interest groups, and labor unions that emerged from the budding civil society. Some of the most important were the influential revolutionary cultural societies of the East, such as the Devrimci Doğu Kültür Ocakları, which were established in Ankara and Istanbul in 1969 and then in Kurdish towns and cities and which published journals and newspapers in Kurdish and Turkish about the "eastern problem."

Like leftist nationalists in Iraqi Kurdistan, Kurdish leftists in Turkey tied their nationalist claims to revolutionary Marxist-Leninist ideology, socioeconomic development, and Kurdish cultural rights. However, in contrast to the highly ethnicized anti-Arab claims made by Iraqi Kurds, their demands were shaped by the economic polarizations caused by the state's industrialization programs, their status as marginalized populations, and the economic neglect of Kurdistan, of which the distinct Kurdish ethnicity, culture, and language were part. During the dozens of meetings held by Kurdish and Turkish intellectuals and working classes during the 1960s, the participants protested against the underdevelopment of southeast Turkey. They demanded "teachers and schools and not police" (Akin 1996, 117). Kurdish nationalists also criticized education without the Kurdish language and life in Kurdistan "without water or food" (Arda 1980; Barnas 1980).

The political space in Turkey also created a fundamentally different relationship between the Kurdish aghas and the central government than that which emerged in the Iraqi state during the Arab socialist years. In Turkey it was not the urban leftists, but the traditional landowning stratum that found favor in the political center. After 1947 and again in 1960 the state elite allowed deported and redeported Kurdish chieftains to return to their lands, honored land deeds from the Ottoman period, and abolished the tax on agricultural production. Whereas Iraq's attempted land reforms weakened Kurdish aghas during the 1960s and 1970s, Turkey's programs allowed them to realize some of their biggest political and economic gains.

Indeed, the mechanization of agriculture favored the Turkish provinces, not the underdeveloped eastern and southeastern Kurdish regions. Only 3.3 percent of state-provided tractors, 4.7 percent of harvesting machines, and 6.5 percent of road transport were available in Kurdistan, reinforcing economic inequalities between ethnically Turkish and Kurdish provinces (Beşikçi 1992, 87; Jafar 1976, 60–63). Still, state-supported economic privatization and industrialization programs did not weaken the Kurdish agha. In fact, they strengthened it. The switch from labor- to capital-intensive production benefited tobacco and cotton cultivators in central and western Anatolia; however, from 1950 to 1953 some Kurdish and Turkish farmers realized their highest agricultural yields since the prewar period (Aresvik 1975, 166; Akçay 1988, 11; McDowall 1997, 299).[5]

Additionally, in contrast to Iraqi reforms, Turkish agricultural industrialization programs altered the relationship between labor inputs and land and gave rise to a new Kurdish commercial class tied to conservative Turkish parties, which further stifled Kurdish nationalist potential in the countryside and urban centers. Large landownings turned into capitalist enterprises based on machinery (Ramazanoğlu 1985, 80–82; Keyder 1986, 88; Akçay 1988, 2). Scarcity of land for sharecropping increased its value. From 1950 to 1960 the average piece of farmland rose by 360 percent. These economic transformations supported absenteeism. Kurdish landlords engaged in commercial ventures such as subcontracting land and investing in enterprises in western Turkish cities or abroad. In the Kurdish village of Sinan in the Bismil subdistrict of Diyarbakir, for example, the landlord received his first tractor in 1955. By 1981 he had obtained twelve tractors, two harvesters, eight tractor-driven plows, six disk harrows, four grain drills, six motor pumps, and other equipment. The landowner became a wealthy building contractor tied to commercial enterprises in western Turkey (Akçay 1988, 21–22). Continued support to the Kurdish countryside ensured a constructive relationship among Kurdish aghas, certain tribal chiefs, and the central government.

Kurdish nationalism, therefore, was weak not because Kurdish aghas "stopped being Kurdish," as some have argued, but because the political space in the liberalizing period encouraged integration of the traditional Kurdish stratum into Turkish politics and society (McDowall 1997, 400). Menderes's and Demirel's state-building strategies created symbiotic alliances with conservative Kurdish communities whose leaders became mayors, deputies, and party representatives. As the number of Kurdish

5. The introduction of tractors reduced the amount of land to be sharecropped by human labor and increased the plots cultivated by machines. Most of the lands formerly sharecropped were then "enclosed" by the landlord, which encouraged the switch from labor-intensive crops to cotton and wheat cultivation.

aghas and shaykhs represented in the Parliament increased, so too did their influence in the urban centers. Most used their powers to reinforce patronage links between the state and local election machines, and not to develop ties with Kurdish nationalist leftist groups. Some aghas threatened peasants and villagers, telling them to vote for certain parties or risk losing their jobs and land rights (S. Ayata 1996, 44).

Certainly, co-opted Kurdish aghas and shaykhs who turned to conservative Turkish parties, particularly those individuals who remained in the Kurdish regions, identified as Kurds ethnically in the private sphere. Some moved back and forth between conservative Turkish and Kurdish nationalist circles. Others recognized Kurdish ethnicity as the sine qua non of their participation in Turkish politics (Bozarslan 1990, 2–4). Kurdish deputies of Turkish parties often lived a double life between Kurdish nationalism and Turkish citizenship. In the villages they wore traditional Kurdish clothing and then dressed in secular Turkish attire when traveling to the big cities. These people continued to speak Kurdish and not Turkish among themselves, especially in the geographically isolated areas, maintaining a sense of Kurdayetî without manifesting it publicly.

Still, given the ethnically restrictive nature of the political space in Turkey and support mechanisms for the agha class, it was economically advantageous and safer for the conservative, traditional Kurdish stratum to emphasize alternative political identities than Kurdish ethnonationalism. Some attained high-level political posts. Abdülmelik Fırat, the grandson of Shaykh Said, returned from exile as a youth and later, in 1957, became a representative in the Democratic Party at Menderes's personal request. Necmettin Cevheri, a Kurdish agha from Urfa, served in the AP and its successor party, the Doğru Yol Partisi, and had been minister of tourism, minister of agriculture, and minister of state under Demirel and Tansu Çiller. Prominent Kurds also joined the ranks of the Democratic Party, including Shaykh Kasım Küfrevi, Halis Öztürk Agha, Celal Yardımcı, Selahattin İnan, Shaykh Gıyasettin Emre, and M. Remzi Bucak. Others responded to the new overtures toward Sunni Muslim communities by turning to Islam. Kurdish Sufi shaykhs, including Osman Siraj al-Din from Iraq, established large followings in Istanbul, crossing ethnonationalist identities for Islamic ones (Zarcone 1998, 122).

The diversification of Kurdish communities into new socioeconomic and political groupings created a less representative form of Kurdayetî than that which emerged in Iraqi Kurdistan during the 1960s. Sons of aghas who supported Menderes did not participate in the opposition and later Kurdish leftist movement. Rather, they became the target of renewed criticisms from urban, educated Kurdish communities, who turned to the secularizing and modernizing Turkish parties in their critiques of Islam and the traditional stratum (van Bruinessen 1998, 32–33). During the 1970s, after the Kurdish aghas had lost some influence, Kurdish leftist nationalists continued to cooperate with Turkey's leftist parties and groups and to support them when necessary or useful, although the tendency to organize separately among themselves became dominant. Conservative Sunni Kurdish aghas and shaykhs joined Turkish center-right parties as part of the anti-communist movement. Some even allied with Türkeş's MHP for its radical stance against communists and Alevis.

One Constantly Ethnicized Political Space: Hostile Kurdish Nationalist-State Relations

In Iraq, Arab nationalist governments ethnicized the political space and militarized Kurdish regions, alienating Kurds from the state on an ethnic basis. However, they also provided economic incentives that co-opted Kurdish nationalists and alleviated the Kurds' social condition. Economic appeasement often dampened the manifestation of Kurdish ethnonationalism. When Kurdish nationalism threatened central government power the Iraqi elite made special efforts to pacify Kurdish communities. Ambiguous political space resulted in an erratic relationship between the Kurdish nationalist and state elites that wavered between hostility and compromise.

These Kurdish management strategies were not part of the Turkish nation-state-building project, which created a fundamentally different relationship between Kurdish leftist nationalists and the state elite. Despite the statist tradition in Turkey and socioeconomic crises caused by urbanization processes, Turkish officials did not attempt to pacify disfranchised Kurdish working-class groups by expanding the state function. Although the political center was marked by internal struggles among the extreme right, army generals, the center-right, and the center-left, none of the coalition governments made any serious effort to assist disfranchised local populations.

In contrast to the Iraqi social-welfare state, in Turkey there was an absence of a redistributive state role or expenditure mechanisms that could have appeased local populations during economic transformations. The Turkish state was not a distributor of wealth that offered free education, food, medicines, and monthly salaries to Kurdish populations (education was free but much less available in the Kurdish provinces than in western and central Anatolia). Rather, it was a regulator of political and market forces, problem solver, price controller, protector of markets, investor, and employer (Keyder 1986; Arat 1991, 144). Alongside the official ideology that denied the existence of Kurds, the state's inability to absorb migrant workers, the uninterest of the right-of-center governments in ameliorating the problem, and the high cost of unionized labor limited the ability of the state elite to co-opt Kurdish leftist nationalist groups the way Iraqi officials did. Whereas a compromising relationship was possible, even temporarily, between Kurdish leftists and Arab socialist governments, it was continuously hostile in Turkey.

The type of ambiguous and variable political space that sporadically appeased Iraqi Kurdish nationalists was also absent in Turkey because the state elite made no effort to accommodate Kurdish ethnic identity. Despite the organizational strength gained from the leftist and youth movements, the political space was limited in content and time, particularly after the 1970 military coup d'état. Although the 1961 constitution remained partially in force, the 1972 Law of Associations limited associational life. The strengthening of right-wing groups in the coalition governments further diminished the possibility of creating an ethnically inclusive political space that could have encouraged compromise between Kurdish nationalists and the state elite.

In Turkey there was no equivalent to Qasim, who initially appealed to Kurdish ethnicity despite the presence of Arab nationalist challengers. Indeed, while in opposition between 1946 and 1950, and then upon assuming the premiership, Menderes tried to gain popular support and an electoral base in Kurdistan by offering Kurds positions alongside Greeks and Armenians. He multiplied promises and personal contacts with prominent Kurds, claiming that his aim was to "re-establish the dialogue between Kurds and Turks and to make a step forward by including in the National Assembly someone from the Shaykh Said family" (Kaya 2003, 104–8). Menderes's party obtained the arrest and condemnation to death of General Mustafa Muğlalı for his leading role in executing the kin of a Kurdish agha, which created a favorable impact on the Democratic Party among the Kurds (Beşikçi 1991).[6]

Still, these appeasement strategies did not alter the ethnicized political boundaries in the state. Co-opted Kurdish communities could not consider themselves Kurds in the public arena; rather, they had to identify as Turkish citizens or Turks ethnically. Even Turkey's so-called center-leftist government made no attempt to recognize Kurdish ethnicity. For instance, when Bülent Ecevit assumed the premiership in 1974, the Cumhuriyet Halk Partisi, which had already shifted leftward during the mid-1960s under İnönü, called for a new opposition strategy based on Scandinavian social democracy (Bianchi 1984, 248, 265). Unlike Qasim, who initially reached out to Kurds as an ethnic group, Ecevit appealed to working classes, peasants, and unions. He negotiated with the Confederation of Trade Unions of Turkey (Türkiye İşçi Sendikaları Konfederasyonu) and the Confederation of Revolutionary Trade Unions of Turkey (Devrimci İşçi Sendikaları Konfederaysonu), but not Kurdish nationalists.

Large gaps emerged between Ecevit's discourse and the political reality, weakening the credibility of the government's proposals and any possibility for a positive relationship with Kurdish nationalists. Although he appointed Serafettin Elçi, a Kurd, as minister of public works in 1977, Ecevit continued to deny Kurdish ethnic identity in the state. He talked about Alevis as an oppressed minority but did not prevent MHP militants and radical Sunni Muslim groups from provoking Sunni populations against the Alevis, instigating divisions within Turkish society and Kurdish nationalist pol-

---

6. The arrest followed a smuggling affair in 1943 by Kurd Memedi Mısto Agha between the Turkish and Iranian border regions. Mısto Agha's kin and villagers on the Turkish side of the border, in the Özalp district of Van, smuggled four hundred sheep to Mısto, who was living on the Iranian side. Forty people were arrested but then freed. General Mustafa Muğlalı detained thirty-three of the smugglers again, brought them to the border, had their hands tied, and executed them. Five years later, in 1947–1948, at the initiative of DP deputies, the "Özalp incident" was brought to the national assembly, where a special commission was convened to establish the facts (the DP had just a few representatives in the Kurdish regions and not one representative from Van). General Mustafa Muğlalı, who eventually admitted to the crime, was found guilty. The military court condemned him to the death penalty but then commuted the sentence to twenty years' imprisonment. The case was supposed to be retried, but Muğlalı died of a heart attack in 1951.

itics. On September 22, 1978, the Young Muslims, a group of radical Turkish nationalist youths, distributed a flyer in the partly Kurdish province of Sivas, promising Sunnis that if they "kill an Alevi they will go to paradise." Additionally, in preparation for the Sunni Muslim holiday Ramadan, the imams of Sivas called Sunni groups to "substitute the blood of a sheep for the blood of an Alevi," warning that "Sivas would become the tomb of the unbelievers (Alevis and Communists)." That same year right-wing paramilitary groups massacred Alevi populations in Maraş, a Kurdish province with a considerable Turkish population of Sunni confession (Coşkun 1995, 289–99).

With increasing violence against opposition groups, the scission of a cohesive ideology within the TİP, and conflicts within the leftist movement, many leading Kurdish leftist nationalists channeled their activities through youth associations such as the Cultural Revolutionary Associations of the People (Devrimci Halk Kültür Dernekleri), the Revolutionary Democratic Cultural Associations (Devrimci Demokratik Kültür Dernekleri), and the Anti-Colonialist Cultural Democratic Associations (Anti Sömürgeci Demokratik Kültür Dernekleri), which were some of the few legal organizational outlets available through the 1970s. In addition to promoting Kurdish cultural and linguistic rights, democracy, and economic development, they advanced Kurdish political interests by presenting "independent candidates" (that is, candidates with no party affiliations) in local elections. These important outlets enabled Kurdish leftist nationalists to become elected mayors in key Kurdish cities, including Medhi Zana in Diyarbakir, Orhan Alpaslan in Agri, and Edip Solmaz in Batman.

In contrast to the early liberalizing period, however, Kurds moved away from Turkish leftist parties and toward distinctly Kurdish nationalist groups that were illegal, including the Socialist Party of Kurdistan in Turkey (Türkiye Kürdistanı Sosyalist Partisi), the Kurdistan Workers' Vanguard Party (Kürdistan Öncü Işci Partisi), and the Liberty Party (Rizgari). Among others, they popularized the slogan "Kurdara Azadi" (Freedom to Kurds) in their manifestations in the big cities and supported Kurdish candidates in local elections. The politically restrictive and unmanageable political space of the late 1970s also gave rise to radical Kurdish nationalist parties such as the National Liberators of Kurdistan (Kürdistan Ulusal Kurtuluşçuları) and the Kurdistan Worker's Party, which manifested a highly ethnicized and violent form of nationalism against the government and each other.

Militarization and Islamization of the Political Space

On September 12, 1980, in response to growing internal insecurity, Turkish military officers staged another coup d'état that dissolved the Demirel government and gave Turkish nationalist military groups control of the political apparatus. This regime change, like the 1968 Ba'thist coup in Iraq, fundamentally transformed the political space. The military elite created a new constitution that elevated the role of the president, terminated the two-chamber Parliament, and assigned new decision-making powers to the National Security Council, now dominated by the military. Article 66 of the 1982 constitution incorporated the racial notion of Turkish identity: "[E]veryone bound to the Turkish state through the bond of citizenship is a Turk" (Gunter 1997, 51–52).

Turkish right-wing factions further closed the political space by removing most legal channels for opposition groups to mobilize. Some democratic institutions remained intact; however, the state elite restricted individual liberties, censored the press, and removed more than one thousand university professors from their posts, replacing them with Turkish nationalists and Islamists. It imposed new electoral laws making it easier for large parties to gain a parliamentary majority, while limiting again the chances of small groups to enter the national assembly (Onis 1991, 35–37; Arat 1991).[7] The Turkish state elite also turned to Western commercial markets to expand military-modernization programs. With a vast military arsenal it became increasingly reliant on the use of force to control the Kurds, just like the Ba'thists did in Iraq. As Kurdish nationalist mobilizations led by the PKK destabilized the border regions and terrorized civilians, the Turkish military establishment was given carte blanche in Kurdistan. After 1984 it employed scorch-and-burn tactics that destroyed

7. The new laws modified the proportional representation system to give more seats to each party with the most votes. In addition to the new 10 percent minimum to gain seats in the Parliament, new barriers were placed on attaining votes in electoral districts. This system made it possible for large parties to gain a smaller number of votes but to obtain a greater amount of seats in the assembly.

villages and farmlands and programs that tortured Kurdish insurgents and massacred civilian populations (Human Rights Watch 1990; Marcus 1994, 19; Jongerden 2002).[8]

While suffocating Kurdish ethnic identity, Turkish state officials opened the political space for Sunni Muslim communities. Upon assuming the presidency in 1984, Turgut Özal, leader of the Motherland Party (Anavatan Partisi), reconfigured the relationship between the state and religion based on the Turkish-Islamic synthesis. He elevated Sunni Muslim brotherhoods in the state's political and commercial networks, supported *imam hatip* schools (secondary schools that offer religious instruction), financed Islamic projects, and created new mosques (Sakallıoğlu 1998, 6–7; Onis 1995; Yavuz 1999; Houston 2001, 85; Yeşilada 1993, 170–75). By Islamizing Turkish nationalism and Turkifying the Islamic tradition Özal slightly altered the boundaries of inclusion and exclusion in the state. That is, in relation to secular groups, to be a Turkish citizen was to be a Turk and a Sunni Muslim.

The Sunni Islamized political space gave the state elite larger opportunities to appease and co-opt Kurdish Sunni communities, just like it did in the late Ottoman period. Özal tried to gain support from Kurdish Sufi orders by pronouncing his Naqshbandiyya origins and appointing Naqshbandiyya shaykhs to high-level government positions. Necmettin Erbakan's Islamic Welfare Party (Refah Partisi) appealed to Kurdish support as well. In presenting the Refah program in 1994, the mayor of Istanbul, Tayyip Erdoğan, promised "to defend the need to break all laws forbidding the recognition and development of Kurdish culture . . . and condemn as well the terror of the PKK as well as that of the state, to oppose Kurdish and Turkish racism" (Bozarslan 1997, 137). Refah offered social-welfare services to poor Kurdish migrant families in urban centers.

Important differences remained, however, between the late imperial period and post-1980 Turkey, which dampened the integrative effects of Islam. Whereas the political space in the Ottoman Empire was based on Islam and an ambiguous sense of ethnicity, in modern Turkey it was clearly and highly exclusionary on an ethnic basis. In fact, as the political space

8. During the course of the war approximately 1,800 Kurdish villages and 6,150 communities were evacuated or destroyed by the Turkish security forces. Some 3 million to 4 million persons fled their villages.

re-Islamized, the Turkish elite continued to promote racist programs. The MHP, having created an alliance with the Welfare Party and Ecevit's Democratic Left Party, used Islam as a surrogate identity for the official state nationalism (Yavuz 2002, 211). Despite the increasing reference to Kurds and the "eastern problem," official state publications denied the authenticity of Kurdish ethnic identity (see, for example, Koçaş 1990, 63–75; Arvasi 1986, 29–31; Giritli 1989, 5–14; Eröz 1975; Çay 1988; Yegen 1998, 216–18; and Akin 1995, 210–13). Turkish nationalist writings argued that the Kurdish Nowruz celebration was really a Turkish holiday. Another popular myth was that Abdullah Öcalan, leader of the PKK, was really an Armenian and that the PKK's goal was to annihilate Sunni Muslims.

The highly ethnicized and militarized political space preempted any possible compromise between the Kurdish nationalists and the state elite. To be sure, in response to European pressures to democratize the political system, Iraqi Kurdish mobilizations, the civil war in the Kurdish regions, and diasporic influences, some Turkish civilian leaders started talking about the Kurds as an ethnic group. On December 8, 1991, in Diyarbakir, Prime Minister Süleyman Demirel claimed, "Those who speak Kurdish, who call themselves of Kurdish origin, who claim their Kurdish identity. It is not possible to oppose these claims" (Akin 1995, 14). In 1992 Özal overturned the 1980 law by allowing limited language opportunities for Kurds and the creation of a Kurdish cultural center in Istanbul. The following year he tried to negotiate a cease-fire with the PKK. Similarly, when she assumed the premiership Tansu Çiller proposed a Basque solution, or a model of limited autonomy, to resolve the Kurdish problem. She attempted to limit the role of the military and check the National Security Council with a special committee of civilians within Parliament (Barkey and Fuller 1998, 144–45). In January 2001 debates recommenced in the national assembly about expanding Kurdish cultural rights. Şenkal Atasagun, the national intelligence chief, claimed it was in Turkey's interest to lift the ban on Kurdish-language broadcasting. The Kurdish issue was also discussed openly at university conferences and in media debates.

Yet in a highly diversified political space dominated by conservative military and radical Turkish nationalist factions and fragmented within the civilian leadership, these overtures were limited in content and time. Despite promises to increase Kurdish cultural rights no group or leader made any effort to de-ethnicize the notion of Turkish citizenship. Large gaps remained between the discourse and the political reality. Demirel talked about a gigantic Turkic world stretching from the Adriatic Sea to the Great Wall of China. Özal, who was more sensitive to resolving the Kurdish problem than any other civilian leader, referred to the post-1980 period as the century of the Turks. Çiller retracted her statement about a Basque solution to the Kurdish problem and permitted right-wing gangs *(ülkücüs)* to form in universities. Conservative Turkish state officials also sponsored radical Islamic groups such as Hezbollah in the Kurdish regions to oppose the PKK and fragment Kurdish society and politics.

Although some Turkish elites promised Kurdish cultural rights, the Turkish Parliament adopted its national program in March 2001 without mentioning the term *Kurd* or education in the Kurdish mother tongue (Yavuz 2001, 19). In the 2002 election campaign Abdülmelik Fırat was arrested in Lice for speaking Kurdish. Murat Bozlak and Akin Birdal, leaders of the Demokratik Halk Partisi (DEHAP) and the Turkish Human Rights Association (HRA), respectively, were prohibited from standing as candidates. By 2004, after the Turkish Parliament passed a language law, permitted limited Kurdish-language broadcasts, and released nine Kurdish deputies from prison, it was still illegal to give babies Kurdish names, speak Kurdish in a political context, or travel with Kurdish-language books without risk of confiscation or arrest.

Violent, Diversified Ethnonationalism

In the highly ethnicized and militarized political space, and in the absence of open political alternatives, Kurdish nationalist sentiment and organizations became highly ethnicized, violent, and diversified. Urbanized Kurdish nationalists produced clandestine journals such as *MEDYA Güneşi, Toplumsal Diriliş, Özgür Gelecek,* and *Vatan Güneşi* that criticized the state's military warfare in Kurdistan and emphasized the distinct Kurdish language. Still prevented from using the term *Kurd,* they created secular, pro-Kurdish parties, including the People's Labor Party (Halkın Emek Partisi [HEP]). In 1993 some HEP representatives even attained seats in the Grand National Assembly after merging with the Turkish center-left Social Democratic People's Party (Sosyaldemokrat Halk Partisi [SHP]). Yet Kurdish parties and their various successor organizations had little opportunity to evolve continuously. The state elite harassed and arrested the leaders, sporadically prohibited their political activities, and closed down their offices.

Other Kurds turned to radical illegal groups such as the PKK, now based in Syria and Lebanon, and engaged in violence and claims for territo-

4. Cover of *MEDYA Güneşi,* a clandestine Kurdish nationalist journal published in Turkey, 1988. From *MEDYA Güneşi,* no. 6.

rial separation. Still committed to socialist principles, after 1989 the PKK replaced its communist symbols with Kurdish nationalist ones. Part of this shift was tied to the downfall of the Soviet Union and a weakening of leftist ideology. A larger part was owing to the political space in post-1980 Turkey. Öcalan stated:

> I did not emphasize Kurdayetî along with other leftists during the 1960s–70s because the extreme left was very strong and the Kurds lost their confidence. Also, there was not a dictatorship in Turkey during this time. We created the PKK in 1978 at the time of the massacres in Karamaraş. Still it was not a party uniquely for the Kurds or for Kurdayetî. It was an idea of the socialists. . . . [O]ur route to revolution was socialism. . . . But after 1980 the "flash" appeared. (Perinçek 1989, 16–33)

Unlike the early Kemalist and liberalizing period, Öcalan's flash, or realization of his distinct Kurdish ethnic identity, became increasingly influential across Kurdish society. The government's refusal to grant real Kurdish cultural and political freedoms, terrorism across Kurdistan, destruction of Kurdish lands, imprisonment of Leyla Zana and seven other moderate Kurdish deputies for speaking Kurdish in the Turkish Parliament, and Öcalan's arrest in Nairobi in 1999 created a growing sense of outrage among the Kurdish masses as an ethnic group, even if they did not support the PKK openly.

Kurdayetî also became salient in the Kurdish countryside. In contrast to Menderes's and Demirel's policies, socioeconomic changes tied to Özal's privatization programs helped transform Turkey from a major agricultural exporter to an industrial one. From 1980 to 1990 the percentage of total exports of agricultural goods declined from 57.5 percent to 18 percent, while industrial outputs doubled, from 40 percent to 80 percent. The state elite closed Kurdish pasturelands used for cattle breeding, resulting in a loss of revenue for certain Kurdish tribes (Houston 2001, 115). Also, after more than fifteen years of civil war Kurdish villages had been depopulated or razed completely, weakening the traditional Kurdish economy and opportunities tied to the land (Eralp 1998; Togan and Balasubramanyam 1996, 90; Saracoğlu 1994; *Turquie* 1985, 9). Kurdish agricultural centers such as Erzurum and Diyarbakir saw their economic advantages decline as wheat-producing regions. These economic transformations ruptured patron-client relations among Kurdish tribal chiefs, aghas, and the central government. Some conservative Kurdish communities turned away from state-supported parties and toward Kurdish nationalist ones. In 2001, after thirty-seven years of political accommodation with Demirel's AP, Abdülmelik Fırat resigned from his post and created a new Kurdish party demanding Kurdish rights, although criticizing the PKK and its violent manner of seeking to resolve the Kurdish issue.

Yet in contrast to the highly salient and influential Kurdayetî in autonomous Iraqi Kurdistan, the presence of a complex political space, even in a weakened form, has ensured a more diversified, and less representative, form of Kurdish nationalism in Turkey. After the 1980 coup d'état there remained a controlled multiparty system and a Turkish civil society. Kurdish groups, unlike their counterparts in Iraqi Kurdistan, still have limited channels to express their political identities outside Kurdish nationalist parties. By the mid-1990s the number of registered voluntary associations rose to 112,000, half of which included cooperatives and unions (Kalaycıoğlu 2002, 254). Indeed, real political participation is limited. Turkey's rigid electoral system discriminates against small parties that do not pass the 10 percent barrier. It has consistently prevented the highly popular DEHAP, which won between 35 percent and 56 percent of the votes in nine different Kurdish regions in the 2002 elections, from attaining seats in the national assembly. Nearly half of the electorate in the 2002 election was not represented in the Turkish Parliament.

Still, the more complex electoral spectrum in Turkey has created greater opportunities for fragmentation of the Kurdish nationalist elite, organizations, and sentiment. Whereas the 2001 municipality election results in Iraqi Kurdistan were largely divided between the two highly influential and representative Kurdish nationalist parties, the Kurdish vote in the 1999 and 2004 elections in Turkey was diffused among five pro-Kurdish parties, the Islamic parties (Fazilet Partisi and Adalet ve Kalkınma Partisi [AKP]), and three center-left parties. In the March 2004 municipality elections DEHAP merged with small socialist Turkish parties under the SHP banner as an attempt to gain greater leverage and political legitimacy with Turkish authorities and society.

Further, some conservative Kurdish constituencies continue to support

Turkish center-right parties for economic and political reasons, even if they consider themselves Kurds ethnically. Economic liberalization weakened the role of agriculture, the village agha, and some tribes; however, it created an entrepreneurial class that integrated into the Turkish political economy. Kurdish landowners who migrated to and reinvested in the western regions profited from Özal's industrialization and privatization programs. They became some of the wealthiest businessmen and most influential politicians in Turkey.[9] Yalım Erez, a Kurd, was president of the Turkish Chamber of Commerce and Industry (Türkiye Ticaret ve Sanayi Odaları). Some Naqshbandiyya shakyhs gained financial capital from the Islamic banking system (which was permitted to install in Turkey under the condition of organizing as mixed societies with Naqshbandiyyas tied to Özal) and became part of a new class of "dervish managers," entrepreneurs, and engineers. Hikmet Çetin, a Kurd from Lice, became deputy in the CHP and its successor party, the SHP, and served as foreign minister in the coalition governments of DYP-SHP in the early 1990s. Abdülkadir Aksu, a Kurd from Diyarbakir, became deputy in the ANAP, the RP, and the AKP and served as minister of internal affairs under Özal, minister of state under Mesut Yılmaz, and minister of the interior under Erdoğan. Kamuran İnan, grandson of Shaykh Shahabeddin, became deputy in the ANAP (after twenty years as deputy in Demirel's AP) and minister of state under Özal. Still other Kurds responded to the central government's divide-and-rule strategies by joining the village guard system, acting as informants against Kurdish activists. In 1992 in the region of Van, for instance, Sedun Seylan, head of the Alan tribe, owned twenty-six villages, retained five hundred village guards, and received a monthly salary of $115,000 (McDowall 1997, 422; Zarcone 1998, 113–14; Besson 1998, 42–49).

Turkey's complex political space has also encouraged the reemergence of Islam in Kurdish nationalist politics. Sunni Kurdish migrants turned to Refah to reap the sociowelfare services it provided to the urban poor. In the early 1990s Refah strengthened its influence in the Kurdish regions, receiving between 14 percent and 25 percent of the vote in Batman, Diyarbakir, Ağrı, Mardin, Şirnak, and Van. In the 1995 elections Kurds in Istanbul

9. The special June 1993 edition of *Nokta* focused on "the one-hundred richest Kurds" in Turkey.

largely voted for Refah, not HADEP. Islamic influences further increased in the March 2004 elections, whereby SHP, of which DEHAP was a part, lost representation in four Kurdish provinces—Ağrı, Bingol, Siirt, and Van—to the AKP *(Bulletin* 2004, 8).[10]

Kurdish nationalists, in turn, have sporadically used religion to advance their nationalist agenda. After 1990 some Kurds in Turkey reconfigured Kurdish liberation in the context of Islam as a way of countering the state's Islamic policies. Öcalan declared the PKK more Islamic than the Islamists and said that "he too, prayed during his youth" (Perinçek 1989, 16). Redefining the Kurdish struggle as a jihad against the Turkish state, he created clandestine groups such as the Patriotic Union of the Mullahs of Kurdistan, the Islamic Party of Kurdistan, and the Kurdish-Alevi Union. Others turned away from Refah, which they associated with statist Islam, and called for a Muslim Kurdistan through armed struggle. Still others regenerated Sufism, maintaining ties with Kurdish brotherhoods and medreses without turning to Kurdish nationalist groups.

An Alevi movement also became salient, creating even greater diversity in Kurdayetî in Turkey. Alevism, which emphasizes the distinct Alevi identity alongside or instead of Kurdish ethnonationalism, became possible because the political space after 1980 increased for Alevi communities. Although it was still illegal to discuss the Kurdish issue in the Grand National Assembly, political officials started to debate cultural rights for Alevis. Özal permitted the construction of *cemevis* (houses of Alevi ritual), cultural organizations, and associations in the big Turkish cities and towns, including the cemevi Hacı Bektaşi Veli Anadolu Kültür Vakfı in Ankara and Istanbul. For the first time in the history of the Turkish republic Alevis had public places to express their distinct cultural and religious identities. Although some Kurdish Alevis joined secular Kurdish nationalist organizations, others responded to the rise of Islamism and turned toward secular Turkish leftist social democratic parties. Still others identified as Alevis first and turned to Turkish and Kurdish Alevi associations (Shankland 1996).

---

10. DEHAP's alliance with the SHP in 2004 may have temporarily legitimated the party with Turkish authorities; however, it was criticized among some Kurdish nationalists. Many protested the DEHAP-SHP alliance, which partially accounts for the high abstention rates in the Kurdish regions in the March 2004 elections.

Conclusions

After 1950 the political space in Turkey remained highly ethnicized, which prevented any possible accommodation between the Kurdish nationalists and the state elite. Yet it also diversified alongside transformations tied to the liberalization period. Consequently, whereas Kurdayetî in Iraq was manifested around two main oppositional identities, in Turkey it diffused along more complex socioeconomic, religious, and political lines. A more economically and politically diversified space has also prevented Kurdish nationalism from becoming as representative as it is in Iraqi Kurdistan. Kurds in Turkey have greater opportunities to merge nationalist and ethnic claims with civic, religious, and localist identities, which in turn creates greater challenges to the emergence of a unified nationalist elite and organization across Kurdish society.

6

Iran's Transition to a
Constitutional Monarchy

The downfall of the Qajar imperial system and rise of a constitutional monarchy reshaped the political space in the Iranian state. Like Iraqi and Turkish officials the Iranian elite redrew political boundaries by ethnicizing, secularizing, and centralizing the government. The Kurds became part of the Other because they were not Persians ethnically. However, the nature and timing of the nation-state-building processes differed from the Iraqi and Turkish projects. By reconstructing myths based on special shared histories between Persians and Kurds, sporadically recognizing Kurdish ethnicity in a limited cultural form, and tolerating Islam in the public sphere, the Iranian elite gave Kurds less incentive and opportunities to manifest Kurdayetî than in early colonial Iraq and Kemalist Turkey.

Transition Period: Segmented Nationalism

As in the Iraqi and Turkish state transition periods, postwar Persia was marked by internal instability and economic havoc. The weak Qajar government was still in power, state financing was in arrears, and tribal revolts and Soviet-backed autonomy movements continued in the outlying regions (Zabih 1966, 13–16). Foreign government penetrations left the country divided politically and administratively. With the signing of the 1919 Anglo-Iranian Agreement Iran became a semicolony of Britain, even though it escaped the mandate system. Further, General Reza Khan, who after the 1921 coup d'état became minister of defense and rising head of state, did

117

not have popular support outside the Conservative Reformer's Party. Tensions continued between constitutionalists and monarchists, British- and Russian-supported factions, and ulema and secularists.

To stabilize the country and consolidate power, Reza Khan, like British and Turkish officials, reached out to the traditional stratum tied to imperial structures. Although he repressed tribal revolts with force, Reza Khan permitted the chiefs to retain relative autonomy in their localities. He also appealed to conservative ulema factions, which reacted against the idea of a republican system in Iran similar to the Turkish model (Cronin 1997, 187). Promising to protect Islam in a constitutional monarchy, on April 1, 1924, Reza Khan met with religious elite in Qom. He affirmed he would "preserve the majesty of Islam and the independence of Iran" and ensure that "the status of our religious leaders is respected and honored" (Lenczowski 1978, 24).

Yet Reza Khan made no appeals to Kurdish nationalism as did British and Turkish officials. Instead of promising Kurdish-Persian fraternity in a future Iranian state or creating committees for the development of southwest Iran, he addressed the Kurds strictly as a tribal community and later criticized foreign governments for stirring rivalry among the Kurdish tribes in Iraq (Burrell 1997, 6:20). Nor did the Iranian elite struggle over Kurdish territories and borders, despite British influences in Kermanshah. The postimperial carving of Kurdistan affected only the former Ottoman Kurdish regions, not Qajar Persia. Iranian Kurdistan was also excluded from a future Kurdish state as envisioned in the Sèvres Treaty. From the outset the colonial powers made it clear that Iranian Kurdistan was an integral part of Iran and that the Kurdish problem centered on Iraq and Turkey.

Indeed, some Iranian Kurdish chiefs, like Kurds in Iraq and Turkey, took advantage of the decentralized transition period to advance nationalist claims. Influenced by cross-border Kurdish mobilizations, independence movements in the Caucasus, and the presence of foreign powers, Kurdish notables such as Seyyid Taha and Hama Rashid met with British officials to discuss a Kurdish state under a British protectorate. Ismail Agha Simko, leader of the Kurdish Shakak tribe, wrote to Babekr I Selim Agha, the *qaimaqam* (mayor) of Qaladiza in Iraqi Kurdistan, arguing in favor of enlisting the assistance of the British government. "He who does not realize this, Simko wrote, is a fool" ("Translation of Letter" 1921). Kurdish chieftains such as Mahmoud Bey, and the khanate of Maku turned to Soviet networks to secure their nationalist interests, and personal ambitions, and economic opportunities.

Still, the manifestation of Kurdish nationalism was not influential or representative across Kurdistan. In contrast to the transitioning Iraqi and Turkish states, whereby Kurdish nationalists accessed semilegal associations, modernizing political parties, tariqa orders, and external support to influence local populations, Iranian Kurds could rely only on disorganized tribal militias. Foreign officials made vague promises to the Kurds; however, they did not encourage Kurdayetî. There were no Major Noels traveling through the Iranian Kurdish countryside promising Kurdish statehood, creating local administrations, and elevating Kurds to legitimate local leadership positions.

Even if a nationalist elite and organizations were available, imperial structures that elevated the traditional stratum would have limited Kurdish nationalist potential anyway. The agrarian-based, segmented Kurdish society was more interested in protecting tribal, religious, and landowning interests, particularly in response to the 1906 reforms that confiscated lands and replaced the tuyul system with private ownership, than in manifesting Kurdish nationalism. Most Kurds aligned with the monarchy, Islam, tribes, and localities. Others remained politically inactive in their isolated provincial enclaves. Tribal leaders such as Sardar in Khorasan, Akram in Kermanshah, and Simko in Urmiya made no serious effort to manifest a cohesive ethnonational sentiment. Although considering himself a Kurdish nationalist, Simko ensured that his grand council of Kurdish chiefs excluded Kurds from Mahabad. Kurds from Kurdistan and Kermanshah refused to mobilize for any type of nationalism unless they were paid. The Kurdish khan of Maku tried to prevent a Simko-Turkish alliance by selling his grain surpluses to the Kemalists.

Appeals to Islam also failed to unify the fractured Kurdish tribal community. Whereby Sunni Kurdish nationalists in the former Ottoman territories joined Arabs and Turks to save the caliphate, Iranian Kurds made no serious attempts to manifest a cohesive Islamic Kurdish nationalism. Indeed, Simko warned, "[I]f a nation does not protect its nationhood now, its religion too, will go under" and formed a "pan-Islamic alliance" with Shaykh Taha in Turkey ("Translation of Letter" 1921). This effort, however, had marginal influence across Kurdish society. Sunni Kurds in Kurdistan Province refused to join Simko's band that mobilized Sunni Turks against Christian groups.

The absence of a standardized Kurdish language and developed communications and transportation systems kept Kurdish communities further separated from one another, just as they did in colonial Iraq and Kemalist Turkey. Kurdistan Province was an isolated Sunni Kurdish region. West Azerbaijan and Kermanshah, mixed with Kurds, Shi'a Azeris, and Persian communities, had marginal contact with populations outside their localities. Sorani-speaking Kurds in the Iranian border regions had greater attachments to Iraqi Kurds in Sulaimaniya Province than to Kurds in Kermanshah and Urmiya. Consequently, rather than seeing themselves as an imagined community, most Iranian Kurds identified as Sanandaji, Kermanshahi, Mahabadi, Hamadani, Sunni, and Shi'a Muslims and as members of the Shakak, Mamash, Pishdar, Jaf, Kalhur, and Shamdinan tribes.

The Iranian Constitutional Monarchy

After removing the last Qajar king from power, declaring Iran a constitutional monarchy, and assuming the position of *shahenshah* in 1925, Reza Khan, now called Reza Shah, commenced his nation-state-building project. Like the British, Iraqi, and Turkish elite, the shah tried to unify the fragmented country by creating an official state nationalism based on an ethnicized, modernized, and secular notion of Iranian identity. Assisted by the Iranian cultural academy and Society of Public Guidance, he "Persianized" the Iranian language, altered school curricula, dedicated architectural images to pre-Islamic Sassanid and Achaemenid kings, and defined non-Persian languages as local dialects of Persian. Reza Shah militarily coerced and repressed non-Persian ethnic communities into the state-defined Persian culture and arrested some Kurdish communities for speaking the Kurdish language (Hushyar 1992, 92–94; Lenczowski 1978, 37; Higgens 1986, 174–75; Mojab and Hassanpour 1995, 231–34).

Centralizing and modernizing the state also meant terminating the tribal way of life. Like Atatürk, Reza Shah labeled non-Persian traditions as tribal lifestyles, killed and forcibly resettled tribal chiefs, prohibited winter migrations, and confiscated tribal territories. His militarily repressive and centralization policies destroyed essential socioeconomic structures and political organization in Kurdistan (Vali 1994a, 157; Katouzian 1981, 130; Akhavi 1986b, 209). In doing so he prevented the Kurdish tribal stratum from any potential role it could have played as a nationalist elite, just as had been done in Turkey. Following Atatürk's secularization policies, Reza Shah also limited Islam in the public sphere. Except for the Luri king Karim Khan Zand, he removed all official references to the Islamic period. Although the shah initially promised the ulema that the constitutional monarchy would guarantee Islamic principles, after 1924 he closed Qur'anic schools, curtailed religious holidays, and transferred ulema power, wealth, and status to the Ministry of Education. The Majlis-approved 1928 civil code was based on the French system, which placed the ulema outside the judiciary.

Given these apparent similarities in political spaces, what accounts for the differences in the manifestation of Kurdayetî in Iran? In colonial Iraq Kurdish nationalism emerged alongside semilegal local governments and sporadic revolts against the British, and in early Kemalist Turkey it was violent, highly ethnicized, and Islamized. However, in early constitutional Iran Kurdayetî was still barely existent.

Although Reza Shah followed Atatürk's example, his nation-state-building project incorporated elements of the Iraqi case, which created a particular type of political space that limited incentives and opportunities for Kurds to manifest their ethnonational identity. As in Turkey, militarization and centralization policies made it unsafe or impossible to organize as ethnic communities. Yet the boundaries of inclusion and exclusion were also less alienating for Kurds ethnically and certain subgroups in the traditional stratum, which constrained the emergence of a salient sense of Kurdayetî across Kurdistan.

In contrast to Kemalist Turkey and like colonial Iraq, the early official Iranian nationalism was partially ambiguous. Emergent and competing ideological currents were nationalistic; however, they were based on modernism, Islam, and rejection of foreign penetration in the country, not solely ethnicity. Unlike Atatürk, Reza Shah's objective was to destroy the political and military organization of the Kurdish tribes, not their ethnic identity (Vali 1994a, 157; Katouzian 1981, 80; Fawcett 1992, 82). Reza Shah de-ethnicized Iranian identity at politically expedient moments, such as during his attempt to repossess the Arab-populated Bahrain islands from Britain, which he considered part of Iran. The particular myths tied to the official state nationalism were also more inclusive for Iranian Kurds as an ethnic group. Whereas qawmiyya Arab nationalists in colonial Iraq talked about a pan-Arab state and the Kemalist elite denied Kurdish identity by calling Kurds Gökturks, the Iranian elite emphasized the Aryan nature of Persian identity. Reza Shah's notion of pan-Iran was based on the union of all Iranians, including the Pars in India, Afghans, Armenians, and Jews, under a single nation (Dr. Afshar 1927, 564; Tabrizi 1927).

One of the shah's popular claims was based on the idea of the natural cultural similarity between Kurds and Persians as descendants of the Medes and speakers of a shared Indo-European language. According to one leading Iranian nationalist of the period, the problem of Iranian unity centered not on the Kurds, who were similar to Persians, but on non-Persian communities racially linked to Arabs and Turks, including Azeris (Dr. Afshar 1927, 564). Modern nationalism supported by Reza Shah was also pre-Islamic and Zoroastrian. It emphasized distinctions with Arabs, which Reza Shah blamed for the Islamization of Iran (Katouzian 1981, 82). Ambiguous discourses and policies weakened, but did not remove the ethnicized boundaries between Persians and non-Persians. Iranian Kurds may have faced discriminations as a non-Persian community; however, they had a special place in the official state nationalism that was unavailable to Kurds in Iraq or Turkey, or to Iran's other non-Persian communities, such as Arabs and Turks.

Reza Shah's modernization and secularization programs were also less drastic than the Turkish reforms, giving the traditional stratum larger opportunities to maintain their privileged positions in the Iranian power structure (Vali 1993; Floor 1984, 45–57; Abrahamian 1982, 378; Firoozi 1976, 10–11, 28–30; Akhavi 1986b, 206–7). Despite the 1923 financial administrative reform, the state's increasing role in managing the economy, sedentarization of tribes, and improvement in some peasants' status, agrarian relations in Kurdistan favored medium and large landowners. Reza Shah's economic and agricultural policies reinforced the power of Kurdish khans by creating wheat-purchasing schemes, state-supported investment projects, and tax exemptions for landowners. Rather than using land for revenue-generating purposes like Qajar leaders, he encouraged private ownership through land registrations, which resulted in greater land titles for the aghas. Agricultural production declined during World War II, yet the abolishment of the agricultural land tax, creation of state subsidies and monopoly law, and addition of new taxes extracted by tribal chiefs reinforced patron-client relations among landowners, some remaining tribesmen, and the state (Lambton 1969, 34; Koohi-Kamali 1992, 173–4).

However, in contrast to Atatürk's statism and industrialization policies that elevated a commercial bourgeoisie tied to Western capitalist markets, Reza Shah's programs built the infrastructure but limited benefits for commercial classes, including bazaaris, sarafs, and moneylenders. Manufacturing commenced in the private sector and encouraged small industries, yet it did not become autonomous like it did in Turkey. Iranian merchants had to fund the construction of factories, whereas the trade monopoly law protected state-run industries. Even after the termination of foreign capitulations and opening of the Trans-Iranian Railway in 1930, which improved trade and commerce, the Iranian elite sheltered the growing industrial sector from foreign manufacturers (Floor 1984, 19; Akhavi 1986b, 206–7). The absence of an independent, influential Persian commercial class linked to international financial capital prevented the type of ethically defined economic polarizations that emerged in Kemalist Turkey from becoming salient in constitutional Iran. By the late 1930s it was not the Persian and Azeri merchants, industrialists, or bureaucratic elite that enjoyed a privileged position in the Pahlavi court, but the landowning stratum, many of whom were Kurdish khans, former tribesman, and leading Shi'a ulema. From 1909 to 1941 landlord seats in the Majlis increased from 21 percent to 58 percent. The merchants' representation decreased from 41 percent to 18 percent and the clergy declined from 20 to 8 percent (Najambadi 1987a, 221; Burrell 1997, 6:438).

Additionally, although he repressed the leading tribes, Reza Shah tempered smaller and settled tribesmen by giving them semilegitimate authority in their localities. In the fall of 1926 the minister of war, General Abdullah Amir Tahmasseb, visited Sanandaj to negotiate with Kurdish tribal chiefs (Arfa 1965, 204). The minister of the interior received Hani Bab Shaykh in his office in Tehran. State officials gave Kurds government positions: Saifullah Khan Ardalan in Saqqiz, Mahmud Kanisanan in Meriwan, and Qazî Muhammed in Mahabad (Burrell 1997, 2:470). In addition, certain tribes such as the Kalhur, Jaf, and Pishdar maintained access to labor markets and summer grazing rights. Others continued to profit from smuggling activities on the Iraqi border. Most settled tribes, however, were reorganized into the landowning stratum, allowing them to reconsolidate power in the countryside. Others assimilated into Iranian social and political structures in the urban centers through the shah's military conscription and centralized education policies.

The political space in early constitutional Iran was also more institutionally accommodating for Islamic communities than it was in early colonial Iraq or republican Turkey, particularly for the Shi'a majority. Even though Reza Shah campaigned against the religious establishment and his secularization policies weakened Islam in the public sphere, he had to accommodate the ulema in the state apparatus. The Supplementary Law separated religion and politics, and a 1939 decree authorized the state to assume vaqf lands. However, in contrast to the political and Sunni religious institutions in colonial Iraq and Kemalist Turkey, the Majlis assumed a role of real political importance and the ulema retained autonomy, which often required the shah to seek parliamentary support from ulema factions. The special parliamentary committee and Iran's dual legal system also guaranteed legal and formal status of the ulema in the political arena. Shi'a Muslim law had influence in the civil code based on the principles of Ja'fari rights, which incorporated Islamic laws into issues such as crop sharing, inheritance, and property rights (Lambton 1953, 194).

The institutionalized and autonomous role of Shi'a Islam in the Iranian power structure alongside the secularization policies created a particular relationship between the central government and the religious establishment that was not present in the Iraqi and Turkish cases. In fact, Reza Shah appealed to the Islamic leaders when he needed to strengthen his power base. For instance, to convince the ulema of his commitment to Islam, in 1936 he purged Baha'is from the army and government posts and closed Baha'i schools, affecting some ten thousand students (Avery, Hambly, and Melville 1991, 181–82).[1] Medreses and ulema centers for learning, including in Qom and Mashhad, operated with a degree of autonomy from the monarchy. Muslims continued to worship in provincial and urban centers. Whereas the Sancta Sophia mosque in Istanbul became a tourist museum, the Sepahsalar mosque in Tehran remained an open legal space for Muslim worship. Although the shah Europeanized the dress code in 1936, some women in rural areas continued to wear the hejab.

Consequently, whereas Islam gradually lost its saliency in late colonial Iraq and was ruptured from the political space in Kemalist Turkey, it was

1. The Baha'is are the followers of Sayyid Ali Muhammed, a young merchant from Shiraz. He reinterpreted Shi'a beliefs, clashed with the traditional ulema, and was executed in 1850.

significantly weakened in early constitutional Iran but continued to shape the boundaries of inclusion and exclusion. All groups applying for military positions had to designate their religious affiliation (Abrahamian 1982, 145–70; Higgens 1986, 173; Burrell 1997, 10:213–14). Majlis representation was based on religious groupings, not ethnicity. Zoroastrians and Armenians had special reserved seats in the government; however, they did not have full rights as Muslim Iranians. Majlis debates over the compulsory closing of all shops on Fridays were directed at Armenian and Jewish shopkeepers. Bazaar-shop signs warned those customers who were not Muslim to wash their hands.

In the political space that repressed opposition, acknowledged some form of Kurdish identity, elevated Kurdish khans, and tolerated limited Islam, most Kurds had little opportunity and less reason to revolt against the government than did Kurds in Kemalist Turkey. Instead of expressing a highly ethnicized, Islamic, or violent sense of Kurdayetî, the Kurdish nationalist Mihemedê Qazi blamed Kurds for their ignorance, which allowed them to be dominated by others. "Look at the English nation," he wrote in 1928–1929, "which due to science and knowledge, has advanced before other nations." Like Jaf in early colonial Iraq, Qazî affirmed that only by acquiring knowledge could the Kurds end their condition as victims (Çira, no. 13 [1998]: 92).

Moderate Ethnonationalism

Although Kurdayetî was quiet, it did not remain that way. Reza Shah talked about the Iranian people and a shared Aryan culture; however, his policies favored Shi'a Persian-speaking groups. Most high-level positions, local governorships, and military posts were reserved for Persian nationals. In this ethnicizing space and influenced by the Azerbaijani autonomy movement and Iraqi Kurdish nationalist parties, Kurdayetî became salient and ethnicized. Iranian Kurdish nationalism also gained significance because in contrast to the transition and early constitutional periods, Kurds had the necessary opportunity structures to advance their nationalist claims. By the early 1940s weak government power created a political vacuum in Iran. Foreign power penetrations during World War II temporarily removed political restrictions against Kurds in certain provinces and offered new forms of external resources and support. With Soviet backing

and new printing presses Kurdish nationalists in the Mahabad region created the Kurdish nationalist party, the Komeley-i Jineweh-i Kurdistan (JK),
in 1942, which became the Kurdistan Democratic Party of Iran (KDPI).
They also had an educated nationalist leader, Qazî Muhammed, a notable,
judge, and clergyman from Mahabad, to mobilize Kurdish populations in
the outlying provinces. Qazî Muhammed and his nationalist circles even
created a government called the Kurdish Republic of Mahabad.

The presence of a modernizing nationalist elite, semilegal nationalist
party, Kurdish publications, and quasi-autonomous government urbanized
the Kurdish movement and spread nationalist ideas, just like it did in Iraqi
Kurdistan. One of the dominant themes of Kurdish nationalist sentiment
was the need to protect the distinct Kurdish ethnic identity. The Kurdish
national anthem, for instance, claimed that "the Kurdish-speaking people
still exist and that their flag will never fall" (Ghassemlou 1976, 19; Eagleton
1991; Ezat 1995; Yassin 1995, 143–85). Kurdish publications also became
ethnicized. The Iranian Kurdish nationalist Hêmin (Muhammed Amin
Shaykh ul-Islam [1921–1995]) reacted to the shah's repressive policies by
proclaiming his attachment to his ethnic identity. In his well-known political poem of the period, "Kurdim Amin" (I am a Kurd) he wrote:

5. The cultural committee of the Mahabad Republic in Iran, 1946. Photograph
courtesy of Rafiq Studio.

Although I am taken in by desperation, regret, and sufferance, never in face of this ungrateful destiny I will let myself be battered. I am not in love with the sensual eyes or open neck of great beauty. I am in love with the mountains, hills, and rocks. Even if I freeze today because of hunger and nudity, I will not submit to the settlements of the foreigner as long as I am on this land. I am not afraid of chains nor cords nor sticks nor prison. Cut in pieces until they kill me, I will still say that I am a Kurd. (1974, 49)

Similarly, in an article in the JK organ, *Nishtiman,* the author reprinted the discourse of Shaykh Said during the 1925 revolt in Turkey. He claimed that dying for Kurdistan was better than living without freedom, which would be equivalent to living without honor ("Wutarêikî Shaykh Said" 1943).

Although Kurdayetî became highly salient and ethnicized, it was more accommodating than Kurdish nationalism in colonial Iraq and Kemalist Turkey. JK members certainly were hostile to the central government and made claims for a free and independent Kurdistan; however, their political strategy for manifesting Kurdayetî was not based on violence (Vali 1994a, 162). Even with Mullah Mustafa Barzani as the general commander of the Mahabad Army and his tribal militias in Iran, most Kurdish nationalists, including Qazî Muhammed, did not engage in militarily violent ethnonationalism. Influenced by foreign powers, some demanded a free Kurdish nation within a shared state culture and permission to use the Kurdish language. Others refused to accept Germany's wartime propaganda that emphasized the shared Aryan identity of Persians, Kurds, and Germans, but they supported the notion of a Kurdish empire based on the Aryan nature of all Kurds. Still others defined and defended Kurdish national identity in Iran as part of the strong Aryan race *(Kurdistan,* Jan. 11, 1946, 1, 3; *Nishtiman* Aug.-Sept. 1946; "Qawmî Kurd layqî Jian" 1943; Lenczowski 1978, 160–61).[2]

Nor was Kurdayetî highly representative or influential across Kurdish society. Most Kurds may have considered themselves ethnically Kurdish, yet they did not manifest a coherent Kurdish nationalism in the public sphere. It was not possible, given the nature of the political space. The militarization of Iran, foreign occupations, and administrative constraints hin-

---

2. Under the Nuremberg racial laws the Reich cabinet promoted new Aryan legends, using the swastika to emphasize the special relationship between Aryans and Zoroastrians.

dered open transportation and communication between Kurdish regions. Kurdish communities in outlying provinces remained geographically isolated from one another. Although the Mahabad government welcomed all Kurds, its representation did not include Kurds in Saqqez, Sanandaj, and Kermanshah, the three largest Kurdish-populated cities. Also, given the underdeveloped nature of Kurdistan, Qazî Muhammed and his small group of Sunni supporters and Kurdish notables had marginal influence among the Iranian Kurdish masses, the majority of whom were poor, illiterate, and tied to traditional social structures. Mahabad may have had a government, but there was not one secondary school in the province. The few families that could afford to sent their children to Tabriz to be educated.

Hostility to the central government was made on not only an ethnic basis but also an economic one. Reza Shah's poorly planned industrialization policies ignored agricultural markets so that by the early World War II years, wheat silos were empty and the shah was importing wheat, which further discouraged production at home. His modernization programs resulted in overtaxation, conscription, and prohibition of smuggling and trade in certain border regions (Burrell 1997, 10:470). In this militarized, centralized, and undeveloped political space it was often economically advantageous and politically safer to emphasize local, provincial, or socioeconomic identities than ethnonationalist ones. For instance, the Soviets' offer to purchase the 1945 wheat harvest gave Kurdish farmers, including members of the nationalist JK party, an additional $80,000 above the 10 percent that the Iranian government already paid (Burrell 1997, 11:539–40). Rather than forming a redistribution system that could have supported Kurdish communities during the wheat crisis or using their profits to back the Mahabad government, some Kurdish farmers hoarded their goods, raised prices, and gained financially. Other Kurdish khans criticized progressive nationalists who wanted to remove feudal structures.

The shah's policies, like the tactics in Iraq and Turkey, made no effort to weaken intra-Kurdish dichotomies. Uneven modernization programs reinforced socioeconomic distinctions between Sunni and Shi'a regions and created new ones between urbanizing centers and the Kurdish countryside. Centralization policies subdivided Kurdish regions and treated them differently from one another. For example, the Sunni Kurdish region of Kurdistan was called a Kurdish province; however, other ethnically Kurdish towns were tied to Persian provincial centers and administered as such. The 1956 administrative reforms separated Ilam and Hamadan from Kermanshah and placed them as districts under Tehran's jurisdiction. Urmiya became part of West Azerbaijan, but the mixed Kurdish-Persian Shi'a majority province of Kermanshah was linked to the southwest oil-producing region of Khuzestan and gained limited opportunities from the Anglo-Iranian Oil Company (Clarke and Clarke 1969, 10–55). By 1976 Kermanshah was nearly twice as urbanized as Kurdistan Province and had the highest number of people working in the tertiary sector, with the exception of Tehran.

In Kurdistan and the ethnically and religiously mixed West Azerbaijan Province, however, the situation was different. The state elite supported the traditional stratum without modernizing the infrastructure. Although Tehran's medreses more than halved and Kermanshah's declined from forty to four from 1926 to 1941, medreses in Kurdistan and parts of West Azerbaijan increased from seventeen to twenty-eight and from zero to seventy-four, respectively (Aghajanian 1983; Clarke and Clarke 1969, 55; Akhavi 1980, 190–91, 208).

Continued attachment to traditional power structures and uneven modernization policies further polarized socioeconomic groups and reinforced divisions between the town and country, just like they did in colonial Iraq. Instead of advancing claims against Persians, working-class rights, or Islam, modernizing Kurdish nationalists focused on the negative role of the traditional stratum in the Kurdish movement. In analyzing why the Kurds did not have a state, articles in *Nishtiman* blamed Kurdish mullahs, landowners, and tribesmen, calling them "traitors . . . Sufis with beards and beads, thick necks and big bellies . . . begging bowls and poverty" who were unable "to push forward the Kurdish cause or serve in a Kurdish state" (Vali 1994a, 160; McDowall 1997, 238). Certainly, at politically expedient moments JK members emphasized their Muslim identity as a way of convincing conservative factions and ulema groups they were not communists or atheists. However, Sunni Kurds did not make important demands as a Muslim minority. Although Qazî Muhammed was a cleric and his assistant was the Naqshbandiyya shaykh Abdullah Gilani, he did not emphasize a common Sunni Muslim identity or attempt to create an Islamic Kurdish nationalism. Kurdayetî in early constitutional Iran was defined by its secular and ethnicized sentiment, just as it was in colonial Iraq.

Democratizing Political Space: Diversified Nationalism

After the 1946 Soviet withdrawal and reoccupation of Kurdistan by Iranian military forces, Kurdish nationalists lost important resources that could have ensured the survivability of their nationalist project. Iranian officials sporadically tried to negotiate with KDPI leaders; however, they repressed the Mahabad Republic with force, arrested and hanged the nationalist elite, outlawed the KDPI, and restricted Kurdish nationalist activities. Kurdayetî ceased, went outside the country, or became clandestine, just like it did in Kemalist Turkey. Yet although the political space contracted for Kurds as an ethnic group, it did not close entirely. Reza Shah ruled by firman, prevented an open political party system, and prohibited Kurdish nationalist activities; however, he could not dissolve the Majlis. The commitment to parliamentary rule continued under Reza Shah's son, Muhammed Reza Shah (1941–1979), which allowed competing power centers to crystallize in the government. In fact, during the Iranian nationalist leftist movement under Dr. Mohaddes Mosaddeq (1941–1953), the political space in constitutional Iran decentralized and expanded.

As in Turkey, liberalization encouraged the democratization of law, social reform, and emergence of a civil society, political parties, and opposition groups. Political opening, in turn, created a more diversified and less representative form of Kurdayetî. Kurds were still prohibited from mobilizing as an ethnonationalist group; however, they had alternative channels to organize without joining the Persian equivalent of the Arab Ba'th Party. Even before the downfall of the Mahabad Republic in 1946, some Kurdish nationalists, mainly intellectuals, turned to the Iranian Communist Party (Tudeh) and its Kurdish Communist Committee. The Tudeh, like Iraqi and Turkish Communist Parties, was the only legal Iranian party that recognized minority rights and incorporated them into the democratic movement.

The alliance between Kurdish nationalists and the Iranian leftist movement led to the leftward shift of Kurdish nationalist leadership, organization, and sentiment, just as it did in colonial Iraq and Turkey. In September 1949 Tudeh's Kurdish Communist Committee issued "Mellat and Meliyet," linking the Kurdish problem to the larger issue of social democracy (Cottom 1988, 31; Abrahamian 1982, 397). The Tudeh created the Committee for Kurdistan and Azerbaijan (KAK), with Sarmaddin Sadeqh Vaziri, a Kurdish lawyer from Sanandaj and KDPI representative, as director. For several years after Mahabad's suppression the KDPI became a local branch of Tudeh. Alongside Tudeh support, some Kurdish peasants in the Urmiya and Sanandaj regions reacted to oppressive landlord policies by turning to peasant unions and peasant leftist groups. Still, in contrast to the large Kurdish representation in the Iraqi and Turkish leftist movements, by the early 1950s Kurdish membership in Tudeh was less than 3 percent (McDowall 1997, 250–56). Tudeh appeals to Persian-speaking Marxists, its weakening after 1953, and the 1958 Iraqi revolution encouraged most Kurdish nationalist cadres to return to the KDPI, the only available Kurdish nationalist organization, although it remained underground.[3]

Most Kurdish khans, however, backed the shah and conservative Iranian parties. Others turned to Mosaddeq's popular movement, the National Democratic Front, which accommodated Iranian leftism with moderate Islam, suspended land reforms, and allowed Kurdish khans to control village economies.[4] Two leading Kurdish landowners from Kermanshah, Abdul Hamid Zanganeh and Karim Sanjabi, attained important posts in Mosaddeq's cabinet and became leading participants in the Iranian nationalist movement (Katouzian 1990, 49; Lenczowski 1978, 133, 241; Zabih 1966, 50–60; Mottahedeh 1985, 217–38; Akhavi 1988; Atabaki 1993, 95).

Fluctuating Kurdish Nationalist-State Relations

As in the Iraqi state, the political space in constitutional Iran varied over time. This variability was linked to power struggles among the monarchy, leftist reformist movement, and clerical establishment. It created a relationship between Kurdish nationalists and the central government, including the shah and the Majlis, which fluctuated between compromise and hostility. For instance, in response to rising Kurdish nationalism, Azerbaijani autonomy movement, lawlessness in the countryside, and competing influences from foreign powers, the Iranian elite attempted to appease and

3. After Qasimlu's expulsion from Prague in 1968 he started to criticize the Soviet Union and distanced KDPI relations from Tudeh.

4. Qom did not challenge Mosaddeq during his early campaign. However, the religious center shut down for one week after the visit of the influential Ali Akbar Burqai to the Soviet-sponsored World Peace Conference and the demonstrations of other leftist clerics who chanted, "Long live Stalin."

co-opt Kurdish communities to secure power (Atabaki 1993, 129–78; Fawcett 1992). In 1941 it established a committee to hear land grievances by Kurds and reinstitute lands appropriated unjustly (Burrell 1997, 11:426). During the unstable World War II period Prime Minister Qavam es-Saltaneh sent government representatives to a conference in Baku to negotiate autonomy with the Kurdish elite. Qavam also attempted to lead social reforms and aligned with the leftist movement. These efforts semilegitimated Kurdayetî and encouraged negotiation among Kurdish nationalists, Qavam, and his supporting factions in the Majlis.

Compromise was possible but only to a point. As the shah attempted to reassert monarchical power, and as other ethnic and tribal groups started making claims for autonomy and landowning rights, Qavam was pressured to retreat from his Kurdish-appeasement and leftist policies. Like Qasim and al-Bazzaz in Iraq, he shifted rightward and pacified conservative constituencies by bringing tribal leaders into the government, including the Kurdish Qubaidan of the Kalhur, as well as Qashqai and Bakhtiari chiefs (Entessar 1992, 24–25; Abrahamian 1982, 235–38). Qavam was eventually expelled from office, terminating possible negotiation between the Kurdish nationalists and state elite. Similar patterns of behavior occurred during the premierships of General Razmara (a Kurd from Kermanshah [1950–1951]) and Mosaddeq (1951–1953). Razmara talked about administrative decentralization for the Kurds. Mosaddeq tried to accommodate leftist and minority populations. However, pressures from conservative groups in the Majlis and British and U.S. influences blocked their efforts. Razmara was assassinated, and Mosaddeq was overthrown in a CIA-led coup d'état. What followed were more communist witch-hunts, closure of leftist organizations, restrictions of political liberties, and renewed repressions against Kurdish nationalists and opposition groups. Potentially compromising relations between the Kurdish and state elite turned to antagonism once again.

Erratic relations between Kurdish nationalists and the central government continued after the downfall of Mosaddeq and reassertion of monarchical power. To hasten the demonstration effects of the 1958 Iraqi revolution and Qasim's liberal Kurdish policies, and counter the Soviet's Kurdish-language broadcasts, the shah slightly opened the political space for Kurds. Although restrictions remained on political parties, he permitted Kurdish cultural organizations, association for the Kurds at the University of Tehran, and international Kurdish conferences. The state-run security agency, SAVAK (Sazmani Ittila'at va Amniyat Keshvar), sponsored a Kurdish radio station, a weekly Kurdish television program, and a Kurdish-language newspaper called *Kurdistan* (Samii 1996; Burrell 1997, 6:470). During this period, the Iranian minister of health visited the Kurdish regions, promising to implement development projects. Still prevented from manifesting a politicized sense of Kurdish nationalism, some Kurds took advantage of state-supported resources to develop the cultural aspects of their national identity. Publications in Kurdish journals were ethnicized and culturally accommodating, focusing on Kurdish literary scholars, Kurdish history, and the Kurdish language inside the territorial boundaries of Iran *(Kurdistan,* June 12, 1959, 6–7; July 9, 1959, 2).

Yet the political space in Pahlavi Iran was limited in content and time, terminating any durable accommodation between Kurdish nationalists and the central government. During the 1950s and 1960s Iran became the recipient of massive U.S. aid, including military and economic assistance, oil concessions, and important petroleum revenues after having nationalized the petroleum industry. From 1949 to 1961 U.S. military assistance to Iran increased from about $17 million to $436 million, while economic aid increased from $16.5 million to $611 million. Petroleum receipts and shifts in regional politics encouraged the shah to negotiate defense contracts with the West, finance grandiose industrialization projects linked to foreign capital that mainly benefited Tehran and central and Isfahan provinces, expand the state arsenals, and strengthen the government's coercive power.[5] From 1962 to 1972 defense and security spending, which made up 25 percent to 30 percent of total government disbursements, increased from $210 million to $1.4 billion, giving Iran the fifth largest military budget in the world (Karimi 1986, 33; Fesharaki 1976, 190; Firoozi 1976; Ramazani 1975, 261–62; Katouzian 1981; Lenczowski 1978, 388).

5. An analysis of the differences in Iraqi and Iranian petroleum markets cannot be made here. It is important to note, however, that even though Iran became a rentier state and quadrupled its oil revenues after 1973, the petroleum industry had an overall smaller impact on Iran's economic growth than it did in Iraq. Also, whereas the Iraqi petroleum industry was based on complete state ownership, Iran's nationalized industry centered on joint-venture agreements among Western oil companies, multinational enterprises, and Iranian firms.

The consolidation of monarchical power, militarization of the state, and domination of right-wing factions in the government significantly reduced the political space for Kurdish communities, just as it did in Ba'thist Iraq and Kemalist Turkey. Although the government created the Religious Corps in August 1971 and supported the Shi'a establishment, new studies of Iranology made it clear that Persian language and identity tied to secular Western culture would be the prominent aspect of Iranian citizenship. For example, to market the grandiose celebration of the fabricated 2,500th anniversary of the monarchy, the Pahlavi elite disseminated images of ancient Iranian warriors alongside the shah; his unveiled wife, Queen Shahbanu; and U.S. multinational corporations *(Tamashah,* no. 31 [1971]: 3–9; no. 3 [1971]: 3–13). The shah continued to claim that "the Kurds are Aryans, and the Aryans are the purest Iranians that exist" (Hushyar 1992, 97; Mojab and Hassanpour 1995, 231). However, the emphasis on Cyrus the Great as the symbol of Iranian identity favored Persian, not Kurdish, history. The shah also militarized strategic Iranian provinces, including parts of the Kurdish regions, and used SAVAK forces to terrorize local populations. By the early 1970s constitutional Iran had become a closed police state.

Collective Identities

"Persianization" programs heightened ethnic distinctions and reinforced the Kurds' sense of Otherness. Despite discourses about shared Aryan cultures, the Azeris, and not Kurds, became the favored non-Persian community. Some Kurds received political positions, but important government posts such as the provincial governorships were still reserved for Persian nationals. By the late 1970s Iranian Kurds still did not have one Kurdish school for Kurdish-language instruction. Yet a mass, unified Kurdish national identity was not forged or manifested at this time. In fact, from the mid-1950s to 1978 Kurdish nationalism ceased in the public sphere. What happened to Kurdayetî in Iran during this period, particularly during the peak of Pahlavi ethnicization and militarization programs?

Like Ba'thist Iraq and Turkey, the highly restrictive political space in the Pahlavi police state prevented the open manifestation of Kurdayetî. As the political space ethnicized, centralized, and militarized it became increasingly unsafe for Kurds to publicly express their ethnic identity. Indeed, the Majlis retained its role in the political system, allowing some form of constitutional rule and a limited associational life. However, in contrast to the Mosaddeq period, the absence of democratic institutions, personal freedoms, and rights for opposition groups stifled open political expression. The shah arrested those individuals suspected of harboring Kurdish nationalist tendencies. In the 1952 elections, for instance, KDPI candidates received about 80 percent of the votes in the Kurdish regions, yet they were prohibited from attaining seats in the Majlis.

Kurdayetî certainly remained salient for Kurdish nationalist cadres. Although Vaziri was director of Tudeh's KAK, he ran as the "Kurdish candidate" from Mahabad in 1952 in his bid for a seat in the Majlis. During the mid-1950s KDPI members, clandestinely expressed a highly ethnicized nationalism tied to the liberation of all of Kurdistan and creation of a Kurdish government (McDowall 1997, 251). Still, Kurdish nationalism was unable to develop openly and legitimately on an organizational level. Whereas Barzani and Talabani maintained semilegitimate status and external support, even during the revolts of the 1960s, the Iranian Kurdish nationalist elite and its political parties went underground. Most progressive leaders in the KDPI, including Ghani Boulourian and Aziz Youssefi, were arrested. Abdul Rahman Qasimlu eventually assumed the KDPI leadership, yet he, like other Kurdish nationalists, was placed under SAVAK surveillance and prevented from engaging in open political activities.

In the absense of legal parties and ideological splits with the Tudeh, some Kurds, like counterparts in Ba'athist Iraq and Turkey, remained active in or returned to clandestine Kurdish nationalist activities. Others radicalized their demands against the shah by joing mass movements in the city centers. The opposition included different combinations of secular, leftist, and ulema factions, which appealed to Kurdish nationalists because they were nonethnicized and based on the notion of a future Iranian state that rejected the West and of which the Kurds were a part (Chehabi 1990; Abrahamian 1993, 27–30; Kub 1974, 27–47; al-Ahmad 1997, 21–23; Milani 1988, 79–82).

Lack of opportunities, fear of repression, and internal fragmentation were not the only reasons Kurdish nationalism did not become highly salient. As in post-1950 Turkey, socioeconomic transformations encouraged new collective identities to emerge in urban and rural areas. Industrialization and modernization programs weakened tribal structures so that by 1976, less than 5 percent of Iranian society were tribalized and about 50 percent were living in city centers (Najambadi 1987a, 222). Modernization trends gave rise to urban, educated, and professional classes that integrated into Iranian society. Kurds became famous singers, Majlis representatives, and professionals. Shi'a Kurds such as Gholam Rashid Yasemi, a large landowner from West Kermanshah and professor at the University of Tehran, integrated into society as Iranians first. Yasemi wrote a book against the Kurdish nation, arguing that Kurds were really Persians (Yasemi 1937, 186–88).

Economic development and modernization programs also involved rural restructuring and the creation of agricultural cooperatives to increase production. Land reforms affected the Kurdish nationalist trajectory by altering land-tenure relations, opportunity structures, and political identities. The 1962 reforms, the 1966 provision of the Municipality Law, and new urbanization planning expropriated the large class of noncultivating small landowners. The *khoshneshin,* or populations without traditional land-use rights, and small peasant farmers who could not compete with large agribusinesses and sold their unproductive plots migrated to towns and cities. The dispossessed also included urban middle classes and petty bourgeoisie who had invested savings in land (Majd 2000, 124–27; Hooglund 1982, 113–15).

Some migrants were absorbed into the state's expanding service sector that penetrated towns and villages. From 1956 to 1976 the percentage of Iran's population employed in agriculture declined from 56 percent to 34 percent. Those individuals working in industry, construction, and services increased from 44 percent to 66 percent (Khatib 1994; Parvin and Taghavi 1986; Najambadi 1987a, 214; Bharier 1977, 331–36; Moghadam 1996, 79–98). Others, however, became seasonal agricultural workers or part of the unemployed, marginalized urban poor. Although the government used oil revenues to develop the infrastructure and became the largest public employer, the shah made no real effort to alleviate the socioeconomic condition of disfranchised groups. Instead of strengthening state ties to society, he drew them further apart.

In this increasingly harsh socioeconomic order some Kurdish migrants may have become sensitized to their ethnic identity; however, they did not necessarily abandon tribal and village identities for ethnic ones. Expropriated landless peasants and seasonal workers maintained ties to villages and lived between provincial and urban centers. Also, even though most disfranchised Kurds migrated to cities and towns within Kurdistan, economic problems were not concentrated in the Kurdish regions as they were in Turkey. Non-Kurdish provinces such as Yazd, Sistan, Baluchistan, and Büshar were also underdeveloped relative to Tehran and Isfahan, and often more so than Kurdistan. Alongside or instead of ethnic consciousness, a sense of collective hardship emerged among marginalized populations living in squatter settlements in Tehran and its outskirts. Unlike Kurdish migrants in Turkey, however, they were not displaced to factories where a working-class consciousness breeds. In fact, only 16.5 percent of the income of Kurdish peasant proprietors in the khoshneshin came from wage labor (Koohi-Kamali 2003, 152).

Certain communities had other reasons not to manifest a highly ethnicized sense of Kurdayetî. Although the shah repressed Kurdish nationalism, he sporadically appeased some conservative groups. Still committed to secularism, the shah tried to convince the ulema of his loyalty to Islam by vowing to uphold religion in Iranian politics and denouncing Tudeh as the enemy of Islam. He created the Society for Propagation of Islam in Shi'a urban centers, including the Kurdish regions of Kermanshah, Ilam, and West Azerbaijan; reopened Maktab schools; invited the exiled Hajo Agha Housayn Qum to Tehran; and visited Shi'a shrines in Mashhad, Qom, and Mecca (Mottahedeh 1985, 217–38; Akhavi 1988; Lenczowski 1978, 241; Abrahamian 1982, 421). Additionally, like Demirel in post-1950 Turkey, the shah released Kurdish tribal chiefs from detention and allowed them to return to their localities. Although landowners declined in the Majlis from 58 percent to 35 percent and lost some privileges after 1963, the shah invited tribal chiefs into conservative Iranian political parties, where they expanded client-state networks and gained influence in urban areas. He also appointed Kurdish notables to high-level local posts. Abbas Qabudian was "elected" to the Majlis and joined the Majlis Tribal Commission. The Kurdish general Rahimi Saghez became the military commander in Tehran; Ali Guli Khan of Ardalan was the Iranian chargé d'affaires in Washington, D.C; and Colonel I. Pejman assumed a leading position in SAVAK (Afkhami and Nasr 1991, 8–14, 34–39).[6]

---

6. Pejman, a Kurd from Sanandaj, played a key role in the Iranian government's counterintelligence activities against the Tudeh Party. While in Iraqi Kurdistan Pejman offered special incentives to the Iraqi Kurdish Jaf tribe, negotiated with Jelal Talabani, and helped

Further, some parts of the Kurdish countryside benefited from the land reforms. In contrast to Iraqi and Turkish programs, Iranian reforms terminated the traditional *boneh* system and turned about 92 percent of sharecroppers into peasant proprietors and small farmers (Lambton 1969; Hoogland 1982, 4; Moghadam 1996, 58–69, 86–88; Nattagh 1986, 32–50; Amini 1978; Najambadi 1987b, 99–117). The reforms destroyed most feudalist land relations and disfranchised masses of peasant landowners; however, the results varied across regions.[7] In Urmiya new peasant contracts with government cooperatives helped increase tobacco and sugar beet production. Some villages involved in the Dez agricultural project in Khuzestan gained electricity and irrigation systems (Salmanzadeh 1980, 5; Lambton 1969, 127, 182–83).

In other regions Iranian officials purchased the land and then leased it to state-run agribusinesses, cooperatives, and large landowners. Government compensation for the expropriated land was minimal, yet the Kurdish regions were among the highest paid for their land, except for parts of Kurdistan Province. In Kermanshah, Hamadan, and parts of Sanandaj, where there were alternative means of income generation or where the tax rate and land value were high, landowners profited from the land sales (Majd 2000, 126; Lambton 1969, 121–22). Half the village in Kermanshah was transferred to the peasants but later acquired by two large landowners. Consequently, some rural communities became or remained the shah's strongest supporters, even though they may have considered themselves Kurds ethnically.

Conclusions

The rise of an exclusionary nationalist project in constitutional Iran ethnicized Kurdayeti, just like it did in the Arabized Iraqi police state and in Kemalist Turkey. Still, the political space was less repressive against Kurds

---

Iraqi Kurdish chiefs across the border to ensure their support for the Iranian government. I thank Vali Nasr for bringing this source to my attention and Gholam Afkhami for discussing this issue with me at the Foundation for Iranian Studies in April 1999.

7. Land-tenure relations and ownership differed by region. In the Kurdish town of Sanandaj two main factions rented the land. In Azerbaijan large landowners controlled the land, except for in Urmiya where peasants were also the proprietors.

as a distinct ethnic group than it was in Iraq and Turkey, resulting in a less hostile expression of Kurdayetî across Kurdish society. Iranian Kurds became increasingly conscious of their ethnonationalist identity but did not turn to the type of violent ethnonationalism as did Kurds in Turkey. They also lacked a semilegitimate modernizing nationalist elite and organizations that could have advanced Kurdish nationalist sentiment. What emerged instead was an ethnicized, more culturally adaptive form of Kurdayetî that had limited influence across the underdeveloped Kurdish society.

7

Iran's Transition to
an Islamic Republic

After the Iranian Revolution of 1978–1979, which transformed the
constitutional monarchy into an Islamic republic, the political space
was reshaped by religion.[1] Whereas the official state nationalism was previously defined by its secular, ethnicized, and Westernizing tendencies, it became tied to an Islamic identity independent of the West. New boundaries
of inclusion and exclusion developed based on conservative Shi'a Islam,
alongside ethnicity, reducing opportunities for Kurds, non-Shi'a communities, and secular groups in the state. Yet the presence of a reforming faction
in the Majlis, even in a weakened form, prevented the political space from
closing completely. Kurds still had limited opportunities to acknowledge
their ethnic identity within a narrow cultural milieu, resulting in a salient but
more accommodating form of ethnonationalism than the Iraqi and Turkish cases.

A Transitioning Islamic State

During the initial months after the revolutionaries took power in February 1979, the political space was large in content and size. No one faction

1. The beginnings of the 1978–1979 revolution can be identified with the demonstrations and attacks on the holy city Qom in response to a newspaper article in January 1978
against Khomeini. The period followed with mass demonstrations and anti-U.S. slogans
from September 1978 to January 1979 (Keddie and Hooglund 1986, 3–4).

controlled the Provisional Revolutionary Government, which was directed by the left-leaning Mehdi Bazargan and composed of civilian leftists, moderates, and secular and Islamic nationalists. Two Kurds received posts in the first cabinet: Kareem Sanjabi as minister of foreign affairs and Ali Ardalan as minister of economy. Nor was ulema power institutionalized in the transitional political system. The office of the spiritual leader was nonexistent, the role of the Guardian Council was limited, parliamentary powers were safeguarded, and the president was not obliged to have religious authority. The provisional constitution neither discussed the notion of *velayat-e faqih* (the rule of the Islamic jurist) nor ensured positions for the clergy except in the new Guardian Council. Rather, it recognized the equality of all ethnic groups—Persians, Azeris, Turks, Arabs, Kurds, Baluch, and Turkomen—non-Persian languages, and the four Sunni schools of Islam (Schirazi 1997, 22–23; Milani 1988, 143–46).

Even Ayatollah Sayyid Ruhallah Khomeini, spiritual leader of the provisional government, created space for leftist, moderate, and Kurdish nationalist groups. He needed to, given the fragility of his power base and the upcoming March 1979 referendum. Although he was backed by conservative factions and the Islamic Republican Party (IRP), Khomeini was challenged by radicalized leftist, secularized, and liberal Islamic parties, increasing tensions in Kurdistan. Khomeini thus started to fight harder for support from opposition groups. After the revolution he declared May Day a paid public holiday, increased the minimum wage and housing allowance for workers, and sponsored leftist activities (Abrahamian 1993, 60–87). Forty-six Kurdish political prisoners arrested by the shah were also the first to be liberated after the revolution.

An integral part of Khomeini's early discourses was the shift from ethnicity to religion as the defining aspect of "Iranianness." Instead of discussing the importance of the Persian language and culture like the Pahlavi shahs, or turning to some of his earlier writings that were critical of Sunni groups, Khomeini emphasized the pan-Islamic character of Iran that included Sunni and Shi'a communities alike. After winning the referendum and declaring Iran an Islamic republic on April 3, 1979, Khomeini called all Islamic countries of the world to "unite under one big Islamic state and under one flag" (Khomeini 1980, 50–53). He invited Shi'a Muslims to participate in the ritual prayer with their Sunni counterparts and paid special salaries to Sunni ulema. Moderate and conservative members of the Shi'a clergy visited Sunni Arab countries, talking about the struggle against Western imperialism and discrimination against Muslim peoples.

The idea of an Islamic identity, however, was still unclear, wavering between different forms of democracy and a theocratic government. Political boundaries were based on the oppressed and the oppressors, not between Shiʻas and Sunnis or Persians and non-Persian groups. To bridge the gap between Shiʻa Muslims and non-Muslim and secular communities, Khomeini advocated general notions of social justice, equality of people and provinces, consciousness, guidance, and honor within an Islamic state (Menashri 1988, 217; *Ayandegan* 1979a, 1979f; Khomeini 1980, 2–3). The absence of an ethnicizing tendency gave the perception of ethnic equality in a future Iranian state. In one public radio speech Khomeini affirmed:

> I say to all groups of the nation that in an Islamic Republic there are no privileges between the rich and the poor, the white and the black, Sunni and Shiʻa, Arabs and non-Arabs, Turk and other than Turk. . . . The rights of religious minorities will be preserved. . . . Islam respects all groups, the Kurds and other groups who have a different language are all our brothers. . . . We are brothers with the Sunnis and we must not claim to be better than they are. (Khomeini 1980, 5–11)

Although he criticized independence for ethnic communities, Khomeini accepted the proposal of *showras* (local councils) that were established after the revolution and managed by leftist groups.

Additionally, to stabilize outlying regions and consolidate power, Iranian officials in the transitioning Islamic state attempted to negotiate with Kurds, which semilegitimated the nationalist elite and their organizations. Khomeini offered the Kurdish regions one day's oil revenues, or $75 million (Koohi-Kamali 2003, 185). Bazargan invited Kurdish leaders to Qom and sent delegations to Kurdistan. He also discussed the Kurdish autonomy issue in the Majlis and promised Kurds a plan for self-determination within the Islamic republic. After visiting Kurdistan Province the labor minister, Daryush Foruhar, promised that Kurdish rights would be ensured within a constitution guaranteeing fundamental rights for all Iranians. Foruhar stated, "After fifty years of having their demands repressed the Kurds have the right to some type of autonomy" *(Keyhan* 1979c; see also *Ayandegan* 1979b, 1979e).

Similarly, the Islamic modernist Ayatollah Taleqani acknowledged that his "deprived Kurdish brothers and sisters have suffered . . . by sending their taxes to the men of pleasure in northern Tehran." Taleqani claimed that if "Kurdistan becomes independent then Iran becomes independent." Calling to the "noble, pure Kurdish race," he asserted that "autonomy is the same thing that we want. Each individual is autonomous and knows that the Islamic order is free. . . . What person is able to deny cultural freedom, the destiny, and the language of the people of Kurdistan. . . ?" *(Ayandegan* 1979d; see also *Keyhan* 1979d). To make his promises appear real Taleqani created a proposal that recognized the Kurds in the fundamental laws, protected Kurdish culture, and promised high-level political appointments and Majlis representation for Kurdish leaders. He further promised to establish an administrative council in Sanandaj composed of eleven Kurdish ulema.

Moderated Ethnonationalism

Despite claims of ethnic tolerance and promises for Kurdish autonomy, gaps emerged between the state elite's discourses and the political reality. Government proposals for Kurdish self-administration did not include cultural or political autonomy in Kurdistan. Khomeini argued that all ethnic groups were equal; however, he prevented the KDPI from establishing bureaus in certain cities. The Iranian elite talked about a Sunni-Shi'a partnership, yet it labeled Sunni Kurdish leftists as communists. It also allowed Shi'a Kurdish landlords to create Islamic-revolutionary committees in their regions, authorized the eviction of peasants from their lands, and further militarized the Kurdish regions.

Reacting to these discrepancies and taking advantage of the decentralized period, some Kurds manifested a highly ethnicized form of nationalism. Because Kurdish nationalist parties were semilegalized and the press was open, they disseminated their own nationalist newspapers, reopened Kurdish organizations, and published Kurdish textbooks in preparation for a Kurdish university. Free to discuss its political views, the KDPI came out of thirty years of clandestine existence and made public claims for political autonomy (Koohi-Kamali 1992, 183). It even published an open letter to Ayatollah Khomeini in early 1979, criticizing the Iranian government's negative propaganda against the Kurds. Other Kurds revolted in the streets, staged demonstrations in mosques, and engaged in violence to make nationalist claims as a distinct ethnic group.

Even though Kurdayetî became salient and ethnicized, it fluctuated between hostility and compromise. Instead of radicalizing their claims alongside demonstrators in Sanandaj, demanding territorial separation, or turning to the various Iraqi Kurdish parties based in the mountainous Iran-Iraq border regions, the Kurdish nationalist elite initially attempted to negotiate with the new Iranian leaders. Despite its criticisms of the regime, in its early postrevolutionary public discourses the KDPI called itself an authentically national and Iranian party. The central committee of the KDPI sent Khomeini a letter asking for an autonomous Kurdistan as part of a federated Iran that could benefit all of the country's minority groups *(Lettre ouverte* 1979; Chaliland 1993). In fact, KDPI officials criticized Kurds who demanded independence as traitors of the revolution and people of Iran. The Kurdish shaykh Husayni 'Izz al-Din from Mahabad demanded an autonomous Kurdistan that included all regions where there was a majority of Kurds, but within the territorial borders of Iran. Employing the cultural-similarities argument he affirmed: "We are all Iranians and we are not separate from Iran. It is incontestable that we are brothers and in other lands Kurds are brothers with Iranians because we are all Aryans. And before that we all lived together in the land of Iran. . . . However, the rights to autonomy inside Iran must be given to the Kurds" *(Mamosta Cheikh Ezzedine Hosseini* 1984, 13). Husayni demanded an autonomous region to include a Kurdish regional government tied to the central government, schools to teach the Kurdish language alongside Persian, and a portion of the national budget for economic development.

The nature of Kurdayetî differed, however, from the secular Kurdish ethnonationalism tied to the constitutional monarchy. In the attempt to accommodate the transitioning Islamic government, Kurdayetî became slightly Islamized. Sunni Kurdish shaykhs who played a marginal role in Kurdish politics before the revolution became popular on a national level, including Ahmad Muftizadeh in Sanandaj and Husayni in Mahabad, each of whom had his own local following. Kurdish nationalist leaders also started emphasizing their Muslim identity as a salient aspect of Kurdayetî, just like some Kurdish nationalists did in the Islamized space in Turkey after 1980.

For instance, although he was part of the Sunni minority, the conservative Muftizadeh argued that Kurdish autonomy did not mean a change in borders, but was a "natural right in one Islamic country and within an Islamic framework." Shaykh Husayni, who was tied to the secular, leftist Komala Party and opposed the idea of an Islamic state, claimed he "did not know the opposition of religion to socialism." Emphasizing the compatibility between Sunni and Shi'a groups he stated in an interview with the Tehran newspaper *Ayandegan* in April 1979: "There are different tastes among Shi'as and Sunnis, but they should not lead the people to oppose one another. . . . If we say Islam we say the spirit of Islam, there is no Shi'a and Sunni" (1979g). Even leftist, secular Kurdish nationalists such as Qasimlu talked about a Muslim Kurdish identity tied to the state. Alongside his claims of democracy for Iran and autonomy for Kurdistan, Qasimlu said he was prepared to accept Islamic autonomy for Kurdistan. During negotiations with Islamic leaders he claimed that "the Kurdish people wait for the guidance of the Iranian revolution's Imam Khomeini . . . which will assure that . . . all of the people of Iran are defended" *(Ayandegan* 1979c, 1979h; Ghassemlou 1981, 11–12).

Indeed, power rivalries continued, heightening intra-Kurdish divisions and weakening the overall influence of Kurdayetî, just as they did in Iraq, Turkey, and the Iranian constitutional monarchy. Instead of creating a cohesive Kurdish nationalist movement, some Kurdish leaders such as Husayni's brother, Shaykh Jalal, accepted Iraq's military assistance and formed a Sunni militia opposed to the Iranian government and Kurdish nationalist parties. Qasimlu differentiated his real Kurdish nationalist party from "traitors" within the KDPI. Others, such as the prominent Ghani Boulourian, tried to negotiate with the central government. After the revolution some Shi'a Kurds from Ilam, Kermanshah, and West Azerbaijan turned away from Kurdish nationalists and toward non-Kurdish Shi'a communities. Sunni Kurdish leftists continued to direct the nationalist project from their enclave in Kurdistan Province, having marginal influence over Shi'a Kurds in other regions.

Like Iraqi, Turkish, and Pahlavi Iranian officials, instead of weakening these dichotomies the new state elite heightened them by implementing divide-and-rule policies. Even though Qasimlu was the leader of the semilegal KDPI, Iranian officials recognized the former Kurdish SAVAK agent Shaykh Osman Naqshbandiyya as the representative of the Kurds. While promising Shaykh Husayni a leadership position in the showra of Mahabad, they called him *zed al din* (antireligious) and backed an alternative Kurdish leader, Muftizadeh from Sanandaj and his Iraqi Kurdish supporters (Mojab and Hassanpour 1995, 237). In Kurdistan Province they stirred personal jealousies among Moftizadeh, Husayni, and Mustafa Barzani's faction, the Provisionary KDP Leadership (Qiyada-ye Movaqqat), which took refuge outside Tehran during the revolution. Also, despite promises of Islamic equality the state elite gave Shi'as privileged economic, professional, and religious opportunities.

Kurdish nationalism in postrevolutionary Iran, however, was more complex than traditional dichotomies between Kurdish political party leaders or religious differences between Shi'a and Sunni groups. In the decentralized transition period, Kurdish national organization and sentiment became part of more diversified political space among heterogenous leftist opposition groups and socioeconomic classes. In addition to protecting Kurdish ethnic identity, the KDPI promised to end unequal landownership and weaken the power of the dependent bourgeoisie. The Kurdish Komala Party allied with the Iranian (Tudeh) Communist Party in the attempt to wage an armed struggle against the Islamic regime. Political opportunities also became available for rural communities, creating greater complexity in nationalist organization at the local level. After 1979 the multiplication of national election processes encouraged massive participation by village and peasant groups in national politics. The early Islamic government tolerated, but did not legalize, Kurdish leftist-nationalist parties and Kurdish peasant unions, which became outlets for secular, leftist, working-class, and peasant communities. Some Kurdish leftists turned to Masud Rajavi's National Resistance Council, demanding Kurdish autonomy in a republican and democratic Iran *(Komala* 1980, 5; *Declaration commune* 1981, 33–35; *Resistance* 1981, 8; Hourcade 1988, 166; Alaolmolki 1987, 230). Others supported Komala, the KDPI, Husayni, and the Feda'yin-e Khalq, which promised to protect the toiling masses and the oppressed people of Iran and wipe out feudalism *(derebegayeti)* in Kurdistan *(Set Up Peasants* 1981, 3–17).

Cross-cutting relationships also reemerged between Sunni Kurds and the Shi'a government. To ensure their landowning privileges, former pro-shah Sunni Kurdish landowners started emphasizing their Muslim identity tied to the Shi'a state. After the Islamic revolution Sunni Kurdish landlords in the Divandarreh region in Sanandaj "became die-hard Muslims ... overnight." Firuz Khan and his brothers started calling themselves the humble servants of Rahbar Ali Ghadr (the great leader), promising to fight a jihad against communists and unbelievers. Other Sunni Kurdish landowners wrote letters to the state elite pledging their lives in the service of the Islamic republic (*Trial* 1981, 2–5). Many supported their Shi'a government patrons over Sunni Kurdish urban leftists, mechanized cooperatives, and small peasant farmers. The constructive relationship between certain Sunni Kurdish landowners and the Shi'a political center was reinforced by the government's failure to implement land reforms in 1982.

A Conservative Shi'a Islamic State: Restrictive Political Space

Although Iranian Kurds had large cultural and political space in the transitioning Islamic state, their opportunities were short-lived. The March 1979 referendum gave the IRP a parliamentary majority and awarded the Council of Guardians final veto power. Still, Khomeini had not consolidated his political power. Pockets of secular groups remained politically active, the commitment to parliamentary rule continued, prerevolutionary secular laws remained in force, and the Majlis retained its leftist tendencies. Tensions between the leftist, moderate, and secular and Islamic nationalist groups became fierce, leading to the resignation of the Bazargan government in late 1979, assassinations of liberal government leaders, and terrorist incidents against the IRP (Arjomand 1988, 135–42; Ehteshami 1995, 7–12; Rose 1983; Hooglund 1986, 18–20; Akhavi 1987, 186–98; Akhavi 1986a, 57–65; and Mottahedeh 1985, 105–6).

To rescue his state-building project Khomeini strengthened the role of conservative Shi'a ulema groups in the political system. In November 1979 he replaced leftist factions in the government with conservative clerics. After annulling the provisional constitution Khomeini approved an Islamic constitution, which centralized the government and strengthened the role of the president (Omid 1994; Schirazi 1997, 64–133; Ehteshami 1995, 46–53). He also replaced the constitutional assembly with the Council of Experts and increased the powers of extraparliamentary institutions such as the Security Council and the Guardian Council. Although the Majlis survived, real government power now belonged to the Revolutionary Council, which became the state's highest decision maker and administrative organization. Other events, such as the U.S. hostage crisis, weakened leftist-Islamic groups and elevated conservative ulema factions in the various government agencies. The Soviet invasion of Afghanistan, an influx of Afghan refugees to Iran, the 1980 military coup in Turkey, and the Iran-Iraq War further encouraged reactionary Islam promoted by conservative Shi'a clerics.

The domination of conservative right-wing factions in the government resulted in new nation-state-building strategies that reduced the political space for Kurdish nationalist communities, just as it did in Ba'thist Iraq, republican Turkey, and Pahlavi Iran. Conservative Islamic elite emphasized an exclusionary notion of Iranian identity based on Shi'a Islamic principles as interpreted by maktabi jurists. A big part of Khomeini's new programs involved desecularizing the political and cultural systems. Government appointments required approval by local mosques, a background check by the ulema-controlled Ministry of Information, and an exam in Islamic sciences. Courses in Islamic studies and the Arabic language were introduced into school curricula and institutions of higher education. Hezbollah groups became active in university programs. The state elite required women to wear the hejab in public (Hooglund 1986, 24). Khomeini also replaced the Safavid principle of *zullullah,* that the shah is God's shadow on earth, for velayat-e faqih, or rule of the Islamic jurist, which was incorporated into the new constitution. He declared the Ja'far school of Twelver Shi'ism as the official state religion, and emblazoned the words *Allahu Akbar* on the national flag (Higgens 1986, 176). To legitimate an active Shi'a establishment Khomeini employed the myths of Karbala and the succession of the Mahdi as part of the official Shi'a Islamic identity.

The clear emphasis on Shi'a Islam as the dominant identity marker in the state favored Shi'a Muslim groups, just as it had during certain periods of Qajar rule. Yet whereas the political space in the Qajar period was Islamicized but not ethnicized, the post-1979 Islamic state retained the modern and ethnicized component of Iranian identity. Certain Qajar kings gave Kurdish Sufi shaykhs positions in the political hierarchy and allowed Sunni Kurdish tribal chiefs to access the court; however, the conservative Shi'a ulema made no attempt to integrate Sunni Kurds into the government. Although the Islamic constitution ensured the equality of all Iranians no matter what ethnic group or tribe, the state elite continued to favor Persian nationals in high-level posts. Persian nationalist tendencies were encouraged by Iranian patriotism that emerged during the Iran-Iraq War. Echoing other Iranian nationalists, Mahmud Afshar wrote, "[A]ll of Kurdistan, in-

cluding the neighboring province of Azerbaijan . . . in reality, is Iran itself"
(M. Afshar 1990, 250–51). Consequently, political power did change among
ethnic groups, but shifted within the dominant Persian community. After
1980 political boundaries became more particularly defined to benefit Shiʻa
Muslim Persian communities.

Indeed, some Sunni Kurdish landowners continued to enjoy socioeconomic and political power in their localities and Tehran. The conservative
Islamic elite tried to give the impression of political tolerance by conducting new studies of the outlying provinces and paying greater attention to
tribal cultures. It disseminated publications about the Kurds, Baluchis,
Qashqais, and Bakhtiaris as tribal communities with distinct cultural traditions (Moslem 1999, 80–85; Menashri 1988, 217; Abrahamian 1982, 51;
Hourcade 1988, 167).

Still, Khomeini did not attempt to de-ethnicize the official state identity,
incorporate minorities into the state-defined nationalism, or make it any
safer for Kurds and opposition groups. In fact, after 1979 the political
space became more restrictive and dangerous for Kurdish nationalists. As
right-wing ulema factions consolidated their rule, government policies toward the Kurds became increasingly uncompromising and militant, just as
they had in Baʻthist Iraq, the post-1980 militarized Turkish state, and the
Pahlavi police state. After having "won" the referendum, Khomeini terminated negotiations with Kurdish leaders, banned discussions of Kurdish
autonomy, and removed Kurds from their political posts. Qasimlu was labeled seditious and expelled from the Council of Experts (McDowall 1997,
270). Using the new Islamic Revolutionary Guard Corps (Sepah-e Pas-
daran-e Enqelab-e Islam), the secret police, and security guards (Basij-e
Mustaz aʼfiri), the state elite employed new methods to control Kurdish and
opposition groups. Violence and coercion escalated as the government increased its military and security forces from 5,000 to 250,000 from 1979 to
1986 (Entessar 1986, 56–74). Kurdistan, Hamadan, Kermanshah, and key
Kurdish border and transportation routes were placed under military rule
and became integrally tied to the Iran-Iraq War.

Secular, Leftist Ethnonationalism

The increasingly restrictive and militarized political space created a
highly salient and ethnicized Kurdish nationalism. The complicity that

once existed between the Kurdish countryside and the central government had virtually disappeared. In contrast to the transition period, whereby Kurdayetî slightly Islamized as a way of accommodating the central government, in the conservative Shi'a Islamic state it turned away from religion and toward secular, leftist ethnonational ideology. In late 1979 the KDPI no longer identified itself as an Iranian organization, but rather as a revolutionary party of the Kurdish people. Using their media privileges, other Kurds wrote about the distinct ethnic and territorial nature of Kurdish identity. In a two-part series called "Kurd?" in the Kurdish literary journal *Sirwe,* the author wrote, "Today, this place called Kurdistan. . . , divided into four countries, Iran, Iraq, Syria, and Turkey, with a history of more than three thousand years, . . .is the motherland *(nishtiman)* and well-known place of the Kurdish people" (Husayni 1987a, 21). At no point did Kurdish leftist nationalists attempt to link their sense of Kurdayetî to conservative Shi'a Islam. Kurdish nationalism also became violent. About 100,000 Kurdish peshmerga forces, as well as training stations and communications systems, had been formed to develop and defend Kurdayetî in the mountainous border regions (Koohi-Kamali 2003, 179–80).

Still, Kurdayetî was not highly influential or representative across Kurdish society. The dangerous political space in the conservative Shi'a state prevented Kurds from manifesting their sense of ethnonationalism in the public arena. An official election process was instituted in the Islamic constitution; however, the government's repression of opposition groups and Kurdish parties, the militarization of Kurdish regions, and the near absence of democratic structures made it unsafe to organize as a nationalist community. Nor did Iranian Kurds have an effective leader to mobilize the Kurdish masses. Unlike the semilegal Iraqi Kurdish elite, which were sporadically called to Baghdad to negotiate with the government, Iranian Kurdish nationalist leaders had been killed, arrested, or placed under government surveillance. After the Islamic transition period, conservative Shi'a officials forced Kurdish parties to close, return to secrecy, or relocate outside the country.

The absence of a cohesive sense of Kurdayetî was not entirely owing to a repressive political space. As in Iraq, Turkey, and Pahlavi Iran, the dichotomous Kurdish society, reinforced by the state's divide-and-rule policies, impeded the continuous evolution and institutionialization of Kurdayetî. Shi'a Kurds in Kermanshah may have considered themselves ethnically Kurdish; however, their Kurdish national identity coexisted alongside their Persian Shiʻa brethren and against the central government's disastrous economic policies. After 1980 Kurdish Islamic sects such as the Ahl-e Haqq started to emphasize their distinct group identity. Although Ahl-e Haqq leaders considered themselves the purest Kurds and their Howreman region as the center of Kurdish nationalism, they made claims to protection as a religious minority.[2] Instead of turning to Qasimlu's secularized KDPI or Husayni's leftist-democratic nationalism, the Ahl-e Haqq manifested its political identity alongside its counterparts in the Howreman-Halabja region in Iraqi Kurdistan. Similarly, although the KDPI joined the national resistance council in Paris in 1981, a united front against the Islamic government then controlled by the Mujahidden-e Khalq, Komala criticized this alliance and refused to cooperate (Koohi-Kamali 2003, 180–81).

Socioeconomic transformations in the conservative Islamic state encouraged alternative political identities to become salient alongside or instead of Kurdish ethnonationalism. Marginalization processes that commenced with the modernization programs under the Pahlavi shahs continued. During the 1980s new waves of urban migration brought more than half the Kurdish populations to the large towns and cities outside Kurdistan. Tehran, including Qaraj, became the second largest Kurdish-populated city after Kermanshah. Urbanization trends altered traditional living patterns, shifted the state's incentive structures, and changed the way that Kurds identified in the public sphere, just as they did in the Iraqi rentier state, liberalizing Turkey, and late Pahlavi Iran.

Iranian officials attempted to manage disfranchised populations by increasing the state's social welfare function. As part of its nationalization policies they passed a series of prolabor laws that ensured permanent employment for seasonal workers and prohibited certain companies from reducing their workforces. Within several years new state-owned institutions, renamed *boniyads* and *nahads,* controlled about 70 percent of the gross domestic product and assumed new social welfare activities, such as refugee assistance, land allocation, and Islamic education. Under the direction of the Reconstruction Crusade (Jehad-e Sazandegi) the government engaged

2. Interview with Mr. Mehmet in Kermanshah and Paweh, Iran. I also thank Mr. Medhi for discussing this issue with me and providing me access to videotapes of his personal interviews with Howremani leaders, in Qaraj, Iran, in March and April 1998.

in rural development and infrastructure projects. By 1991 it had become the largest patron in the state, employing one-third of the total workforce.

Even though the Shi'a ulema paid greater attention to social services than any other Iranian government, its economic reforms, food rationing, and austerity measures worsened the conditions of the new working poor and unemployed masses over the long term (Rashid 1994, 46–55; Loeffler 1986, 96; Karimi 1986, 42). Iranian Kurdish rural communities that had migrated en masse to the cities became part of the growing urban squatter settlements. Although the settlements were constructed around ethnic communities, a new type of segregation system emerged based on socioeconomic identities. Kurdish migrants may have considered themselves ethnically Kurdish, but in their economically precarious condition they also identified and were categorized as part of *zaghehnishinan, alounaknishinan,* and *mardum-i hashiyenishin,* that is, settlers of shacks and shanties and residents of city margins (Bayat 1997, 30–31).

The Kurds' sense of collective hardship was reinforced by the Iran-Iraq War. Although Persian nationalist tendencies heightened during this period, they were muted by the effects of the war itself. Because all of Iran's ethnic and religious communities were mobilized to the war front, they developed a shared sense of personal loss that transcended ethnic boundaries. Most Iranian citizens experienced the tragedies of losing family members, seeing villages bombed, or having businesses destroyed (Marten-Finnis 1995, 256). War-affected Kurdish families became part of the cult of the martyrs *(shahid)* that represented the communal sentiment of suffering in Iranian society after the war. Alongside the traditional expressions of martyrdom tied to Shi'a beliefs, the cult of the martyrs, symbolized by contemporary shrines and institutions, included all ethnic groups alike. At the Behesht-e Zahra cemetery in Tehran, for example, the Kurds were given a special place called Halabja, commemorating their own martyrs in the Iraqi Anfal campaign.

Iranian Kurdish masses had other reasons to refrain from radical ethnonationalism. In Islamic Iran, there were no ethnic cleansing programs like the ones that became part of the political space in Ba'thist Iraq and republican Turkey. Although state officials closed liberal newspapers, arrested Kurdish nationalists, and silenced opposition groups, they tolerated Kurdish cultural organizations, events, and certain publications. Kurds were able to wear traditional clothing in the public sphere. Important Kurdish and Persian holidays such as Nowruz remained part of the Iranian heritage, despite attempts to weaken secular Persian culture. The official state nationalism also continued to acknowledge the various peoples of Iran and their cultural traditions. In postrevolutionary school textbooks the idea of Iranian citizenship was based on the notion of various groups living in an ethnically diverse, unified Islamic territory (Yavari-d'Hellencourt 1988). These texts reaffirmed the Kurds' place in the official national identity as an ethnic community, even though they had no rights to mobilize as a national group.

Limited tolerance of Kurdish ethnic identity, despite prohibitions against Kurdish-language instruction and political parties, resulted in a more culturally adaptive form of Kurdayetî than the extreme Kurdish ethnonationalist sentiment that emerged in Ba'thist Iraq and republican Turkey. The post-1980 Iranian Kurdish formula was based on the notion that Kurds and Iranians shared special ethnic, cultural, and linguistic ties that could not be constructed among Arabs, Turks, and Kurds. Although Kurdish nationalist writings referred to a larger Kurdistan composed of four states, they claimed that Kurdayetî was part of the Iranian identity and that the Kurdish *nishtiman* (motherland) was based inside the territorial boundaries of Iran. Some Kurdish nationalists continued to argue that the Kurds were of the Median race and Kurdish was part of the Iranian language group (Husayni 1987a, 1987b).

Variable Political Space: Fluctuating Kurdish-State Relations

Had Iranian officials maintained a constant and clearly restrictive political space, then a continuously violent and highly ethnicized sense of Kurdish nationalism might have become salient as it did in Turkey. However, the political space in the conservative Islamic republic varied over time, resulting in a relationship between the Kurdish nationalists and state elite that fluctuated between compromise and hostility. As in Iraq and Pahlavi Iran, variable relations between Kurdish nationalists and the state elite were tied to regime-consolidation processes. When central government power was fragile, the conservative Islamic officials made special efforts to pacify Kurds by expanding the political space. During these brief periods Kurdish nationalist-state relations became constructive and political negotiation was possible. Yet the Iranian elite was ultimately unwilling to cross the

6. Page from a school textbook in the Islamic republic of Iran representing all ethnic groups within the territorial boundaries of Iran. From *Ta'limat-e Ejtema'i* (charim dabistan), 128.

threshold of real Kurdish political autonomy, which resulted in resumed hostility between Kurdish nationalists and the central government.

For instance, even though conservative Shi'a ulema factions gained control of the government, by 1980 Khomeini had still not consolidated power. The commitment to parliamentary rule remained, and struggles continued between left- and right-wing factions.[3] Khomeini's power was further challenged by Iran's international ostracization tied to the Iran-Iraq War, oil and trade embargoes, high unemployment, U.S. support of the Pakistani and Afghan governments, the arming of Iraq and Arab countries by the West, and hostilities with Israel. In these regime-threatening circumstances it became politically expedient for the conservative Shiʻa elite to reach out to Kurdish communities.

Khomeini tried to pacify Kurdish nationalist and opposition groups. After 1983 conservative ulema factions started receiving Sunni Muslim delegations in Tehran, emphasizing similarities between Shiʻas and Sunnis. In a public speech to Sunni Kurdish communities Hojjat al-Islam Seyyid Ali Khamenei claimed, "[W]e have the Qur'an, the same Ka'ba, the same religious obligation and the same prayers. . . . Despite the marginal differences between us, that which unifies us is great" (Menashri 1988, 218–21). State officials even appealed to Kurdish nationalism. Six years after removing Qasimlu and Kurdish nationalists from the political arena they tried to negotiate with the KDPI. The Majlis legalized the publication of a Kurdish journal, commenced development programs in Kurdistan, created new Kurdish cultural centers, and enforced a quota system that included undeveloped regions such as Kurdistan, Ilam, and Kermanshah in state universities.

Accommodating policies encouraged compromise between Kurdish nationalists and the state elite, just as they did in Iraq, the liberalizing period in Iran, and the transitioning Islamic state. Even though Qasimlu appealed to the "Iranian people terrorized by the Islamic regime," he welcomed Khomeini to Sanandaj for negotiations. During his various meetings with state officials Qasimlu argued for a federal form of government that recognized autonomy for Kurds and all minority groups. Restating the cultural-similarities argument, he argued that Iran was his motherland and that from

---

3. The clerical establishment fractured over the notion of *velayat-e faqih* and the nature of the Islamic government. Although most ulema supported the imam's line (maktabi), leftists and moderates wanted to limit the ulema's political powers while leaving political affairs in the hands of state functionaries. Conservative factions, such as Ayatollahs Khomeini and Hossein Ali Montazeri, Hojjat al-Islam Seyyid Ali Khamanei, and Hojjat al-Islam Ali Akbar Hashami Rafsanjani advocated a more active political role for the ulema.

the point of view of history, language, and culture, Kurds had Iranian roots (Copy of notes 1989). Efforts to negotiate, however, could not be sustained in a political system controlled by conservative *maktabi* jurists. After Ayatollah Hossein Ali Montazeri's resignation in March 1989, Khomeini's death, and Ayatollah Khamanei's rise to the Supreme Faqih, conservative Shi'a factions gained even greater influence in the government. Upon taking power Khamenei reformed the constitution, replaced the five-member Judicial High Council with an appointed chief justice, removed the prime minister, created new centralized bodies, and rejected Majlis legislation, arguing that it was un-Islamic (Ehteshami 1995, 46–49). Despite the weakening of the Expediency Council's monopoly power and constitutional changes in the position of the *faqih,* the Iranian elite strengthened the role of the spiritual leader and Guardian Council at the expense of parliamentary institutions.

The reinforcement of hard-line clerics in the government removed any possibility for durable compromise between the Kurdish nationalists and conservative Shi'a elite. To be sure, during the presidency of Hojjat al-Islam Ali Akbar Hashemi Rafsanjani state officials reached out to Kurdish nationalists once again. Upon taking office Rafsanjani claimed that "the rights of the Kurds, whether in Iran, Turkey or Iraq should be given to them . . . and that they should feel they are a part of the country and be treated on an equal footing" (Nader 1995, 13). Yet Rafsanjani's political survival depended upon support from conservative constituencies and right-wing ulema factions. Instead of granting Kurdish nationalists the opportunity to learn the Kurdish language or increased autonomy, Rafsanjani censored Kurdish parties and sponsored radical Islamic groups in the Kurdish border regions. Qasimlu was assassinated during a meeting in Vienna in 1989, and his successors in the KDPI were killed in Berlin in 1994.

Contradictory and erratic policies further weakened the credibility of the government discourses and resulted in renewed antagonisms between Kurdish nationalists and the central government. In the June 1993 elections Kurdistan was the only province in which a majority of the electorate did not support Rafsanjani for president. Kurdish nationalist organizations also became less accommodating. Although the KDPI still demanded democracy for Iran and autonomy for Kurdistan, it no longer attempted to compromise with the Shi'a ulema. Instead, the KDPI and Komala turned to small radical Iranian parties and reengaged in military activities in the mountainous border regions.

Even during Iran's reform movement led by the political moderate Hojjat al-Islam Muhammed Khatami, the dominant influence of maktabi power prevented a constructive relationship from being sustained between Kurdish nationalists and the central government. One of Khatami's main efforts was to address the Kurdish problem, which by 1997 had become increasingly affected by Kurdish mobilizations in Iraqi Kurdistan, Turkey, and Europe. Although he emphasized Islam as the pillar of Iranian identity, Khatami appealed to the Kurds as a distinct ethnic community ("President" 1998). Redeploying the cultural-similarities argument Khatami reinforced myths about the Kurds' Median ancestry and the natural affinity between Kurds and Persians. He also increased the political space for Kurds as an ethnonational group. In 1997 Khatami authorized a new Kurdish radio station and permitted the creation of Kurdish publications, a Kurdish-Persian-language newspaper, and Kurdish cultural centers. Backed by reformers in the Majlis, Khatami promised to construct Kurdish schools and develop the Kurdish regions (*Awiyar* 1996, 1997a, 1997b). Not surprisingly, he gained the overwhelmingly support of Kurds, particularly in the Kurdistan region.

As with Qasim in Iraq, Qavam and Mosaddeq in Pahlavi Iran, and Bani Sadr and Bazargan in the transitioning Islamic state, conservative rightwing factions pulled Khatami back from his pro-Kurdish policies. To protect his position, he started criticizing the opposition movement and made new political appointments of conservative ulema in the government. These concessions did not, however, close the political space entirely. Instead of being removed from his post Khatami stayed in power. The presence of an ulema reform faction and functioning Majlis, even in a weakened form, allowed some Kurdish journals and cultural organizations to survive. An active student opposition movement also continued, keeping the notion of political consciousness, modernity, and interior revolution alive among the Iranian youth (Khosrokhavar 1997, 54–62).

Still, the failure of the conservative Islamic state elite to maintain a credible, open political space that seriously addressed Kurdish nationalist claims, while allowing the economic situation to deteriorate across Kurdistan and the country, encouraged growing hostility across Kurdish society.

By the late 1990s even Shi'a Kurdish groups started to openly criticize the Islamic government and emphasize their Kurdish ethnic identity. Some demanded the government to change the name of Kermanshah back to its Kurdish name, Kermashan.[4]

Given the nature of the political space in conservative Islamic Iran, these demands have no chance of becoming as politically influential or significant as they have in autonomous Iraqi Kurdistan or post-1980 Turkey. Iranian Kurds still do not have a semilegal nationalist elite, highly representative political party, or sufficient resources to propel Kurdish ethnonationalist sentiment in the open public arena. Whereas Kurdayetî in Iraq flourishes in a legal, highly influential nationalist institution and in Turkey is manifested within diverse leftist and Kurdish-influenced political parties, in Iran it remains suppressed and operates clandestinely across borders. The strengthening of conservative Shi'a factions and removal of important reformist groups in the Majlis after the 2004 elections has ensured continued discrimination against Kurds on a religious and ethnic basis. In this restrictive climate the possibilities for compromise between the Kurdish nationalist elite and the central government have declined considerably.

Conclusions

Iran's postrevolutionary state-building policies reconfigured the political boundaries based on conservative Shi'a Islam while maintaining exclusions against Kurds as an ethnic community. Kurdish nationalism became increasingly ethnicized and hostile over time, even among traditionally accommodating Shi'a communities. However, although the Iranian elite repressed Kurdish nationalism and failed to draw the Kurds into the political center, it did not counterproductively ethnicize the political space enough to create an ethnonational sentiment that was highly representative across Kurdish society. Also, in contrast to Iraq and Turkey, by the 1990s the political space in Iran failed to create an influential or semilegal nationalist elite or organization, which hindered the manifestation of Kurdayetî across

4. The name Kermanshah has been changed several times since the state-formation period. From its original Kurdish name of Kermanj Shahr, it became Kermanshah (after the shah separated the region from other parts of Kurdistan and created it as a province), Imanshahr (in official writings), and Bakhtaran (on official maps) after the Iranian Revolution.

Iranian Kurdistan. Kurdish nationalism became highly salient, but it continued to be expressed alongside the Iranian opposition movement and small radical leftist and Kurdish groups, not an influential mass Kurdish nationalist party.

8

Transnational Space

Reconfiguring Kurdayetî

As the three case studies have shown, different forms of Kurdayetî
have evolved in Iraq, Turkey, and Iran as a function of the political
space in each state. Variations in political spaces have resulted in a semilegal, fractured, and changing ethnonationalist movement in Iraq; an illegal,
highly ethnicized, urban-based leftist nationalist movement in Turkey that
became tied to Islam; and a more adaptive form of Kurdish ethnonationalism in Iran represented by a secular, leftist Sunni nationalist elite. However,
the different expressions of Kurdayetî that crystallized in each state started
to alter after the early 1990s, even when some political spaces remained relatively unchanged. During this period globalization and transnational
processes facilitated the movement and communication of Kurdish communities across borders. Kurds living in the diaspora and the homeland
gained access to international nongovernmental organizations, transnational networks, and open societies in host-country settings. External influences reinforced ethnonationalist sentiment, while creating greater
complexity in the nationalist projects at home.

Transnational Space: External Opportunity Structures

Transnational space has added a new dimension to Kurdayetî in Iraq,
Turkey, and Iran. More complex than foreign government penetrations or
cross-border support to Kurdish groups, it refers to externally based op-

portunity structures such as diasporic networks, international nongovernmental organizations, host-country democratic systems, and advanced telecommunication systems that provide new forms of support or constraint to Kurdish nationalist projects. In contrast to political space inside the state, transnational space is a deterritorialized arena where cross-border cultural flows transcend state boundaries and where Kurds can openly renegotiate or reinvent their national identity (Koopmans and Statham 2001, 64–71; Munch 2001, 13–17; Peteet 2000, 183–84; McAdam, McCarthy, and Zald 1996; Goldring 1999, 164; Faist 2000, 198–200). Transnational space can encourage the emergence of new political identities and reshape existing ones based on shared migration experiences, international organizations, and ties to new community leaders in host-country settings.

Resources linked to transnational space, alongside ongoing restrictions at home, have reinforced the ethnicized sense of Kurdayetî that has emerged since the state-formation period. They have also established new alliances between Kurdish groups where they never before existed. In contrast to Bedir Khan and his small circle of intellectuals that were disconnected from the uneducated Kurdish masses, the more than one million Kurdish refugees, guestworkers, and asylum seekers that compose the Kurdish diaspora have established thick transnational networks between host countries and the Kurdish homeland. Transnational linkages have merged different Kurdish communities on a political, personal, and institutional level. During and after Abdullah Öcalan's arrest in Nairobi, for example, Kurds manifested throughout European cities and the Kurdish regions, coming together as an imagined community.

Transnational space has also helped institutionalize Kurdayetî at an international level. In contrast to restrictive or limited political space inside the state, transnational space offers Kurdish nationalists access to a larger legal political arena to make their nationalist claims without fear of repression and for a relatively continuous period of time. Kurdish communities mobilize alongside the wide range of transnational social-movement organizations that have emerged with democratization processes and increased public participation in international policy processes (Kriesberg 1997, 4–5; Ball 2000, 55–56). The Kurdish Human Rights Association, Amnesty International, Handicap International, Mines Awareness Group, and Human Rights Watch have implemented awareness campaigns and development programs in the Kurdish regions. These efforts, as well as shifts in international norms, have increased international attention for the Kurdish problem and the saliency of Kurdayetî in Kurdistan and abroad.

Even if Kurdish nationalism is reconstructed on a transnational scale, it is less certain as to how transnationalism has affected Kurdayetî in different homelands. If transnational space is another opportunity structure contributing to increasingly uniform methods of contention over highly local issues, then we should see similar manifestations of Kurdish nationalism across state borders. Instead, new variations in Kurdayetî have emerged across Kurdistan.

The asymmetrical nature of transnational space has created greater diversification in Kurdish nationalism across borders. Depending on the character of transnational space, Kurdayetî can become increasingly salient, but it can also shift in form. For instance, when the nationalist elite is given international legitimacy, access to international organizations, and foreign government support, Kurdayetî can flourish within the cadre of international norms. When the Kurdish nationalist elite is arrested and its organizations proscribed at home and abroad, Kurdish nationalist activities are likely to cease, turn to clandestine operations, or become violent. External opportunity structures also interact with domestic ones, creating a nexus between the global and local that can advance or constrain the nationalist potential. Since the early 1990s it has been easier for Iraqi Kurdish diasporic communities to become active in homeland activities than Kurds from Turkey or Iran, who are limited by restrictive political spaces at home.

Thus, although the foundation of Kurdayetî remains tied to the distinct historical trajectories that evolved inside each state, the new expressions it has assumed after the early 1990s, whether it becomes moderate or hostile or informed by democratic, religious, or socioeconomic ideologies, will be shaped, to different degrees, by opportunity structures outside the state's territorial borders. In Iraq, the large transnational space has helped create a legitimate and democratized sense of Kurdayetî. In Turkey, the Europeanized transnational space tied to the human rights regime has "juridicized" Kurdayetî on an international level, although Kurdish nationalism remains illegal inside the Turkish state. In Iran, the restrictive transnational space has crippled Kurdayetî, weakening the significance of Iranian Kurdish nationalism on an international level and inside Iranian Kurdistan.

Autonomous Iraqi Kurdistan: Large Transnational Space

Since the 1991 Persian Gulf War, Iraqi Kurds have accessed a large transnational space that has encouraged the economic and political development of Kurdistan. Preventing the "Saddamization" of the North, investigating weapons of mass destruction, and mobilizing the Iraqi opposition meant rallying the international-policy community against Saddam Hussein and maintaining stability in Iraqi Kurdistan. Under the protection of coalition forces the northern Kurdish region became an internationally recognized, autonomous safe haven. The once remote border post of Zakho became a regional hub for oil smuggling and its lucrative related industries.

Iraqi Kurdistan also benefited from generous international humanitarian-relief aid. Whereas international NGOs played little role in Kurdish politics in the early state period, immediately after the Gulf War they became essential actors in Kurdistan. Dozens of NGOs and donor agencies, in conjunction with the KRG, reconstructed villages, demined farmlands, rebuilt the infrastructure, restarted the economy, and created employment opportunities for local populations. They also developed institutional linkages between the Kurdish governorates, the KRG, headquarters' offices, and donor organizations. NGOs started lobbying foreign governments and providing information about the Kurdish situation to the international-policy community. Even after the abortive uprising against Saddam in 1995 and the withdrawal of coalition forces from Iraqi Kurdistan in 1996, international support for Iraqi Kurds as victims of Saddam Hussein continued.

The United Nations assumed a key role in rehabilitating Iraq and Iraqi Kurdistan. The controversial oil-for-food program (UNSCR 986), implemented by the UN from March 1997 to November 2003, alleviated the adverse effects of the trade embargoes for Iraqi populations. Indeed, the program was rampant with accountability problems, disproportionately taxed the Kurdish North, and failed to pay the Kurds their full 13 percent share of the total proceeds of Iraqi oil sales. However, it provided Iraqi Kurdistan with about four billion dollars' worth of humanitarian goods and services, further encouraging reconstruction and rehabilitation programs in Kurdistan. Despite the disappearance of most international

NGOs and termination of the oil-for-food program in November 2003, the transnational space for Iraqi Kurds remains large. In fact, the British-U.S. intervention in Iraq and overthrow of Saddam Hussein in April 2003 has reinforced the role of transnational influences in Iraqi Kurdistan. Kurdish nationalist politics remains tied to the Iraqi reconstruction and U.S. security agenda.

In contrast to the early state period, whereby foreign intervention reinforced Kurdish factionalization, external penetrations in Iraqi Kurdistan after 1991 encouraged compromise and stability. After the Kurdish infighting from 1994 to 1996, UN and U.S. officials sponsored reconciliation efforts with KDP and PUK representatives in European capitals and Washington, D.C. They negotiated political, economic, and security agreements among the KRG, foreign governments, and international organizations. Changing international norms, and in particular the emphasis on democracy and federalism in Iraq, helped legitimate Kurdish nationalist institutions. Whereas the creation of the KRG in 1992 was virtually ignored by U.S. and European governments, it eventually gained international attention and foreign government support. At the thirty-fourth conference of the International Federation of Human Rights in Casablanca in January 2001, a resolution was passed calling for international protection of Kurdish rights to self-determination. That same year the Swedish Parliament reaffirmed the need to support Iraqi Kurds and protect their self-government.

Even the skeptical U.S. government offered tacit support to the Iraqi Kurdish Regional Government. Following the reopening of the unified Kurdish Parliament in October 2002, U.S. Secretary of State Colin Powell sent Iraqi Kurdish leaders a letter congratulating them on their efforts to sustain democracy and stability in Iraq. During his trip to Iraqi Kurdistan in January 2003, French senator Aymeri de Montesquiou affirmed that "a free spirited nation lives here in Iraqi Kurdistan whose affairs are administered competently by an authority representing them . . . which confirms the ability and success of the people of Kurdistan to manage their own affairs" ("Visiting French Senator" 2003). Three months later, in April 2003, Lord Nazir Ahmad, a member of the British House of Lords, addressed the KRG, calling for international support for Kurdish self-government within a federated Iraq.

The creation of a protected, autonomous region encouraged the transfer of people, ideas, and resources to Iraqi Kurdistan, all of which helped advance the notion of Kurdish self-rule. Since the early 1990s influential Iraqi Kurdish diasporic communities have become engaged in transnational nationalism, exporting their nationalist ideas, skills, and financial support to their homeland. Legitimated as victims of Saddam's regime, recognized institutionally in host-country systems, and free to return to the autonomous North, politicized Iraqi Kurdish communities in Europe and the United States have sponsored cultural and educational activities. They have improved research centers in Iraqi Kurdistan by donating materials for schools, libraries, and laboratories. By 2003 three members of the ministerial cabinet in the KRG in Arbil (Hawlêr) were European Kurds.

Legitimate, Democratized Kurdayetî in Iraq

Access to an autonomous safe haven and generous humanitarian-relief aid has created structural changes in the Iraqi Kurdish political economy and new opportunities for Kurds to mobilize as a national group. From 1991 to 2000, in conjunction with NGO and UN support, the Ministry of Reconstruction and Development of the KRG reconstructed more than 65 percent of the villages in the North that were destroyed by the Iraqi government. With international donor funds it implemented fifty million dollars' worth of reconstruction and humanitarian-relief projects, while providing much needed jobs for Kurdish civil servants and private entrepreneurs. External opportunity structures also encouraged alternative forms of income generation: the underground petroleum economy, telecommunication industry, private contracting, exchange markets, and foreign remittances, all of which have been the source of economic development and growth inside Iraqi Kurdistan.

New financial resources have enabled the Kurdish nationalist elite to reformulate and propel their nationalist agenda. Kurdish entrepreneurs have reinvested their revenues inside Iraqi Kurdistan by developing distinctly Kurdish institutions: the Kurdish Regional Government, Kurdish lobbying networks, Kurdish postage stamps, and Kurdish institutions of higher education. Since 1991 the nationalist elite has established new government agencies to address demands made by NGOs, the UN, international organizations, and donor agencies. With the emergence of a Kurdish civil society and generous international support, Kurdish local organizations have become active in humanitarian relief, reconstruction, and human rights, alongside new Kurdish ministries tailored for these activities.

Kurdish nationalist sentiment in Iraqi Kurdistan has also shifted. Instead of linking their nationalist project to socialist ideology or talking about a free Kurdistan like they did immediately after the 1991 Gulf War, Iraqi Kurdish officials have reframed their nationalist project as a democratic one. Taking advantage of the democratization efforts across the globe, and hoping to attract the political support of the West, former diasporic Kurds and the Kurdish nationalist elite redefined their government as an experiment in democracy. Kurdish nationalist organizations and sentiment have become tied to Western liberal ideology, norms, and institutions. These transformations, and their linkages to humanitarian relief and Western liberal democracy, have legitimated Kurdayetî on an international level. Since 1992 the KRG has transformed from a quasi-legal entity to a legitimate model for democracy in the Middle East.

The presence of democratizing nationalist institutions, even in a developing form, has encouraged compromise between the Kurdish nationalist elite and Baghdad. After the British-U.S. intervention Kurdish officials attempted to renegotiate Kurdish autonomy within the Iraqi state. Barzani

7. The Parliament building of the Kurdish regional government in Arbil (Hawlêr), Iraqi Kurdistan, ca. 1995. Photograph taken by the author.

drew up a constitution based on a federal structure, recognizing Baghdad as the political center. Even the politically sensitive issue of Kirkuk became open for negotiation, at least between Kurdish and U.S. officials. Although they still consider Kirkuk an essential Kurdish city, Barzani and Talabani stressed its multinational aspect. After the April 2003 intervention, they started advising Kurds to coexist in the spirit of fraternity with Assyrian, Arab, Chaldean, and Turkoman communities. Talabani addressed Turkey's concerns about the Turkoman populations. Although threatening to "open the door to Diyarbakir" during his visit to Kirkuk on April 14, 2003, Talabani asserted that the Kurds "support the rights of the Turkomen more than we support the rights of the Kurds because the Turkomen have suffered a great injustice" ("Talabani Remarks" 2003). In the provisional Iraqi constitution (transitional law for the administration of Iraq [TAL]) signed in March 2004, the Kurdish elite even agreed to share Kirkuk's oil revenues with the future Iraqi central government.

Although transnational space has advanced Iraqi Kurdish political autonomy, it has also placed limitations on it. The nature of international aid, for instance, has helped and hindered Kurdish self-sufficiency by creating new types of dependent relationships between Iraqi Kurds and the international donor and NGO community. Since 1991 the overly inflated dollar and extreme wage differentials turned most highly skilled and educated Iraqi Kurds toward NGOs or U.S.-financed projects for jobs, instead of the KRG. By the mid-1990s about 70 percent of active Kurdish populations were dependent on international humanitarian relief and its related income-generating activities (Bozarslan 1996a, 110; Leezenberg 2000).

Also, international relief programs have been framed by post-Gulf War regional politics and in particular the Turkish government's quest to constrain Kurdish autonomy. With control of the only legal open border into Iraqi Kurdistan until 2003, the Turkish government limited the movement of personnel, goods, and services to and from Kurdistan. After 1991 Turkey became the economic and political lifeline into Iraqi Kurdistan, which demanded certain compromises between Iraqi Kurds and Turkish officials. Donor organizations also refused to directly fund the KRG, despite its de facto status and defunct government in Baghdad. From the wheat buy-back program to reconstruction projects and food distributions, the KRG was prevented from directly implementing externally funded development programs. Consequently, instead of establishing long-term development planning, the Kurdish ministries functioned on six-month contingency plans that were dependent upon international donors, the United States, and Turkey (Natali 1999).

Indeed, since the 2003 Iraqi war international humanitarian relief has encouraged greater economic and political autonomy in Iraqi Kurdistan. With the transition of the remaining UN oil-for-food account ($1.5 billion) to the Kurdish Regional Government in November 2003 and a Baghdad-approved regional budget, the KRG has obtained much needed revenue to increases salaries for civil servants and implement economic-development programs.[1] This financial injection into the Kurdish political economy, as well as international investments from private companies, has created new linkages among the Kurdish nationalist elite, the KRG, local institutions, private contractors, diasporic communities, and the U.S.-led reconstruction of Iraq.

Further, despite influences on Kurdish nationalist organizations, sentiment, and center-periphery relations, transnational space has not significantly altered the representation of the nationalist elite inside Iraqi Kurdistan. International humanitarian aid and the British-U.S. intervention have advanced economic and political development without encouraging social restructuring at the local levels. Even though the Kurdish nationalist elite has accepted some type of federal structure for a post-Saddam Iraq, the notion of federalism has little meaning for the majority of Iraqi Kurds still tied to traditional sociopolitical structures. Most Iraqi Kurds remain loyal to Barzani and Talabani and their political parties, alongside and as an integral part of the KRG. Photographs of both Kurdish leaders are found throughout Iraqi Kurdistan—in baklava shops in local markets, village clinics, ministerial offices, and administrative buildings. Local political identities and power-sharing issues also remain salient. Talabani may have increased his international status, but he has not gained popularity in the Barzani-controlled regions of Iraqi Kurdistan. Nor has Barzani increased his influence in the PUK-influenced Sulaimaniya region.

1. After the overthrow of Saddam Hussein and the Ba'thist government in April 2003 the UN terminated its oil-for-food program and transitioned its remaining funds, or about $1.5 billion, to the Coalition Provisional Authority, which then transferred the funds to the Kurdish Regional Governments in Arbil (Hawlêr) and Sulaimaniya to complete the unfinished projects in Iraqi Kurdistan.

Juridical Transnational Space in Turkey

Like Iraqi Kurds, Kurds from Turkey have benefited from a relatively large transnational space. Instead of U.S. backing, however, they have accessed the European Parliament and its commitment to the Geneva Conventions. In contrast to Iraq, Turkey is a member of the Council of Europe and signatory of the European Convention on Human Rights. In 1987 and 1990 the Turkish government recognized the rights of individuals to appeal directly to the European Court and acknowledged the court's binding jurisdiction. Europe's decision to grant Turkey membership status in the European Union (EU) has also led to new pressures on the Turkish government as defined by the 1993 Copenhagen criteria to democratize its political system.

Turkey's EU candidacy has transnationalized its Kurdish problem. Access to European Union institutions has reinforced ties to the international network of human-rights organizations and created a new legal political arena for Kurdish nationalist claims. International organizations such as Amnesty International, the International Federation of Human Rights in Turkey, Helsinki Watch, the International Pen-Writers in Prison Committee, the United Nations Convention Against Torture, and the Convention on Civil and Political Rights have raised the visibility of the Kurdish problem in Turkey. Although some have presented Kurdish rights as an ethnic issue, most focus on its legal aspects: arbitrary killings, freedom of expression, independence of the judiciary, and random disappearances of individuals. These organizations make claims to the European Court of Justice, European Convention on Human Rights, and the Organization for Security and Cooperation in Europe on behalf of Kurdish clients.[2] What has emerged in Turkey and is absent in Iraq is a "juridicization" of Kurdayetî at the international level (Bertrand and Rigoni 2000, 413).

---

2. Given the complexities involved in the human-rights litigation it is difficult to extract precise numbers of Kurdish cases brought to the European Court of Human Rights. The ethnicity of the applicant is added only in some cases (to allege that human-rights violations were discriminatory), but not all. The first cases concerning Kurdish human-rights violations in Turkey were introduced by the Kurdish Human Rights Project (KHRP) in 1993 and decided in 1996 (*Akdivar v. Turkey* [99/1995/605/693] and *Aksoy v. Turkey* [100/1995/606/694]). I thank Rochelle Harris at the KHRP for this information.

Although they condemn PKK terrorism, European institutions have semilegitimated Kurdish leaders from Turkey and their nationalist activities. The Turkish government's arrest of Layla Zana and eight other Kurdish deputies for speaking Kurdish in the Turkish assembly in 1993 created an uproar in Europe and human-rights circles. Turkey labeled Zana a PKK terrorist and sentenced her and her colleagues to fifteen years in prison. However, the European Parliament awarded Zana the Sakhorov Peace Prize. The European Court of Justice in Strasbourg, influenced by the legal findings of the Kurdish Human Rights Association and the Human Rights Association (HRA) of Turkey, has also effectively intervened on behalf of persecuted Kurdish families. European governments continue to pressure Turkey to democratize its political system, which includes improving its human-rights record.

Like Iraqi Kurds, Kurdish diasporic communities from Turkey have taken advantage of open European democratic systems by establishing Kurdish cultural and political organizations that sponsor language training, cultural symposia, and academic conferences on the Kurdish problem. Supported by European governments, diasporic communities have published Kurdish-language books and journals that have been distributed throughout Europe. L'Institut Kurde de Paris has assumed an important networking role for international organizations and human-rights groups in Turkey and Europe. It presented Akin Birdal as president of the Human Rights Association of Turkey and established the Committee for the Defense of National Democratic Rights of the Kurdish People in Turkey. The president, Dr. Kendal Nezan, a physicist from Diyarbakir, interacts frequently with high-level French government officials, which has helped further legitimate the Kurdish nationalist project on a European level.

Quasi-Legal Ethnonationalism in Turkey

Large transnational space has helped reshape and increase the significance of Kurdayeti in Turkey, just as it has in Iraqi Kurdistan. It has also semilegitimated Kurdish nationalist claims. Instead of appealing to humanitarian-relief organizations, the U.S. government, or influential lobbying networks, Kurds in Turkey have linked their nationalist project to the international human-rights agenda and its European-backed political institutions. Over the past decade many have taken their claims to the HRA in

Turkey, which has established thirty-four offices throughout the country. HRA coordinates casework with the Kurdish Human Rights Project (KHRP) in London, the European Parliament, and international human-rights monitors.

As in Iraqi Kurdistan, changing international norms and access to international organizational support have also reshaped the nationalist sentiment. Instead of demanding Kurdish independence or continuing to engage in violence, the Kurdish nationalist elite from Turkey has reconfigured their claims based on democracy and human rights inside Turkey. Since 2000 the PKK has twice changed its name and political program in the hope of shedding its illegitimate international status. Given these new transnational opportunities, why then have Kurds from Turkey failed to create the type of autonomous nationalist organizations that Iraqi Kurds have done after the Gulf War? With a diasporic community representing 80 percent of all Kurds in the diaspora, including seven hundred thousand in Germany alone, Kurds from Turkey should have developed a highly representative and influential nationalist elite and organizations that could mobilize and unify the Kurdish masses. Yet this has not been the case.

Although the transnational space for Kurds in Turkey has been large, it is more limited than the opportunities made available for Iraqi Kurds. Whereas international organizational support has encouraged the development of Iraqi Kurdistan, its absence inside Turkey has allowed the Kurds' economic and political marginalization to continue. Kurds from Turkey have had no comparable opportunities to rebuild their schools, democratize their regions, or create a self-administered government under the protection of coalition forces. Whereas dozens of NGOs established operations in the Kurdish autonomous zone after the Gulf War, only five relief organizations became temporarily active in the underdeveloped southeastern and eastern Kurdish regions since the early 1990s. The sixty thousand Iraqi Kurdish refugees that were resettled in Turkish camps in 1991 did not even gain access to UN refugee status or humanitarian assistance.

Indeed, after the Gulf War Danielle Mitterand and her France Libertés visited Iraqi Kurdish refugee camps in Turkey and reported on its deplorable conditions. The United Nations High Commission for Refugees (UNHCR) assisted twelve thousand Kurdish refugees from Turkey inside Iraqi Kurdistan and gave them refugee status, as well as food rations and medicines as part of the oil-for-food program. The international human-rights regime and conditions tied to its EU candidacy have also pressured Turkey to modify its Kurdish policies at home. Moderate Turkish civilian leaders have become increasingly attentive to Turkey's abysmal human-rights record by compensating Kurdish families for past abuses sanctioned by the European Parliament.

Still, Kurds from Turkey have not received the same type of international recognition or political support as have Iraqi Kurds. Whereas Iraqi Kurdish leaders, organizations, and sentiment have been legitimated internationally and at home, their counterparts from Turkey have been criminalized abroad and delegitimated inside the state (Fernandes 2001). The asymmetrical nature of transnational space has created a "good Kurds-bad Kurds" dichotomy that has inhibited political and institutional development in the Kurdish movement in Turkey. When the U.S. assistant to humanitarian affairs visited Turkey in 2000 to assess the situation in the Kurdish regions, he underplayed the gravity of the Kurdish problem so as not to jeopardize U.S.-Turkish relations. Even the Kurds' access to the international human-rights regime is in jeopardy, particularly as the European Court attempts to reform its penal system owing to the backlog of cases and costs. If passed, the penal reform will minimize the number of cases heard from Turkey.[3] Without a condemnation from the court, it may reduce pressures on the Turkish government to implement necessary human-rights reforms while encouraging EU affiliation.

Turkey's privileged relationship with Western governments also limits opportunities for Kurdish diasporic communities to mobilize as a national community. Most Kurdish associations from Turkey are monitored with suspicion, regardless of their political affiliations. European governments, pressured by the Turkish state elite, have closed Kurdish television stations several times. Even after reprogramming its broadcasting to focus on cultural and educational issues, the renamed MEDTV is continually harassed through airwave blocking, legal complaints, and destruction of property. Certain cities in Germany and Belgium have refused to register newborns with Kurdish names, just like state officials do in Turkey (Rigoni 1998, 209). Prohibitions against Kurdish organizations from Turkey have become particularly serious since September 11, 2001, as antiterrorist groups have

---

3. To improve judicial efficiency the court has proposed to accept only those cases that raise new issues, becoming more of a constitutional court.

placed greater restrictions on PKK/Kongra-gel-affiliated organizations, many of which have been put on the international terrorist list. Others have been closed or have lost funding from host-country governments.

Even if Kurds from Turkey had access to an equally generous transnational space, they would still be constrained by a restrictive political space at home. The absence of a positive nexus between the global and the local limits the influence of transnational space inside Turkey. Whereas Barzani and Talabani have gained access to high-level Western officials and become legitimate Kurdish elite inside Kurdistan, Öcalan, Zana, and other representatives have been arrested or killed. Whereas diasporic communities and international NGOs can freely circulate in Iraqi Kurdistan, they have no serious chance of mobilizing in Turkey. Human-rights organizations and their representatives have been imprisoned and harassed by government officials. The former president of the Human Rights Association in Turkey, Akin Birdal, has been the victim of assassination attempts and eventually resigned from his post.

Additionally, in contrast to Iraqi Kurdistan, the transnationalization of political Islam and the Islamization of the political space inside Turkey and in host countries have encouraged Kurds to emphasize their Muslim identities, alongside or instead of Kurdish ethnonationalism. For instance, although the German government contains extreme Kurdish nationalist activities, it has allowed Turkish government-supported *diyanets* (departments of religious affairs attached to the prime minister's office) and Islamic organizations to become institutionalized in German cities and towns. Increasing Islamic influences in diasporic settings, as well as the Sunni-inspired July 1993 fire in Sivas, Turkey, that killed Alevi intellectuals, has given rise to an influential transnational Alevi movement. Alevi communities have created five federations in Europe and more than one hundred associations in Germany. Some organizations are solely Kurdish. Others bring Kurds and Turks together under a shared Alevi identity.

Alevi influences have been reexported to Turkey, creating new dynamics in Kurdish politics and diversifying nationalist mobilizations at home. In the spring 1999 parliamentary elections in Turkey, for instance, two functionaries of the Federation of Alevi Communities in Europe (Avrupa Aleviler Birlikleri Federasyona [AABF]) became candidates for the newly founded Alevi Party (Bariş Partisi) in Turkey. When the Turkish government introduced a new law against nonorthodox tariqa orders, which included Alevis, in the summer of 1998, the AABF sent a delegation from Germany to protest in numerous Turkish cities (Sökefeld and Schwalgin 2000, 13–21). This type of transnational religious and political fragmentation has not become part of Kurdayetî in Iraq, which evolves within a geographically confined region hostile to Islamic influences in nationalist politics.

Restrictive Transnational Space in Iran

In contrast to the large transnational space for Iraqi Kurds and the juridical space for Kurds from Turkey, external opportunity structures for Iranian Kurds have been more restrictive. Although Iraqi Kurds have benefited from generous humanitarian relief and security assistance and their counterparts in Turkey have gained access to the European Parliament, Iranian Kurds have had no such international institutional support. When the Iranian Kurdish regions were militarily attacked and placed under martial law during the 1990s, there were no available coalition forces, international organizations, or influential diasporic communities that lobbied on behalf of Iranian Kurdish populations. The absence of a legal framework defining the conditions under which NGOs can operate and uninterest from conservative Islamic leaders have limited transnational penetrations in the country.

Indeed, international humanitarian-relief agencies have assisted the Iranian government with its significant refugee problems (Rajaee 2000, 46–49). Ongoing work by the UNHCR, in cooperation with other UN agencies, the Iranian Red Crescent Society, and local NGOs, has supported sixteen thousand Iranian Kurdish refugees in camps in southern and central Iraq. International organizations encourage Iranian Kurds to voluntarily repatriate and integrate into Iranian society, while continuing to support their needs as refugees. Also, the World Bank's approved loans to Iran for $232 million and $145 million to finance health care and sewage programs provide much needed aid to poor rural areas and may include the Kurdish regions. Iranian Kurds have also attracted attention from human-rights organizations, which has increased their significance as a minority group. As part of their fact-finding missions on the human-rights situation in Iraqi Kurdistan in the early 1990s, the Federation International des Ligues des Droit de l'Homme, Amnesty International, and France Libertés reported on threats made by Islamic agents against Iranian Kurdish refugees. These findings helped internationalize the Iranian Kurdish problem, giving the Iranian Kurds, like Kurds in Iraq and Turkey, semilegitimacy as political dissidents and refugees.

Yet the transnational space for Iranian Kurds is still far more restrictive than it is for Kurds in Iraq and Turkey. In contrast to Iraqi Kurdistan, whereby international humanitarian-aid programs have encouraged the autonomous region's economic and political prosperity, UN programs in Iran have focused on resettling and repatriating refugees. Even then, support is limited. Of the ten thousand Iranian Kurds inside Iraqi Kurdistan, only four thousand have received UNHCR refugee status, with no assurance of being resettled to a safe third country. In fact, since February 13, 1997, the UNHCR has altered it humanitarian policies toward Iranian Kurdish refugees fleeing Iraqi Kurdistan to Turkey, refusing them access to third-country asylum. Nor have international organizations made any serious attempt to develop the infrastructure, reconstruct villages, or rehabilitate agricultural lands in the Iranian Kurdistan as they have in Iraq. The restrictive space in Iran also prevents political exchanges among international organizations, diasporic communities, and Kurdish nationalists in the homeland, just as it does in Turkey.

Whereas Kurds in Turkey benefit from seven hundred thousand influential diasporic Kurds who have raised international consciousness and given significance to their nationalist agenda, Iranian Kurds have less developed diasporic networks. In striking contrast, only about fifty thousand Iranian Kurds have taken exile in Europe since the Iranian Revolution, leaving the nationalist cadres at home at an institutional and organizational disadvantage. The five hundred thousand Iranian Kurds who left their towns and villages in southwest Iran after the revolution migrated to Tehran and its outskirts. Thousands more took exile in Iraq and Iraqi Kurdistan. Another four thousand fled to the Kurdish regions in Turkey, where they temporarily resided in UNHCR camps ("Fact-Finding Mission" 1995, 36–37).

The regionalization of the Iranian Kurdish diaspora, as opposed to the Europeanization of Kurdish diasporic communities from Iraq and Turkey, has created a much different migration experience for Iranian Kurds abroad and opportunities for nationalist communities at home. Refugee status in Iraqi Kurdistan has not accorded Iranian Kurds easy access to international organizations and their legitimating functions or use of sophisticated telecommunication systems. Instead of interacting with human-rights networks or European educational and professional systems, the sixteen thousand Iranian Kurdish refugees in the al-Tash Camp outside of Baghdad and thirty-two hundred in the urban areas of Arbil (Hawlêr) and Sulaimaniya live in isolated areas and are dependent on UNHCR support. Even the small Iranian Kurdish diasporic community in Europe has failed to mobilize like its Kurdish counterparts from Iraq and Turkey. The KDPI and Komala Parties have established legal representation in European cities. However, they do not have internationally recognized leaders or influential transnational networks that could advance Kurdayetî from afar. Key nationalist elite, such as Qasimlu and Sadeqh Sharafkandi, have been assassinated by agents hired by the Iranian government in different European cities.

Crippled Ethnonationalism in Iran

Like Iraqi Kurds and Kurds in Turkey, Iranian Kurds have taken advantage of transnational space by mobilizing on behalf of their ethnonational identity. In conjunction with diasporic communities, they have organized educational and cultural activities, including musical events in the homeland and in Europe. Many have created Internet sites and political party offices to represent the larger Iranian Kurdish community's claims as an oppressed minority. The Iranian Refugees Alliance, for instance, has established an Internet-based quarterly journal that examines different aspects of Iranian Kurdish refugees. The KDPI and Komala Parties have created offices throughout Europe, generating information and sponsoring events for their Kurdish constituencies, alongside Kurdish communities from Iraq and Turkey. New transnational relationships have also developed between some Iranian Kurds and the PKK. In February 1999 Kurds in Sanandaj, Mahabad, and Urmiya mobilized against the Islamic regime and in support of Öcalan.

Still, Kurdish nationalism inside Iran has not attained the legitimacy and significance it has in Iraq and Turkey after 1990. The absence of an influential nationalist elite, even symbolically in prison, has left Iranian Kurdish nationalists at an institutional and political disadvantage. Those nationalists who continue to mobilize have turned to radical cross-border groups, not international organizations or influential diasporic communities that could have semilegitimated their claims.

Whereas Kurdayetî in Iraq and Turkey has become democratized and tied to human rights, in Iran it has been crippled on an institutional level. The restricted transnational space has also impeded Iranian Kurds from creating sophisticated lobbying networks and public relations campaigns that could have increased the significance of Kurdayetî at home and abroad. For instance, after Öcalan's arrest, tens of thousands of Kurds mobilized across Europe and Kurdistan, soliciting responses from European governments and international human-rights organizations. In comparison, after the 1992 Mikonos affair, in which the Iranian Kurdish nationalist elite were assassinated in Berlin, international media attention and reaction by Kurdish communities and human rights groups did not generate the type of large-scale organizational response needed to mobilize the Kurdish nationalists over the long term.

With limited transnational mobilizing structures and a large transborder community in Iraqi Kurdistan, it would seem that Iranian Kurds could have turned to the KRG to advance their nationalist claims. About one thousand Iranian Kurds travel back and forth daily to Iraqi Kurdistan for personal and cultural activities. Many live in the PUK-influenced Sorani regions and can easily communicate with Iraqi Kurds. Political party representations have also increased cross-border contacts between the Iranian and Iraqi Kurdish communities. Since the 1990s Iranian Kurdish nationalist parties such as the KDPI, Komala, the Union of Revolutionary Toilers of Kurdistan, and the Organization for National and Islamic Struggle of Iranian Kurdistan (known as Khebat) have established offices and communication networks to advance their nationalist claims. These Iranian Kurdish dissident groups have issued press releases, trained peshmerga, and sponsored military campaigns that would otherwise have been prohibited inside Iran. Even after the KDPI was expelled from Iraqi Kurdistan and lost access to communication networks, it reestablished offices elsewhere in the autonomous Kurdish North, where it coordinates activities with its supporters inside Iran.

Yet Iranian Kurds have not attempted to integrate their activities with the Iraqi Kurdish nationalist project. Even across borders, opportunities to mobilize as a national group are limited. The autonomous region has hardly been a safe haven for the majority of Iranian Kurdish refugees and dissidents. Whereas Kurdish diasporic communities from Iraq and Turkey live in relative security in open political systems in European cities, Iranian Kurds living in Iraqi Kurdistan have been subject to political pressures and military assaults from the Iranian government, Iraqi Kurdish parties, and radical Islamic groups. In fact, the autonomous North has become so dangerous for certain Iranian Kurds that demands have increased for resettlement in a safe third country. Nor is the Iraqi Kurdish elite interested in jeopardizing its nationalist project for Iranian Kurds, even if it considers them ethnic brethren. Talabani and Barzani have often succumbed to Iranian government pressures by closing down KDPI telecommunication stations and permitting Iranian military incursions along the border in exchange for economic and political concessions. These restrictions have further crippled Iranian Kurdish nationalist potential, despite the fact that most of the refugees consider themselves Kurds first.

In the absence of alternative legal local institutions, legitimating structures, and influential diasporic communities, some groups, such as the KDPI and Komala Parties based in Sulaimaniya Province in Iraqi Kurdistan, have become further isolated, though secretly active. Instead of reframing their nationalist sentiment according to federalism or the international human-rights regime, Iranian Kurdish nationalists have become less accommodating in local and regional contexts. For instance, exiled Komala leader Ibrahim Alizadeh claimed that although Komala supports autonomy and federalism, it does not seek these political options as a final end point. Rather, according to Alizadeh, "they are tactics to creating a Kurdish state. Komala's first objective is to overthrow the Islamic republic."[4] The KDPI continues to seek democracy for Iran and autonomy for Kurdistan; however, radicalized peshmerga remain militarily active from their isolated and unprotected enclaves in Iranian-Iraqi border regions.

Still, the transnational space that helped cripple Kurdish nationalism has left Iranian Kurds no real political outlet to manifest their sense of nationalism like their counterparts in Iraq and Turkey. Instead, they make claims as oppressed minorities inside Iran alongside other opposition groups. Others have turned to leftist parties in Europe, which offer a safer and more expansive space to gain political influence. For instance, despite

4. Interview with Ibrahim Alizadeh, head of Komala Iran (exiled in Iraqi Kurdistan), and Aziz Mamle, former KDPI representative, Paris, Mar. 6, 2003.

the presence of Komala offices throughout Europe, most of the twenty-five hundred Iranian Kurdish cadres that were sent by the Komala Party to Germany during the 1980s have integrated into European socialist systems. These leftist communities, as well as other Iranian Kurdish refugees, affiliate with Iranian cultural organizations and Iranian associations in Europe, not the uninfluential Iranian Kurdish political parties.

Conclusions

In each case, transnational space has increased the significance and legitimacy of Kurdayetî, helping to reshape Kurdish nationalism at home. Yet its asymmetrical nature has elevated some Kurdish nationalist projects over others. Iraqi Kurds have gained a monopoly on Kurdish autonomy, whereas their counterparts in Turkey and Iran have barely acquired political rights. Whereas Kurdayetî in Iraq has been legitimated internationally and institutionalized inside Iraqi Kurdistan, for Kurds in Turkey it has been semilegitimated abroad and prohibited at home. Iranian Kurds have had even less opportunities to advance their sense of Kurdayetî. Asymmetrical transnational space has also created greater complexity and diversification in Kurdish nationalist organizations and sentiment across borders. This diversification, alongside distinct historical trajectories that have emerged in conjunction with different states, limits the likelihood of a unified Kurdish nationalist project from emerging at the local, regional, or international level.

9

Conclusion

Rethinking Nationalism, Ethnicity, and the Kurdish Problem

Variations in the character of Kurdayetî underline the importance and limitations of regime-created contours of political space in national-identity formation. Political space matters in creating sets of motives, ideas, and mobilization potential for Kurdish communities. It shapes the nature of the nationalist elite, organizations, sentiment, and relationships between Kurds and central governments. However, political space is not constant across space and time. Variations have created differences in the manifestation of Kurdayetî in three different settings over a period of 150 years. For instance, whereas tribal leaders became nationalist elite in Iraq, they played no significant role in the Kurdish leadership in Turkey and Iran. Kurdish organizations in Iraq were influential and semilegitimated; however, in Turkey and Iran they were diversified, illegal, and less representative across Kurdish society. Kurdayetî was also defined by tribalism, ethnoreligious-inspired claims, leftist ideology, and highly ethnicized nationalist sentiment. In Iraq and Iran the relationship between the nationalists and the state elite fluctuated between compromise and hostility. In Turkey it was continuously hostile.

Each case history also reveals a direct relationship between ethnicized political boundaries and Kurdish ethnonationalism. That is to say, as political space becomes ethnicized, so too does Kurdayetî. Kurdish communities "Kurdified" what the state elite Arabized, Turkified, and Persianized. In each setting, ethnic identity, language, and territory became a shared and integral aspect of Kurdayetî. However, the nature and timing of nationalist claims varied depending upon the ethnicization processes and opportunity structures. Iraqi Kurds waited until the 1960s to make highly ethnicized and violent nationalist claims. In Turkey, where the political space was clearly ethnicized, militarized, and restrictive, Kurdayetî became highly ethnicized and violent in the early 1920s. When Kurdayetî became ethnicized but relatively accommodating in Iran during the 1940s, it remained dormant in Turkey and ambiguous in Iraq.

Similarities and variations in Kurdayetî across space and time show that nationalism is a more finely tuned process that extends beyond a single relationship between a political center and a minority group. Kurdish nationalism is not just a consequence of a repressive state acting against a helpless periphery or a by-product of political institutions and structure. It is the result of an active and diverse periphery responding in different ways to the state's varying economic and political incentives. The emergence, formation, and re-formation of Kurdish ethnonationalism over time involve multiple relationships between different factions in the central government and various subgroups in the periphery, which are marked by their own political tensions.

Indeed, these tensions are partially tied to the dichotomous nature of heterogeneous, ethnically diverse societies. Alongside a deeply rooted and shared sense of Kurdish ethnicity, Kurdish nationalist communities have cultural particularities linked to the states in which they live that define their repertoire of political identities. They also engage in power struggles against one another that constrain the emergence of a cohesive sense of Kurdayetî. In fact, despite the presence of exclusivist nationalist projects in Iraq, Turkey, and Iran, many Kurds failed to mobilize on behalf of Kurdish ethnonationalism. After the Iraqi regime's Arabization programs and chemical attacks in Kurdistan, Kurdish ethnonationalism was still fractured. It was not until the late 1980s, some fifty years after the early state revolts, that Kurds in Turkey manifested openly their ethnonational identity. Even then, their nationalist sentiment and organizations were fragmented. Kurdish nationalists had to compete with Islamic and Alevi influences, which after 1990 became an increasingly salient part of Turkish and Kurdish politics. Since the downfall of the Mahabad Republic in 1946 Iranian Kurdish nationalism has been most influential among the left-leaning, secular Sunni Kurdish milieu.

Still, fragmentation and internal dichotomies are not a natural aspect of Kurdish ethnonationalism. Nor is Kurdayetî a function of heterogeneous or undeveloped Kurdish societies. Rather, the detailed case studies show that the very nature of political space in ethnically diverse societies often hinders the emergence of a highly representative and continuous manifestation of Kurdish ethnonationalism. As nation-state-building strategies become more finely tuned, favoring some subgroups over others, national communities become increasingly fragmented among themselves. Differentiation and homogenization can occur within the periphery simultaneously because certain political spaces are more beneficial for some communities than for others. Also, as the political space diversifies, so too do the opportunities for Kurds to express their political identities. An increasingly complex socioeconomic and political order gives rise to an increasingly complex, and often less representative, form of nationalism. Consequently, even during nationalist revival periods some group members may emphasize their national identity while others may not, despite the presence of a deeply rooted ethnie.

Nation-state-building strategies and their consequent political spaces also encourage particular types of nationalism to become salient over others. Although Islam was the key identity marker for Kurds in each imperial setting, only in the post-1980 Turkish state did it become part of Kurdayetî, alongside the existing secular ethnonationalism. Islamic tendencies have become increasingly active in autonomous Iraqi Kurdistan; however, they have not significantly reshaped Kurdayetî, which remains tied to a secular sense of nationalism represented by two highly influential nationalist elites. Kurdish nationalist sentiment in Iranian Kurdistan became slightly Islamized immediately after the Islamic revolution; however, Kurdayetî soon resumed its left-leaning, secular, and ethnicized character.

Variable Kurdish nationalism underlines the importance of mobilizing structures such as a modernizing elite, organizational networks, financial resources, and external support in providing the necessary logistics of ethnic revivals. In underdeveloped, transitional, conflict-prone societies such as Kurdistan that lack institutionalized political structures, uneven modernization trends and the consequences of war can unexpectedly impact resource availability. Such shocks can discourage or prohibit a nationalist project. Fear of repression or the absence of legal rights to organize can also impede the evolution of nationalism, even when a group's identity is highly ethnicized. At certain moments it may be safer for peripheral groups to emphasize their civic, religious, tribal, or provincial identities rather than evoke a sense of ethnic nationalism. Highly ethnicized communities respond to restrictive political spaces by terminating activities, taking their organizations underground and across borders, or turning to alternative groups to make nationalist claims. Thus, even if a group is conscious of its deeply rooted ethnie it may not mobilize on behalf of its ethnonationalist identity because the political space impedes it from doing so. Ethnonationalism can wake up and fall dormant again without compromising the authenticity of the nationalist endeavor. Periods of dormancy do not necessarily mean failed nationalisms.

The emergence of globalization and transnational processes adds a new element to political space. In each setting after the early 1990s, Kurdayetî became highly ethnicized across Kurdistan, regardless of the different political spaces inside each state. Kurdish communities reconfigured their nationalist projects in relation to external mobilizing structures, in particular changing international norms and transnational spaces. Kurdish nationalist sentiment and organizations become linked to democracy, human rights, and self-determination, ideological currents imported from outside the states' territorial borders.

Although transnational space has increased the significance of Kurdayetî at the international level, it has not altered the influence and representation of the Kurdish nationalist elite at the local levels inside Kurdistan. Barzani and Talabani have become legitimate Kurdish leaders; however, their influence is confined to their KDP and PUK enclaves inside Iraqi Kurdistan. Federalism has been imported from transnational space, but it has limited influence across Kurdish society, which is still tied to traditional sociopolitical structures. This gap between the global and the local underlines the continued role of domestic political space in shaping Kurdayetî and the increasingly complex nature of post-1990 national-identity formation and nation-building processes.

Managing the Kurdish Problem

The relationship between political space and national-identity formation provides a useful framework for managing ethnonational conflict, and in particular the Kurdish problem. It shows that group identities can be manipulated, to a certain extent, by state leaders or outside actors. Government policies can stifle nationalist potential, either by supporting traditional power structures, by leaving peripheral regions undeveloped, by repressing nationalist activity, or by failing to develop a cohesive, modernizing nationalist elite. Some strategies are also more inclined toward conflict resolution than others. Whereas the nationalist elite is given semilegitimate status and access to political networks, nationalist organizations and accommodating center-periphery relations are likely to develop. In Iraq and Iran the political space was ambiguous and partially compromising, at least until the late 1980s. This ambiguity encouraged the development of nationalist institutions, the integration and exclusion of Kurdish groups, and some opportunities for negotiation between the nationalist and state elites. In contrast, Turkey's highly exclusionary political space created no opportunities for the development of a legal nationalist elite or nationalist organizations. The unchanging, highly ethnicized political space resulted in continuous hostility between the center and Kurdish nationalist periphery, with no opportunities for negotiation.

Conflict-resolution strategies, therefore, require a political space that is large in content and time: real political equality, recognition of the distinct Kurdish ethnic identity, and opportunities to express this identity within the state. The case histories show that accommodationist policies based on pure rhetoric, or strategies that have a limited time span, lose credibility and weaken the government's negotiating power. As the gap between the discourse and reality widens over time, it becomes increasingly difficult to convince national groups that they are an equal and integral part of the state. Positive management can turn to antagonism, creating or re-creating the cycle of hostility between the center and the periphery.

The bigger challenge is erasing the past. Even if each central government opens its political space and recognizes the distinct Kurdish ethnic identity, will Kurds de-emphasize their sense of ethnonationalism and integrate into their political centers as Iraqi, Turkish, and Iranian citizens? After more than eighty years of exclusionary policies, ethnic-cleansing programs, discrimination, and a new world order where small nations become states, is it realistically possible to contain Kurdish ethnonationalism peacefully within each state? Given the ethnicization and increasing complexity of Kurdayetî, what are the prospects of managing the Kurdish problems in each state and across borders?

In heterogeneous states where ethnic boundaries have become institutionalized, it becomes increasingly difficult to weaken ethnonational sentiment over time. Ethnicity, unlike religious, civic, linguistic, or socioeconomic identities, is an unchanging aspect of group identity that does not necessarily lose its saliency with modernization or secularization policies. On the contrary, as each state unevenly modernized, secularized, and centralized the political apparatus over time, Kurdayetî became increasingly ethnicized and salient. Islamic, leftist, and official state countercurrents may have challenged the influence of Kurdish ethnonationalism across Kurdish society. However, they have not diminished the role of ethnicity in defining contemporary Kurdish nationalism. The idea of a distinct Kurdish ethnic identity and the right to some form of political autonomy within each state have become undeniable, undisputed facts among Kurdish communities across borders, despite variations in Kurdish nationalist elites and organizations.

In light of the ethnicized political spaces and unchangeable role of ethnicity in national-identity formation, managing the contemporary Kurdish problem requires readjusting the political threshold to address the ethnic component of Kurdayetî. Instead of trying to create a false sense of ethnic homogenization, the state elites in Iraq, Turkey, and Iran should emphasize ethnic diversity within decentralized political systems that guarantee protection of minority-group rights. Managing the contemporary Kurdish problem demands recognizing the distinct Kurdish ethnicity as an integral part of the official state nationalism; institutionalizing Kurdish ethnic identity into the state's legal, political, and educational systems; permitting Kurdish-language instruction; and according Kurds some form of political and cultural autonomy in their regions.

The distinct notions of Kurdayetî that emerged in Iraq, Turkey, and Iran also demand policy responses tailored to each state and its Kurdish communities. Although it is unrealistic to imagine a future Iraqi state intact without Kurdayetî, it is not necessarily impossible for Kurdish nationalism to flourish inside a future Iraq. However, the only way an accommodating Kurdayetî can be sustained is for the future state elite to reconstruct an Iraqi identity that recognizes both Kurds and Arabs as equal partners in the state and institutionalizes this partnership in the state's educational, political, and social structures. The TAL, signed by the Iraqi Governing Council on March 8, 2004, must be the fundamental basis of a future Iraqi constitution and implemented as such.

Negotiating Kurdish autonomy in a federal Iraq also requires recognition of distinct Kurdish territories, especially Kirkuk, as historically Kurdish, even if the city's oil revenues are to be shared with the central government. Future Iraqi elite must officially recognize the al-Anfal genocide of the Kurds and compensate Kurdish victims and their families accordingly. If opportunities for Iraqi Kurds as an ethnic group remain large in content and time, if there are no gaps between the discourse and reality, and if the Kurdish autonomous region is permitted to develop politically and economically in a decentralized federal state, then an accommodating Kurdish nationalism can possibly flourish inside Iraq. Policies toward the Kurds in any future Iraqi political system, whether it is federalism, a consociation, or beneficent dictatorship, cannot succeed without these fundamental guarantees.

In republican Turkey, where a system of quasi democracy has existed since the 1950s, a real solution to the Kurdish problem demands constitutional changes in the political system. Essential transformations include checking the military's influence in judicial, political, and bureaucratic affairs; strengthening civilian rule; increasing opportunities for small-party representation in the government; and allowing real freedom of expression. A durable and constructive relationship with Kurdish communities and the central government depends upon an alteration in the official notion of Turkish citizenship. Kurds must be acknowledged, alongside Turks and other ethnic communities, as equal partners with rights to express their distinct ethnic identity within the territorial boundaries of the state.

Moreover, the Turkish elite must reduce the gap between the promises and political reality. The fact that the Kurdish issue can be openly debated in the media and that music and certain journals are produced in the Kurdish language are steps in the right direction. However, there are still too many constraints on the day-to-day lives of average Kurds to enable a positive relationship to develop between Kurdish communities and the central government. The Turkish elite should distinguish between violent Kurdish parties and moderate Kurdish communities that acknowledge themselves as Kurds. It must differentiate terrorism from the demands of innocent Kurdish masses. It must legalize moderate Kurdish parties and give Kurds the right to use the name *Kurd* in their organizations and public associations. It must stop impeding journalists and researchers from accessing and disseminating information about the Kurds. As in Iraq, the Turkish government can begin a process of reconciliation with Kurdish communities by economically developing the Kurdish regions, compensating Kurdish families who lost land or family members in the civil war, terminating the village-guard system, and assisting Kurds in returning to their original villages. This measure can include economic resettlement packages similar to others for internally displaced programs in war-affected regions.

The Iranian government has an equally challenging task ahead. Given the shared histories between Kurds and Persians, the institutionalized role of Shi'a Islam in the state, the Persian imperial formula that drew upon Median and Persian histories, and the ethnoheterogeneity of the Iranian territory, Iranian Kurds have access to particular reference points with the dominant Persian ethnic group that encourage ethnic tolerance and accommodation. Although Iraqi and Turkish officials can try to make Kurdish communities believe they are an integral part of Arab and Turkish cultures, their appeals do not have the same credibility owing to the absence of a shared sense of culture among Turks, Arabs, and Kurds.

Despite a common heritage with their Persian cousins, Kurds in Iran do not have equal opportunities to express their distinct ethnic identity. The Iranian government needs to legitimate its claims to cultural similarity by ensuring real political equality between the Persian and non-Persian ethnic groups, as well as between Shi'a and Sunni communities. Negotiating the Kurdish problem in Iran requires political reforms advocated by the moderate reformist Islamic leaders that include legalizing opposition groups, allowing Kurdish parties to participate in the election process, economically developing Kurdish regions, legalizing Kurdish-language instruction, and permitting Kurdish officials to govern the Kurdish regions.

Still, the contemporary Kurdish problem, which has spread from four Middle Eastern countries to most of Europe, has become part of an increasingly complex transnational space including regional and international actors. The continued volatility of the Kurdish regions and creation of diasporic communities have created new security, economic, and political problems outside Kurdistan while fueling nationalist agendas at home. With swelling numbers of Kurds in European cities and ongoing clandestine immigration, the Kurdish issue has become part of Europe's "foreigner problem." It has brought European governments directly inside Kurdish affairs. International nongovernmental agencies, the European Parliament, refugee organizations, and host-country governments are now active players in Kurdish nationalist politics, which since the 1990s has become tied to human rights, clandestine immigration, and integration policies. Increasing diversity has added new claims for minority rights and refugee assistance into the nationalist agendas. Consequently, the distinction between Kurdish politics in the homeland and host countries has virtually disappeared.

Given these globalization and transnationalization processes, the Kurdish problem can no longer be viewed as an antagonism between particular Kurdish leaders within state borders or an internal affair of the Iraqi, Turkish, and Iranian states. It will not go away by conducting meetings with Barzani and Talabani in Western capitals, modernizing Turkey's military bases, or ostracizing Iran as part of the "axis of evil." Managing Kurdish ethnonationalism in an age of transnationalism requires negotiations among European institutions, diasporic networks, Kurdish nationalist leaders across Kurdistan, international organizations, and home-country governments. External actors in particular have gained increasing leverage in setting the rules of the game in Kurdish domestic politics. For instance, the "juridicization" of the Kurdish issue in Turkey has strengthened the role of institutional co-optation in pressuring for structural changes inside Turkey. Through the Council of Europe and the European Parliament, foreign governments and international organizations exert pressure on the Turkish government in making the necessary constitutional changes that will ensure human rights, real democracy, and a degree of autonomy for the Kurds.

In the attempt to manage the Kurdish problem within and across borders, external influences must also minimize the asymmetrical nature of international aid, norms, and support that has created a dichotomy between "good Kurds and bad Kurds." U.S. government involvement in Iraqi Kurdistan since 1991 has made it increasingly difficult to ignore the Kurdish problems in neighboring states. The U.S. and foreign governments need evenhanded Kurdish policies on international, regional, and local levels. Neglecting the Kurdish problem in Turkey, Iran, and Syria; reinforcing Turkey's military-industrial complex; and arresting Kurdish political extremists without rewarding political moderates discredit the international effort to resolve the Kurdish conflicts.

Finally, Kurds themselves must assume greater responsibility for managing their relationships with central governments, cross-border actors, and international organizations. Political extremism may have increased attention on the Kurdish problem, but these tactics have delegitimated part of the Kurdish nationalist movement. After September 2001 violent mobilizations, even if made in self-defense, are regarded and treated as international terrorism. If the Kurds want to play a serious role in international and regional politics outside their victim status, they need to develop professional cadres at home and abroad that can effectively lobby foreign governments, financial institutions, and the world media.

Instead of turning to radical Kurdish nationalist and Islamic groups, including the ones in the diaspora, Kurdish communities should continue to channel their political claims through human-rights organizations, the European Parliament, and foreign governments. They must also take advantage of the transnational space to safeguard and develop Kurdayeti. The Turkish government may have prevented the growth of the Kurdish language and national identity inside Turkey; however, the Kurds have themselves to blame for allowing this condition to continue in the diaspora. Visionary Kurdish leadership is needed to help build consciousness and highly educated Kurdish masses at home and abroad. Kurds themselves should prepare the next generation to protect the distinct Kurdish ethnic identity and mobilize this political objective effectively within the cadre of international norms.

Glossary

Works Cited

Index

Glossary

agha: tribal chieftain, regional nobleman

ahl-e dhimmat: people or groups with contractual rights to practice religious traditions

Ahl-e Haqq: heterodox sect, Kak'ai; literally, people of the faith

akhund: religious preacher

anjoman: society, association, assembly

ayan: notable, landowner, tribal shaykh

ayatollah: highest religious dignitary in Shi'a Islamic clerical bureaucracy

bast: refuge

bazaari: belonging to the market; major source of support for the ulema and religious institutions

boneh: agricultural labor, work team

boniyad: state-owned institution with social welfare function

caliphate: Islamic institution of politico-religious leadership

cemevi: house of Alevi (Bektaşi) ritual

dede: title used by spiritual leaders of Bektaşi brotherhood

devşirme: periodic levy on unmarried male children from the Christian peasantry

dhull: lowliness

diwankhana: court, tribunal

diyanets: departments of religious affairs

emir: leader of a principality or emirate

faqih: jurist specialized in the science of Islamic law

fatwa: religious edict

firman: command, imperial edict

gastarbeiter: guest worker

gecekondu: squatter settlement

Gökturk: true Turk

gunda: village

Hamidiyan forces: Abdulhamid II's gendarme of tribal chieftains to police the eastern regions of the Ottoman Empire

Hanafi: one of four juridical schools of Sunni Islam

hejab: wearing of the veil

Hezbollah: Party of God

hukumdar: governor

ileyet: tribe, tribal

imam Jum'a: leader of Friday sermons and prayers

jash: literally, donkey foal, traitor

jaysh al-'Aqa'idi: ideological army

jihad: holy war

Ka'ba: holy shrine; literally, a cube-shaped stone structure at the center of the sacred mosque of Mecca, around which Haj pilgrims make their circumbulations and toward which Muslim believers face when praying

kadkhuda: office responsible to landlords, landlord appointees, overseers of land production

khaliseh: crown lands

khalk: inhabitants of a region

khatib: leader of Friday sermons

khoshneshin: populations without traditional land-use rights

kuvay-I Islamiye: Islamic militia of Kurdish and Arab tribes

Majlis: Parliament

maktabi: those individuals who follow the imam's line

mashlihat khaneh: consultative assembly

medrese: school that teaches religious science and Islamic jurisprudence

millet: religious community, people, nation

millet-i hakime: dominant people

millet-i mahkume: dominated people

mufti: highest religious dignitary in Sunni Islam that executes religious law

mujamma'ât: southern desert areas or collective towns

mullah: clerical office in Sunni Islam

nahad: state-owned institution with social welfare function

Naqshbandiyya: Sufi brotherhood founded by Baha' al-Dîn Naqshband

Nowruz: New Year

peshmerga: militia; literally, "those who face death"

pishnamaz: prayer leader

qadi: highest religious dignitary in Sunni Islam that preserves and develops religious law

Qadiriyya: Sufi brotherhood founded by 'Abd al-Qader al Jîlanî or Kailanî

qaimaqam: mayor, local responsible

re'aya: peasant

sadah: name given to those individuals who claim to descend from the Prophet (plural, *ashraf*)

saraf: merchants, merchant capitalists

Şaria: Islamic law that takes its sources in the sacred texts and jurisprudence of the hadith

selefdar: land and grain lender

shabanas: irregular military forces in colonial Iraq under the service of England

Shafi: one of four juridical schools of Sunni Islam

shah: king

shahid: martyr

shaykh: holy man, member of Sufi brotherhood, leader of dervish establishment

showra: local council

sultan: head of Ottoman government

taba'i: dependent

tapu: land

tariqa orders: Sufi brotherhood

tekke: dervish lodge, meeting place

tuyul: state landholdings given to people in lieu of payment

ulema: doctor of Islamic law, member of clergy

ülkücü: gang

umma: Islamic community

vaqf: lands for religious or charitable institutions

vatan: fatherland

velayat-e faqih: the rule of the Islamic jurist

vilayet: pre-Tanzimat system of regional administration; large province with small territorial units comprising ethnic linguistic, and tribal communities

wahda: Arab unity

zullulla: notion that the shah is God's shadow on earth

Works Cited

Abbas, A. 1989. "The Iraqi Armed Forces, Past and Present." In *Saddam's Iraq: Revolution or Reaction?* edited by the Committee Against Repression and for Democratic Rights in Iraq, 203–28. London: Zed Books.

Abdel-Fadil, Mahmoud. 1987. "Macro Behavior of Oil Rentier States in the Arab Region." In *The Rentier State,* edited by Hazem Beblawi and Giacomo Luciani, 83–107. London: Croom Helm.

Abrahamian, Ervand. 1982. *Iran Between Two Revolutions.* Princeton: Princeton Univ. Press.

———. 1993. *Khomeinism: Essays on the Islamic Republic.* Berkeley and Los Angeles: Univ. of California Press.

Adamson, David. 1965. *The Kurdish Wars.* New York: Praeger.

"Ada-ye ehteram be Koorosh." 1971. *Tamasha,* no. 30 (Oct.): 3–13.

Afkhami, Gholam Reza, and Seyyid Vali Reza Nasr, eds. 1991. *The Oral History Collection of the Foundation for Iranian Studies.* Bethesda: Foundation for Iranian Studies.

Afshar, Dr. 1927. "Masele-ye miliyat va vahdat-e milli-ye Iran." *Ayandeh* 2, no. 8: 559–69.

Afshar, Mahmud. 1990. "Kurdistan va vehdat-e meli-ye Iran." In *Kurd,* edited by Ihi Mahavi, Ja'fer Shahidi, and Jevad S. Ala-Salami, 249–79. Tehran: Chapkhaneh-e Naqsh-e Jehan.

Ağaoğulları, Mehmet Ali. 1987. "The Ultranationalist Right." In *Turkey in Transition: New Perspectives,* edited by Irvin Cemil Schick and Ertugrol Ahmet Tonak, 177–217. Oxford: Oxford Univ. Press.

Aghajanian, Akbar. 1983. "Ethnic Inequality in Iran: An Overview." *International Journal of Middle East Studies* 15, no. 2: 211–24.

Ahmad, Feroz, and Bedia Turgay Ahmad. 1976. *Türkiye'de Çok Partili Politikanın Açıklamalı Kronolojisi (1945–1971).* Ankara: Bilgi Yayınevi.

al-Ahmad, Jalal. 1997. *Qorb-e zendegi.* Tehran: Chapkhaney-e Ramin.

Akçay, A. Adnan. 1988. *From Landlordism to Capitalism in Turkish Agriculture.* Ankara: Technical Univ.

Akhavi, Shahrough. 1980. *Religion and Politics in Contemporary Iran: Clergy-State Relations in the Pahlavi Period.* Albany: State Univ. of New York Press.

———. 1986a. "Clerical Politics in Iran since 1979." In *The Iranian Revolution and the Islamic Republic,* edited by Nikki R. Keddie and Eric Hooglund, 57–73. Syracuse: Syracuse Univ. Press.

———. 1986b. "State Formation and Consolidation in Twentieth-Century Iran." In *The State, Religion, and Ethnic Politics: Afghanistan, Iran, and Pakistan,* edited by Ali Banuaziz and Myron Wiener, 198–226. Syracuse: Syracuse Univ. Press.

———. 1987. "Elite Factionalism in the Islamic Republic of Iran." *Middle East Journal* 41, no. 2: 181–217.

———. 1988. "The Role of the Clergy in Iranian Politics, 1949–1954." In *Musaddiq, Iranian Nationalism, and Oil,* edited by James A. Bill and William Roger Louis, 91–117. London: I. B. Tauris.

Akin, Salih. 1995. "Designation du peuple, du territoire, et du langue Kurde dans le discours scientifique et politique Turc." Ph.D. diss., Univ. of Rouen.

———. 1996. "Les Mouvements de jeunesse et la formation des élites Kurdes." *AGORA-Débat/Jeunesse,* no. 6: 111–21.

Alakom, Rohat. 1998a. "Di medya tirkî de karîkaturîzekirina serhildana (1930î)." *Çira,* no. 14: 78–92.

———. 1998b. "Said Nursî entre l'indentité Kurde and l'identité Musulmane." In *Islam de Kurdes,* 317–31. Paris: Institut National de Langues et Civilisations Orientales.

Alaolmolki, Nozar. 1987. "The New Iranian Left." *Middle East Journal* 41, no. 2: 218–33.

Algar, Hamid. 1969. *Religion and State in Iran, 1785–1906: The Role of the Ulema in the Qajar Period.* Berkeley and Los Angeles: Univ. of California Press.

———. 1996. "The Naqshbandi Order in Republican Turkey." *Islamic World Report* 1, no. 3: 51–67.

Ali, Ahmet. 1981. *Développement économique en Turquie.* Paris: Éditions Anthropos.

Amara, Hamid Ait. 1987. "The State, Social Classes, and Agricultural Policies in the Arab World." In *The Rentier State,* edited by Hazem Beblawi and Giacomo Luciani, 138–58. London: Croom Helm.

Amini, Siavosh. 1978. "The Origin, Function, and Disappearance of Collective Productive Units (Haratha) in Rural Areas of Iran." *Iranian Economic Review,* no. 5–6: 146–62.

Arat, Yesim. 1991. "Politics and Big Business: Janus-Faced Link to the State." In

Strong State and Economic Interest Groups: The Post-1980 Turkish Experience, edited by Metin Heper, 135–47. Berlin: Walter de Gruyter.

Arda, Serxas. 1980. "Xwendina Bi Zmanê Kurdi." *Tîrêj,* no. 2: 8–9.

Aresvik, Oddvar. 1975. *The Agricultural Development of Turkey.* New York: Praeger.

Arfa, Hassan. 1965. *The Kurds: A Historical and Political Study.* London: Oxford Univ. Press.

Arjomand, Said Amir. 1988. *The Turban for the Crown: The Islamic Revolution in Iran.* Oxford: Oxford Univ. Press.

Arvasi, Ahmet. 1986. *Doğu Anadolu Gerçeği.* Ankara: Türk Kültütünü Araştirma Enstitüsü.

Atabaki, Touraj. 1993. *Azerbaijan: Ethnicity and Autonomy in Twentieth-Century Iran.* London: I. B. Tauris.

Avery, Peter, Gavin Hambly, and Charles Melville. 1991. *The Cambridge History of Iran: From Nader Shah to the Islamic Republic.* Cambridge: Cambridge Univ. Press.

Awiyar. 1996. Feb. 28. "Kurdistan, por talash va ba nashat dar sahne-ye sazandegı," 1.

———. 1997a. Feb. 13. "Kurdistan niazmand-e eltefât-e Islamı ast.," 1.

———. 1997b. June 7. "Yaddasht-e bayaniye'i mandegar-e nevisandegan-e Kurd," 1.

Ayandegan. 1979a. Mar. 7. "Khomeini: Keshvarha-ye Islami zir-e yik dowlat va yik parcham," 2.

———. 1979b. Mar. 10. "Majlis-e mo'asesan dar bareye khodmokhtari-ye Kurdistan tasmim migirad," 1–2.

———. 1979c. Mar. 17. "Khodmokhtari bareye Kurd, demokrasi bareye Iran," 7.

———. 1979d. Apr. 6. "Amelan-e vaqaye-ye khunin-e Sanandaj Moa'rafi mishavad," 6.

———. 1979e. Apr. 14. "Bazargan: Dar pey-e formul va had-e khodmokhtari hastim," 1.

———. 1979f. Apr. 19. "Nedaye yik Irani-ye Muselman be tamam-e ham vatane gerami," 11.

———. 1979g. Apr. 20. "Mobareze ba efkar va aqayed ra az rahe zoor nemipasandam," 8.

———. 1979h. May 20. "Omidvarim masayel-e Kurdistan az rah masalmat amiz hal shavad," 11.

Ayata, Ayşe. 1993. "Ideology, Social Bases, and Organizational Structure of the Post-1980 Political Parties." In *The Political and Socioeconomic Transformation of Turkey,* edited by Attila Eralp, Muharrem Tunay, and Birol Yesilada, 31–49. Westport, Conn.: Praeger.

Ayata, Sencer. 1993. "The Rise of Islamic Fundamentalism and Its Institutional Framework." In *The Political and Social Transformation of Turkey,* edited by Atila Eralp, Muharrem Tunay, and Birol Yesilada, 51–68. Westport, Conn.: Praeger.

———. 1996. "Patronage, Party, and the State: The Politicization of Islam in Turkey." *Middle East Journal* 50, no. 1: 40–56.

Aydin, Zülküf. 1993. "The World Bank and the Transformation of Turkish Agriculture." In *The Political and Social Transformation of Turkey,* edited by Atila Eralp, Muharrem Tunay, and Birol Yesilada, 111–34. Westport, Conn.: Praeger.

Bakhash, Shaul. 1978. *Iran: Monarchy, Bureaucracy, and Reform under the Qajars, 1858–1896.* London: Ithaca Press.

Bakupov, G. 1997. *Kurdan Guran: Masale-ye Kurd dar Turkiye.* Translated by Syrus Izadi. Tehran: Hidari Publishing House.

Ball, Patrick. 2000. "State Terror, Constitutional Traditions, and Human Rights Movements: A Cross-National Quantitative Comparison." In *Globalization and Social Movements,* edited by John A. Guidry, Michael D. Kennedy, and Mayer N. Zald, 54–75. Ann Arbor: Univ. of Michigan Press.

Baram, Amatzia. 1983a. "Mesopotamian Identity in Ba'athi Iraq." *Middle East Journal* 19, no. 4: 426–55.

———. 1983b. "Qawmiyya and Wataniyya in Ba'athi Iraq: The Search for a New Balance." *Middle Eastern Studies* 19, no. 2: 188–200.

———. 1991. *Culture and Ideology in the Formation of Ba'athist Iraq, 1968–1989.* New York: St. Martin's Press.

Barkey, Henri J., and Graham E. Fuller. 1998. *Turkey's Kurdish Question.* Lanham, Md.: Rowman and Littlefield.

Barnas, Rojen. 1980. "Bi Avê, Bi Nan." *Tîrêj,* no. 2: 13–14.

Bassam, Tibi. 1990. *Arab Nationalism: A Critical Enquiry.* Translated by Marion Farouk-Slugglet and Peter Sluglett. London: Macmillan.

Batatu, Hanna. 1978. *The Old Social Classes and the Revolutionary Movements of Iraq.* Princeton: Princeton Univ. Press.

Bayat, Asef. 1997. *Street Politics: Poor People's Movement in Iran.* New York: Columbia Univ. Press.

Beblawi, Hazem, and Giacomo Luciani, eds. 1987. *The Rentier State.* London: Croom Helm.

"Be boney chapbunewey pêshewa." 1959. *Hetaw,* no. 127: 1.

Beck, Lois. 1990. "Tribes and the State in Nineteenth- and Twentieth-Century Iran." In *Tribes and State Formation in the Middle East,* edited by Philip S. Khoury and Joseph Kostiner, 185–225. Berkeley and Los Angeles: Univ. of California Press.

Beglari, Hormoz. 1997. *Tarîkhe Kermanshah dar 'asr-e Qajar.* Kermanshah: Sherafat-e Vaziri.

Belarbi, Louba. 1983. "Les Mutations dans les structures foncières dans l'Émpire Ottoman à l'Époque du Tanzimat." In *Économie et Sociétés dans l'Émpire Ottoman (fin du XXIIIe début du XXe siécle,* 251–59. Paris: Collogues Internationaux du CNRS.

Bensaid, Said. 1987. "Al-Watan and al-Umma in Contemporary Arab Use." In *The Foundations of the Arab State,* edited by Ghassan Salamé, 149–74. London: Croom Helm.

Berberoglu, Berch, ed. 1989. *Power and Stability in the Middle East.* London: Zed Books.

Bertrand, Gilles, and Isabelle Rigoni. 2000. "Turcs, Kurds, et Chypriotes devant la Cour Européene des droits de l'homme: Une contestation judiciare de questions politiques." *Études Internationals* 31, no. 3: 413–41.

"Beshî lawani dimokratî Kurdistan." 1959. *Hetaw,* no. 147–48: 1–3.

Beşikçi, İsmail. 1979. *Doğu Anadolu'nun Düzeni: Sosyo-Ekonomik ve Etnik Temeller.* Ankara: E. Yayınları.

———. 1990. *Tunceli Kanunu (1935) Ve Dersim Jenosidi.* Ankara: Bilim Yöntemi Türkiye'deki Uygulama.

———. 1991. *Orgeneral Muğlalı Olayı/33 Kurşun.* Istanbul: Belge Yayınları.

———. 1992. *Doğu Mitingleri'nin Analizi (1967).* Ankara: Yurt Kitap-Yayın.

Besson, Frédérique Jeanne. 1998. "La Revanche des Naqchbandis." *Les Cahiers de l'Orient,* no. 50: 35–51.

Bharier, Julian. 1977. "The Growth of Towns and Villages in Iran, 1900–66." In *The Population of Iran: Selection of Readings,* edited by Jamshid A. Momeni, 331–41. Shiraz, Iran: Pahlavi Populations Center and East-West Population Institute.

Bianchi, Robert. 1984. *Interest Groups and Political Development in Turkey.* Princeton: Princeton Univ. Press.

Bill, James A., and William Roger Louis, eds. 1988. *Musaddiq, Iranian Nationalism, and Oil.* London: I. B. Tauris.

Bournoutian, George A. 1992. *The Khanate of Erevan under Qajar Rule (1795–1828).* New York: Mazda Publishers and Bibliotechia Persia.

Bozarslan, Hamit. 1988. "Réflexions sur l'économie de l'Émpire Ottoman et le passage à la Révolution Industrielle." *CEMOTI,* no. 5: 73–103.

———. 1990. "The Kurdish Question in Turkish Political Life: The Situation as of 1990." In *Kurdistan in Search of Ethnic Identity,* edited by Turaj Atabaki and Margreet Dorleijn, 1–23. Utrecht: Houtsma Foundation Publication Series.

———. 1992. "Entre la 'umma et le nationalism: L'Islam Kurde au tournant du siecle." Occasional paper no. 15. Amsterdam: Middle East Research Associates.

———. 1996a. "Kurdistan: Économie de guerre, économie dans la guerre." In *Économie des guerres civiles,* edited by Jean François and Jean Christophe Rufin, 105–46. Paris: Hachette, 1996.

———. 1996b. "Le Problème Kurde en Turquie Kemalist." Master's thesis, École des Hautes Études en Sciences Sociales.

————. 1997. *La Question Kurde*. Paris: Presses de Sciences Po.

————. 2003. "Kurdish Nationalism in Turkey: From Tacit Contract to Rebellion (1919–1980)." In *Essays on the Origins of Kurdish Nationalism,* 163–90. Costa Mesa, Calif.: Mazda.

Braude, Benjamin, and Bernard Lewis, eds. 1982. *Christians and Jews in the Ottoman Empire: The Function of Plural Society.* Vol. 1. New York: Holmes and Meier.

"British Embassy and the Kurdish Revolt, The." 1945. Copy of documents from War Department, Military Intelligence Division, Institut Kurde de Paris, no. 219–45, Sept. 5. Paris, France.

Bulletin de liaison et d'information. 2004. No. 228. Paris: Institut Kurde de Paris.

Bulloch, John, and Harvey Morris. 1992. *No Friends but the Mountains: The Tragic History of the Kurds.* London: Oxford Univ. Press.

Burrell, R. M. 1997. *Iran Political Diaries, 1881–1965.* Vols. 1–4, 6, 10–11. London: Archives Editions.

Busse, Heribert. 1972. *History of Persia under Qajar Rule.* New York: Columbia Univ. Press.

Cağlar, Ayse Neviye. 1990. "The Greywolves as Metaphor." In *Turkish State, Turkish Society,* edited by Andrew Hale and Nükhet Sirman, 216–29. London: Routledge.

Çay, M. Abdülhaluk. 1988. *Turkish Festival of Ergenekon "Nevruz."* Ankara: Anadolu Press Union.

Ceyhun, Fikret. 1989. "Development of Capitalism and Class Struggles in Turkey." In *Power and Stability in the Middle East,* edited by Berch Berberoglu, 55–69. London: Zed Books.

Chabry, Laurent, and Annie Chabry. 1987. *Politique et minorités au Proche-Orient: Les Raisons d'une éxplosion.* Paris: Éditions Maisonneuve et Larose.

Chaliand, Gerard. 1993. "The Kurds under Ayatollah Khomeini." In *A People Without a Country,* edited by Gerard Chaliand, 211–13. New York: Olive Branch Press.

Chaqueri, Cosrie, ed. 1979. *Le Social-democracie en Iran: Articles et documents annotés et presentés.* Florence: Éditions Mazdak.

Chehabi, H. E. 1990. *Iranian Politics and Religious Modernism: The Liberation Movement of Iran under the Shah and Khomeini.* London: I. B. Tauris.

"Çifte Standartlık Bir Yarı-aydin Hastalığı." 1991. *Zazaistan,* no. 2: 9.

Cigerli, Sabri. 1991. "Les Kurdes et le Parti Democrat." Master's thesis, Université Paris X.

Clarke, J. I., and B. D. Clarke. 1969. "Kermanshah: A Provincial City." Research Paper Series no. 10. Durham, England: Univ. of Durham, Centre for Middle Eastern and Islamic Studies.

Cleveland, William L. 1991. *The Making of an Arab Nationalist: Ottomanism and Arabism in the Life and Thought of Sati' al-Husri*. Princeton: Princeton Univ. Press.

———. 1994. *A History of the Modern Middle East*. Boulder: Westview Press.

Coakley, John. 2002. "Religion and Nationalism in the First World War." In *Ethnonationalism in the Contemporary World: Walker Connor and the Study of Nationalism*, edited by Daniele Conversi, 269–90. New York: Routledge.

Colville, Thierry. 1994. "Entre l'état et la marché." In *L'Économie de l'Iran Islamique: Entre l'état et le marché,* edited by Thierry Colville, 17–25. Tehran: Institut Français de Recherche en Iran.

"Comitey Estiqlali Kurdistan." 1966. *Kurdish Journal* 3, no. 1: 4–6.

"Confidential Letter from the Council of Ministers to the Political Secretary." 1930. Copy of British Documents, Institut Kurde de Paris, no. 2957, FO 371/14523. Oct. 18. Paris, France.

"Congrey mamosta u wêjewananî Kurd le Sheqlawe." 1959. *Hetaw,* no. 123: 1.

Connor, Walker. 1978. "A Nation Is a Nation, Is a State, Is an Ethnic Group, Is a . . ." *Ethnic and Racial Studies* 1, no. 4: 379–88.

———. 1994. *Ethnonationalism: The Quest for Understanding*. Princeton: Princeton Univ. Press.

———. 2002. "Nationalism and Political Legitimacy." In *Ethnonationalism in the Contemporary World: Walker Connor and the Study of Nationalism,* edited by Daniele Conversi, 24–49. London: Routledge.

Conversi, Daniele. 2002. "Resisting Primordialism and Other -Isms." In *Ethnonationalism in the Contemporary World: Walker Connor and the Study of Nationalism,* edited by Daniele Conversi, 206–25. New York: Routledge.

Copy of a secret memorandum from the political officer, Suleymaniya, to H. E., the high commissioner, Baghdad. 1921. Copy of British Documents, Institut Kurde de Paris, RG P 1954/1/19, Aug. 30. Paris, France.

Copy of notes taken during the negotiations between an Iranian mission and a delegation of the Democratic Party of Iranian Kurdistan. 1989. Tape recording of the meeting in Vienna, July 13. Institut Kurde de Paris, Paris, France.

Coşkun, Zeki. 1995. *Aleviler, Sünniler ve . . . Öteki Sivas*. İstanbul: İletişim Yayınları.

Cottom, Richard. 1964. *Nationalism in Iran*. Pittsburgh: Univ. of Pittburgh Press.

———. 1988. "Nationalism in Twentieth-Century Iran and Dr. Muhammad Musaddiq." In *Musaddiq, Iranian Nationalism, and Oil,* edited by James A. Bill and William Roger Louis, 23–46. London: I. B. Tauris.

Cronin, Stephanie. 1997. *The Army and the Creation of the Pahlavi State in Iran, 1910–1926*. London: I. B. Tauris.

Dadrian, Vahakan N. 1995. *The History of the Armenian Genocide: Ethnic Conflict from the Balkans to the Caucasus*. Providence, R.I.: Berghahn Books.

Danielson, Eric N. 1995. "Kurdish Relations with Other Nations: Great Britain and the Origins of the Kurdish Question in Iraq (1918–1932)." *Kurdistan Times,* no. 4: 49–75.

Dann, Uriel. 1969. *Iraq under Qassem: A Political History, 1958–1963.* Tel Aviv: Praeger.

Davis, Eric. 1991. "Theorizing Statecraft and Society in Oil-Producing Countries." In *Statecraft in the Middle East: Oil, Historical Memory, and Popular Culture,* edited by Eric Davis and Nicholas Gavrielides, 1–35. Miami: Florida International Univ. Press.

Declaration commune de Partie Toudeh d'Iran et de l'Organization de Fedayins du Peuple d'Iran (majoritaire). 1981. Tehran: Partie Toudeh en France et Sympatisants de l'Organization des Fedayin du Peuple d'Iran.

Delistre, Emile. 1959. "La République arabe unie face à l'Irak et au communism." *Orient,* no. 9: 13–22.

Dersimi, M. Nuri. 1990. *Kürdistan Tarihinde Dersim.* Cologne: Komkar Yayınları.

de Sainte Marie, François. 1960. *Irak rouge: Khassem entre Moscou et le Caire.* Paris: Table Ronde.

Devereux, Robert. 1968. *Ziya Gökalp: The Principles of Turkism.* Leiden: E. J. Brill.

Devlin, John F. 1979. *The Ba'ath Party: A History from Its Origins to 1966.* Stanford, Calif.: Hoover Univ. Press.

Dicle-Firat (Stockholm). 1997. No. 1–8.

"Discours du president du conseil d'Irak." 1959. *Orient,* no. 9: 142–44.

"Doğu Davamız." 1963. *Yön,* no. 26: 12.

"Donya az cheshm-e tamasha-ye vahshiha." 1971. *Tamasha,* no. 31: 3–9.

Eagleton, William, Jr. 1991. *La Republique Kurde.* Translated by Catherine Ter-Sarkissian. Paris: Éditions Complexe.

Eaton, Henry. 1965. "Kurdish Nationalism in Iraq since 1958." *Kurdish Journal* 2, no. 2: 10–14.

"Edibiyatî Qurdî." 1932. *Hawar,* no. 5: 1–2.

"Edibiyatî Welatî." 1932. *Hawar,* no. 1: 5–6.

Edmonds, C. J. 1936. "Soane at Halabja: An Echo." *Journal of the Royal Central Asian Society* 22: 622–25.

———. 1937. *A Bibliography of Southern Kurdish, 1920–1936.* London: Royal Central Asian Society.

———. 1957. *Turks, Kurds, and Arabs.* London: Oxford Univ. Press.

Eftekhari, Nirou. 1987. "Le Petrole dans l'économie at la societé Irakienne." *Peuples Méditerranéens,* no. 40: 43–74.

Ehteshami, Anouchiravan. 1995. *After Khomeini: The Iranian Second Republic.* London: Routledge.

Eickleman, Dale F. 1989. *The Middle East: An Anthropological Approach*. Englewood Cliffs, N.J.: Prentice-Hall.

Elçi, Sait. 1997. "Irkçıların Doğu Düşmanlığı." *Dicle-Firat,* no. 1–8: 2.

"Elfabêya Qurdî." 1932. *Hawar,* no. 2: 5–6.

Entessar, Nader. 1986. "The Military and Politics in the Islamic Republic of Iran." In *Post-Revolutionary Iran,* edited by Hooshang Amirahmadi and Manochar Parvin. Boulder: Westview Press.

———. 1992. *Kurdish Ethnonationalism*. Boulder: Lynn Riener.

"Entre identité Kurde et Kémalisme: Un Entretien avec Şerafettin Elçi." 1997. *Espace Orient,* no. 24: 39–42.

Eralp, Atila. 1998. "Turkey and the European Union in the Aftermath of the Cold War." In *The Political Economy of Turkey in the Post-Soviet Era,* edited by Libby Rittenberg, 37–50. Westport, Conn.: Praeger.

Eralp, Atila, Muharrem Tunay, and Birol Yesilada, eds. 1993. *The Political and Social Transformation of Turkey*. Westport, Conn.: Praeger.

Ergüder, Üstün. 1991. "Agriculture, the Forgotten Sector." In *Strong State and Economic Interest Groups: The Post-1980 Turkish Experience,* edited by Metin Heper, 71–78. Berlin: Walter de Gruyter.

Eröz, Mehmet. 1975. *Doğu Anadolu'nun Türklüğü*. İstanbul: Türk Kültür Yayını.

Esman, Milton J. 1994. *Ethnic Politics*. Ithaca: Cornell Univ. Press.

Esman, Milton J., and Itamar Rabinovich, eds. 1988. *Ethnicity, Pluralism, and the State in the Middle East*. Ithaca: Cornell Univ. Press.

"Extract from a Memorandum of a Conversation Between the Secretary of State for the Colonies and the Prime Minister of Iraq." 1925. Copy of British Documents, Institut Kurde de Paris, RG FO 371/11460, Apr. 12. Paris, France.

Ezat, Mahmod Mola. 1995. *Dowleti Jamhuri-yi Kurdistan*. Vols. 1–2. Stockholm: APEC.

"Fact-Finding Mission on the Human-Rights Situation." 1995. In *Iranian Kurdistan*. Paris: Democratic Party of Iranian Kurdistan.

Faist, Thomas. 2000. *The Volume and Dynamics of International Migration and Transnational Social Spaces*. London: Oxford Univ. Press.

Fakhreddin, Azimi. 1989. *Iran: The Crisis of Democracy, 1941–1953*. London: I. B. Tauris.

Farouk-Sluglett, Marion, and Peter Sluglett. 1987. "From Gang to Elite: The Iraqi Ba'th Party's Consolidation of Power, 1968–1975." *Peuples Méditerranéens,* no. 40: 89–114.

———. 1990. *Iraq since 1958*. London: I. B. Tauris.

Fawcett, Louise. 1992. *Iran and the Cold War: The Azerbaijan Crisis of 1946*. Cambridge: Cambridge Univ. Press.

Fearon, James D., and David D. Laitin. 2000. "Violence and the Social Construction of Ethnic Identity." *International Organization* 54, no. 4: 845–77.

Fernandes, Desmond. 2001. *The Targeting and Criminalisation of Kurdish Asylum Seekers and Refugee Communities in the UK and Germany.* London: Peace in Kurdistan Campaign and the Ahmed Foundation for Kurdish Studies.

Fesharaki, Fereidun. 1976. *Development of the Iranian Oil Industry: International and Domestic Aspects.* London: Praeger.

Feyzioğlu, Turhan. 1982. *Atatürk's Way.* İstanbul: Sun Matbaası.

Firoozi, Fereydoon. 1976. "Industrial Activity and the Economy in Iran." *Iranian Economic Review,* no. 1: 1–33.

Floor, Willem. 1984. *Industrialization in Iran, 1900–1941.* Research Paper Series no. 23. Durham, England: Univ. of Durham, Centre for Middle Eastern and Islamic Studies.

Frazee, Charles A. 1983. *Catholics and Sultans: The Church and the Ottoman Empire, 1453–1923.* London: Cambridge Univ. Press.

Frey, Frederick. 1979. "Patterns of Elite Politics in Turkey." In *Political Elites in the Middle East,* edited by George Lenczowski, 41–82. Washington, D.C.: American Enterprise Institute for Public Policy Research.

Galip, Semra. 1989. *De l'empire à la republique: Le Cas Turc de modernization défensive.* İstanbul: Éditions ISIS.

Gallman, Waldemar, Jr. 1964. *Iraq under General Nuri: My Recollections of Nuri Al-Said, 1954–1958.* Baltimore: Johns Hopkins Univ. Press.

Gause, F. Gregory, III. 1994. *Oil Monarchies.* New York: Council on Foreign Relations.

"Gelî Kurd û ereb." 1959. *Kovari Hetaw,* no. 166 (Nov. 30): 1.

Gellner, Ernest. 1983. *Nations and Nationalism.* Ithaca: Cornell Univ. Press.

Georgeon, François. 1980. *Aux origines de nationalism Turc: Yusuf Akçura (1876–1935).* Paris: Éditions ADPF.

————. 1986. "A la recherche d'une identité—la nationalism Turc." In *La Turquie en transition: Disparités, identités, pouvoirs,* edited by Altan Gökalp, 125–53. Paris: Maisonneuve et Larose.

————. 1991. "De Mossoul à Kirkuk: La Turquie et la question du Kurdistan Irakien." *Monde Arabe Maghreb Machrek,* no. 132: 38–49.

Ghareeb, Edmund. 1981. *The Kurdish Question in Iraq.* Syracuse: Syracuse Univ. Press.

Ghassemlou, A. R. 1976. *Iranian Kurdistan.* Paris: Kurdistan Association.

————. 1981. *Report of the Central Committee to the Fifth Congress of the Kurdistan Democratic Party of Iran.* Paris: KDPI.

————. 1993. "Kurdistan in Iran." In *A People Without a Country,* edited by Gerard Chaliand, 95–121. New York: Olive Branch Press.

"Giftugo-i jenabi Qazi Mohammed." 1946. *Kurdistan,* no. 1: 1.

Giritli, İsmet. 1989. *Kürt Türklerinin Gerçeği.* İstanbul: Yeni Forum Yayıncılık.

Gökalp, Altan, ed. 1986. *La Turquie en transition: Disparités, identités, pouvoirs.* Paris: Maisonneuve et Larose.

Goldring, Luin. 1999. "Power and Status in Transnational Social Spaces." In *Migration and Transnational Social Spaces,* edited by Ludger Pries, 162–86. Aldershot: Ashgate.

Goran, [Abdullah Sulayman]. 1943. *Diwanî Goran.* Baghdad: Bilawkirawakanî Nusaranî Kurd la Iraq.

"Goranî-yı Azadı." 1947. *Gelawêj,* no. 5: 1.

Gunter, Michael. 1997. *The Kurds and the Future of Turkey.* New York: St. Martin's Press.

Güzel, Mehmet Sehmus. 1975. "Mouvement ouvrier et les grèves en Turquie: De l'Émpire Ottoman à nos jours." Ph.D. diss., Univ. of Aix Marseille.

al-Hafeed, Salahaddin M. 1993. "The Embargo on Kurdistan: Its Influences on the Economic and Social Development." In *The Reconstruction and Economic Development of Iraqi Kurdistan: Changes and Perspectives,* edited by Fuad Hussein, Michiel Leezenberg, and Pieter Muller, 38–52. Amsterdam: Stichting Nederland-Koerdistan.

Hakim, Halkawt. 1992. "Le Panarabism Irakien et le problem Kurde." *Les Kurdes par-dela l'éxode,* edited by Halkawt Hakim, 124–44. Paris: L'Harmattan.

Hale, Andrew, and Nükhet Sirman, eds. 1990. *Turkish State, Turkish Society.* London: Routledge.

Hamilton, A. M. 1937. *Road Through Kurdistan: The Narrative of an Engineer in Iraq.* London: Faber and Faber.

Harik, Iliya. 1987. "The Origins of the Arab State System." In *The Foundations of the Arab State,* edited by Ghassam Salamé, 19–46. London: Croom Helm.

Harris, George S. 1965. "The Role of the Military in Turkish Politics." *Middle East Journal* 19, no. 2: 169–76.

———. 1974. "The Soviet Union and Turkey." In *The Soviet Union and the Middle East: The Post-World War Two Era,* edited by Ivo I. Lederer and Wayne S. Vucinich, 25–54. Stanford, Calif.: Hoover Univ. Press.

Hassanpour, Amir. 1992. *Nationalism and Language in Kurdistan.* San Francisco: Mellon Research Univ. Press.

Hechter, Michael. 1985. "Internal Colonialism Revisited." In *New Nationalisms of the Developed West,* edited by Edward Tiryakian and Ronald Rogowski, 17–26. Boston: Allen and Unwin.

———. 2000. *Containing Nationalism.* Oxford: Oxford Univ. Press.

Hêmin [Muhammed Amin Shaykh ul-Islam]. 1974. "Kurdim Amin." *Tarîk û Rûn.* Baghdad: Binkay Pêshewe.

Heper, Metin, ed. 1991. *Strong State and Economic Interest Groups: The Post-1980 Turkish Experience.* Berlin: Walter de Gruyter.

Heper, Metin, and Evin Ahmet, eds. 1994. *Politics in the Third Turkish Republic.* Boulder: Westview Press.

Hewrami. 1966a. "The Evolution of Bazzaz's 12-Point Plan." *Kurdish Journal* 3, no. 2: 7–15.

———. 1966b. "Government by Three." *Kurdish Journal* 3, no. 1: 6–7.

———. 1969a. "Shaikh Mahmoud and the Kurdish Question, 1917–1920." *Kurdish Journal* 6, no. 2: 54–64.

———. 1969b. "Shaikh Mahmoud and the Kurdish Question, 1917–1920." *Kurdish Journal* 6, no. 3: 96–110.

Heyd, Uriel. 1950. *Foundations of Turkish Nationalism: The Life and Teachings of Ziya Gökalp.* London: Luzac and the Harvill Press.

Higgens, Patricia J. 1986. "Minority-State Relations in Contemporary Iran." In *The State, Religion, and Ethnic Politics: Afghanistan, Iran, and Pakistan,* edited by Ali Banuaziz and Myron Wiener, 167–97. Syracuse: Syracuse Univ. Press.

Hizb al-Ba'th al Arabi al Ishtiraki. 1970–1971. Baghdad: National Bureau of Culture.

Hobsbawm, E. J. 1994. *Nations and Nationalism since 1780.* Cambridge: Cambridge Univ. Press.

Hoogland, Eric. 1982. *Land and Revolution in Iran, 1960–1980.* Austin: Univ. of Texas Press.

———. 1986. "Iran, 1980–85: Political and Economic Trends." In *The Iranian Revolution and the Islamic Republic,* edited by Nikki R. Keddie and Eric Hooglund, 17–31. Syracuse: Syracuse Univ. Press.

Horowitz, Donald L. 1985. "Ethnic Nationalism." In *Ethnicity: Theory and Experience,* edited by Daniel Moynihan and N. Glazer, 111–40. Cambridge: Harvard Univ. Press.

———. 2002. "The Primordialists." In *Ethnonationalism in the Contemporary World: Walker Connor and the Study of Nationalism,* edited by Daniele Conversi, 72–81. London: Routledge.

Hourani, A. H. 1947. *Minorities in the Arab World.* London: Oxford Univ. Press.

Hourcade, Bernard. 1988. "Ethnie, nation, et citadinité en Iran." In *Le Fait ethnique en Iran et en Afghanistan,* edited by Jean-Pierre Digard, 161–74. Paris: Éditions du CNRS.

Houston, Christopher. 2001. *Islam, Kurds, and the Turkish Nation State.* Oxford: Berg.

Human Rights Watch. 1990. *Destroying Ethnic Identity: The Kurds in Turkey.* New York: Human Rights Watch.

Husayni, A. H. 1987a. "Kurd?" *Sirwe,* no. 14: 21–27.

———. 1987b. "Kurd?" *Sirwe,* no. 15: 20–22.

Hushyar, Mariwan. 1990. *Musaddiq and the Struggle for Power in Iran.* London: I. B. Tauris.

———. 1992. "Un Aperçu de la politique de l'Iran vis-à-vis des Kurdes." In *Les Kurdes par-dela l'éxode,* edited by Halkawt Hakim, 90–105. Paris: L'Harmattan.

al-Husri, Abu Khaldun Sati'. 1959. "Qu'est ce que le nationalism?" *Orient,* no. 9: 216–23.

Hussein, Fuad, Michiel Leezenberg, and Pieter Muller, eds. 1992. *The Reconstruction and Economic Development of Iraqi Kurdistan: Changes and Perspectives.* Amsterdam: Stichting Nederland-Koerdistan.

Hussein, Saddam. 1973. *Propos sur les problemes actuels.* Baghdad: Ath-Thawra.

———. 1977. *Saddam Hussein on Current Events in Iraq.* Translated by Khalid Kishtainy. London: Longman Group.

Ilhan, Kemal. 1991. "La Revolte Kurdes de Dersim (1936–1938)." Master's thesis, École des Hautes Études en Sciences Sociales.

"Interview with Mullah Mustafa, Mir Haj, and Izzat Aziz." 1947. Copies of documents from the Collections of the Manuscript Division, Institut Kurde de Paris, RG European Section, Near and Middle East, North African Transmitter, Library of Congress. June 20. Paris, France.

Iraq: Report on Iraq Administration, October 1920-March 1922. 1922. London: His Majesty's Stationery Office. Archives du Quai d'Orsay, RG Levant, Mesopotamie Irak, 1918–1929. Carton 314, vol. 26, dossier 1, series E. Paris, France.

"Iraq Government: Stages of Its Development from Early Days of British Occupation to Present Date, The." 1927. In *Official Journal,* no. 624, Archives du Quai d'Orsay, RG Levant, Mesopotamie Irak, 1918–1929. Carton 314, vol. 12, dossier 1, series E, July 4, 11–14. Paris, France.

Al-Iraq Yearbook. 1922–1923. Baghdad: Al-Iraqi Press.

Ismael, Tareq Y. 1979. *The Arab Left.* Syracuse: Syracuse Univ. Press.

Issawi, Charles. 1971. *The Economic History of Iran: 1800–1914.* Chicago: Univ. of Chicago Press.

———. 1980. *The Economic History of Turkey: 1800–1914.* Chicago: Univ. of Chicago Press.

Izady, Mehrdad R. 1992. *The Kurds.* Washington, D.C.: Tailor and Francis.

Jaber, Kamel S. Abu. 1966. *The Arab Ba'th Socialist Party: History, Ideology, and Organization.* Syracuse: Syracuse Univ. Press.

Jaf, Ahmed Mukhtar Begî. 1969. *Diwanî Ahmed Mukhtar Begî Jaf.* Arbil (Hawlêr), Iraq: Chapkhaneh Hawlêr.

Jafar, Majeed R. 1976. *Under-Underdevelopment: A Regional Case Study of the Kurdish Area in Turkey.* Helsinki: Studies of the Social Policy Association.

Jamshid, A. Momeni, ed. 1977. *The Population of Iran: A Selection of Readings*. Shiraz, Iran: Pahlavi Populations Center and East-West Population Institute.

Jawad, Sa'ad. 1979. "The Kurdish Problem in Iraq." In *The Integration of Modern Iraq*, edited by Kelidar Abbas, 171–82. New York: St. Martin's Press.

———. 1981. *Iraq and the Kurdish Question*. London: Ithaca Press.

Jongerden, M. Joost. 2002. "Evacuation forcée, deportation, et réhabilitation." *Études Kurdes* 4, no. 17: 35–53.

al-Jundi, Darwish. 1968. "The Foundations and Objectives of Arab Nationalism." In *Political and Social Thought in the Contemporary Middle East*, edited by Kemal H. Karpat, 42–47. New York: Praeger.

Jwaideh, Wadie. 1960. "The Kurdish Nationalist Movement: Its Origins and Development." Ph.D. diss., Syracuse Univ.

Kalaycioğlu, Ersin. 2002. "State and Civil Society in Turkey: Democracy, Development, and Protest." In *Civil Society in the Muslim World: Contemporary Perspectives*, edited by Amyn B. Sajoo, 247–72. London: I. B. Tauris.

Karabell, Zachary. 1995. "Backfire: US Policy Toward Iraq, 1988–2 August 1990." *Middle East Journal* 49, no. 1: 29–41.

Karimi, Setareh. 1986. "Economic Policies and Structural Changes since the Revolution." In *The Iranian Revolution and the Islamic Republic*, edited by Nikki R. Keddie and Eric Hooglund. Syracuse: Syracuse Univ. Press.

Karpat, Kemal. 1975. "The Memoirs of Nicolae Batzaria: The Young Turks and Nationalism." *International Journal of Middle East Studies* 6, no. 1: 276–97.

———. 1978. "Ottoman Population Records and the Census of 1881/82–1893." *International Journal of Middle East Studies* 9: 252–53.

———. 1982. "Millets and Nationality: The Roots of the Incongruity of Nation and State in the Post-Ottoman Era." In *Christians and Jews in the Ottoman Empire: The Function of Plural Society*, edited by Benjamin Braude and Bernard Lewis, 1:141–69. New York: Holmes and Meier.

———. 1985. *Ottoman Population (1830–1914): Demographic and Social Characteristics*. Madison: Univ. of Wisconsin Press.

———. 1988. "Ottoman Ethnic and Confessional Legacy." In *Ethnicity, Pluralism, and the State in the Middle East*, edited by Milton J. Esman and Itamar Rabinovich, 38–53. Ithaca: Cornell Univ. Press.

———, ed. 1968. *Political and Social Thought in the Contemporary Middle East*. New York: Praeger.

Katouzian, Homa. 1981. *The Political Economy of Modern Iran*. New York: New York Univ. Press.

———. 1990. *Musaddiq and the Struggle for Power in Iran*. London: I. B. Tauris.

Kaya, Ferzende. 2003. *Mezopotamya Sürgünü, Abdülmelik Fırat'ın Yaşam Öyküsü*. İstanbul: Anka Yayınları.

Keddie, Nikki R. 1986. "Is Shi'ism Revolutionary?" In *The Iranian Revolution and the Islamic Republic,* edited by Nikki R. Keddie and Eric Hooglund, 113–36. Syracuse: Syracuse Univ. Press.

———, ed. 1983. *Religion and Politics in Iran: Shi'ism from Quietism to Revolution.* New Haven: Yale Univ. Press.

Keddie, Nikki R., and Hooglund, Eric, eds. 1986. *The Iranian Revolution and the Islamic Republic.* Syracuse: Syracuse Univ. Press.

Kedourie, Elie. 1988. "Ethnicity, Majority, and Minority in the Middle East." In *Ethnicity, Pluralism, and the State in the Middle East,* edited by Milton J. Esman and Itamar Rabinovich, 25–31. Ithaca: Cornell Univ. Press.

Kendal. 1979. "Les Kurdes en Iran." Report no. C. Paris: Minority Group Rights.

Kerîm, Mihemmedî Mela. 1998. "Mewlewi: A Great Poet and Alim of Southern Kurdistan." In *Islam de Kurdes,* translated by Homer Dizeyee and Michael Chyet, 59–82. Paris: Institut National de Langues et Civilisations Orientales.

———, ed. 1986. *Diwanî Faik Bêkas.* Baghdad: Dâr Husam Lilnashr.

Kerr, Stanley. 1973. *The Lions of Marash: Personal Experience with American Near East Relief, 1919–1922.* Albany: State Univ. of New York Press.

Keyder, Çağlar. 1986. "A Model of Differentiated Petty Producing Peasantry." In *La Turquie en transition: Disparités, identités, pouvoirs,* edited by Altan Gökalp, 83–96. Paris: Maisonneuve et Larose.

Keyhan. 1979a. Mar. 9. "Az haq-e khodmokhtari-ye Kurdha sarfenazar nemikonim," 3.

———. 1979b. Mar. 9. "Baradaran-e Kurd hamishe dar mahrumiyat bude and," 3.

———. 1978c. Mar. 10. "Khodmokhtari-ye Kurdha rabateyi ba tajzietalabi nadarad," 3.

———. 1979d. Apr. 6. "Showra-ye montekhab-e mardom, Sanandaj ra edare mikonad," 1, 6.

Khadduri, Majid. 1951. *Socialist Iraq.* London: Oxford Univ. Press.

———. 1969. *Republican Iraq.* London: Oxford Univ. Press.

al-Khalil, Samir. 1989. *Republic of Fear: The Politics of Modern Iraq.* Berkeley and Los Angeles: Univ. of California Press.

Khan, Bedir (Sécretaire General de la Comité de l'Indepedence Kurde). 1920. "À Monsieur le President." Archives du Quai d'Orsay, RG Levant, Mesopotamie Irakm 1918–1928. Carton 311, vol. 13, dossier 3, series E, 78. Paris, France.

Khatib, Mohammad Ali. 1994. "Structure of the Public and the Private Sectors in Pre-revolutionary Iran." In *L'Économie de l'Iran Islamique: Entre l'état et le marché,* edited by Thierry Colville, 29–36. Tehran: Institut Français de Recherche en Iran.

Khomeini, Ruhollah. *Selected Messages and Speeches of Imam Khomeini.* 1980. Tehran: Ministry of National Guidance.

Khosrokhavar, Farhad. 1997. *Anthropologie de la Révolution Iranienne.* Paris: L'Harmattan.

Khoury, Philip S., and Joseph Kostiner, eds. 1990. *Tribes and State Formation in the Middle East.* Berkeley and Los Angeles: Univ. of California Press.

"Khweneranî Kurdistan." 1959. *Kurdistan* (June 12): 7.

Kieser, Hans Lukas. 1993. "Les Kurdes alevis face au nationalism Turc Kemaliste: L'Alevite du Dersim et son role dans le premier soulevement Kurde contre Mustafa Kemal (Kocgiri, 1919–1921)." Occasional Paper no. 18. Amsterdam: Middle East Research Associates.

———. 1994. "L'Alévism Kurde." *Peuples Méditerranéens,* no. 68–69: 57–76.

Kimball, Lorenzo Kent. 1972. *The Changing Pattern of Political Power in Iraq, 1958–1971.* New York: Robert and Sons.

Kingston, Paul W. T. 1996. *Britain and the Politics of Modernization in the Middle East, 1945–1958.* Cambridge: Cambridge Univ. Press.

Kinnane, Derk. 1964. *The Kurds and Kurdistan.* New York: Oxford Univ. Press.

Kirkisci, Kemal, and Gareth M. Winrow. 1998. *The Kurdish Question and Turkey: An Example of a Trans-state Ethnic Conflict.* London: Frank Cass.

Koçaş, M. Sadi. 1990. *Kürtlerin Kökeni ve Güneydoğu Anadolu Gerçeği.* Istanbul: Kastaş A. Ş. Yayınları.

Komala and the Kurdish People's Resistance Movement: Speech Made by Komala Member to the People of Mahabad. 1980. Komala Document Series no. 2. Uppsala, Sweden: Esmail Sharifzade Publications.

Koohi-Kamali, Fereshteh. 1992. "The Development of Nationalism in Iranian Kurdistan." In *The Kurds: A Contemporary Overview,* edited by Philip Kreyenbroek and Stephen Sperl, 171–92. London: Routledge.

———. 2003. *The Political Development of the Kurds in Iran: Pastoral Nomadism.* Houndmills, Basingstoke, Hampshire, England: Palgrave Macmillan.

Koopmans, Ruud, and Paul Statham. 2001. "How National Citizenship Shapes Transnationalism: A Comparative Analysis of Migrant Claims-Making in Germany, Great Britain, and the Netherlands." *Revue Européeane des Migrations Internationales* 17, no. 2: 63–100.

Kramer, Martin. 1996. *Arab Awakening and Islamic Revival: The Politics of Ideas in the Middle East.* New Brunswick, N.J.: Transaction Publishers.

Kreyenbroek, Philip. 1990. "Kurdish Identity and the Language Question." In *Kurdistan in Search of Ethnic Identity,* by Turaj Atabaki and Margreet Dorleijn, 52–69. Utrecht: Houtsma Foundation Publication Series.

Kreyenbroek, Philip, and Christine Allison, eds. 1996. *Kurdish Culture and Identity.* London: Zed Books.

Kreyenbroek, Philip, and Stephen Sperl, eds. 1992. *The Kurds: A Contemporary Overview.* London: Routledge.

Kriesberg, Louis. 1997. "Social Movements and Global Transformation." In *Transnational Social Movements and Global Politics: Solidarity Beyond the State,* edited by Jackie Smith, Charles Chatfield, and Ron Pugnacco, 3–18. Syracuse: Syracuse Univ. Press.

Kub, Abdal Hosein Zereen. 1974. *Na sharqi, na qarbi, ensani.* Tehran: Chapkhaney-e Sepehr.

"Kurdish Problem: Foreign Office Research Paper, The." 1946. Copy of British Documents, letter E27821, 104/34, Institut Kurde de Paris, Apr. 2. Paris, France.

"Kurdish Situation." 1945. Copy of documents from War Department, Military Intelligence Division, Institut Kurde de Paris, BID 3144, no. 220–45, Sept. 6. Paris, France.

"Kurdish Situation: Notes on Suleimanya Liwa." 1945. Copy of documents from War Department, Military Intelligence Division, Institut Kurde de Paris, BID 3144, no. 250–45, Oct. 18. Paris, France.

"Kurdistan." 1944. *Roja Nû,* no. 40–42: 1–2.

"Kurdistan: Suisse du Moyen-Orient." 1944. *Roja Nû,* no. 36: 1.

Kurdo, J. 1988. *Kurdistan: The Origins of Kurdish Civilization.* Hudiksvali, Sweden: Tryck-Media.

"Kurds and Syrian Arab Socialism, The." 1968. *Kurdish Journal* 5, no. 1–2: 1–5.

"Kurds and Turks: Last Bonds of Friendship Destroyed." 1925. *Baghdad Times,* Apr. 7. Archives du Quai d'Orsay, RG Levant, Caucause-Kurdistan, 1918–1929. Carton 311, vol. 13, no. 77, dossier 3, series E. Paris, France.

Kutlay, Naci. 2004. "1920'li Yıllar Meclisinde Kürtler." *Özgür Politika,* Jan. 12, 1–8.

Kutschera, Chris. 1979. *Le Mouvement nationale Kurde.* Paris: Flammarion.

———. 1994. "Mad Dreams of Independence: The Kurds of Turkey and the PKK." *Middle East Report* (July-Aug.): 12–15.

———. 1997. *Le Defi Kurde.* Paris: Bayard Éditions.

Laitin, David. 1983. "The Ogaadeen Question and Changes in Somali Identity." In *State vs. Ethnic Claims: African Policy Dilemmas,* edited by Donald Rothschild and Victor A. Olorunsola, 331–49. Boulder: Westview Press.

Lambton, Ann K. S. 1953. *Landlord and Peasant in Persia.* Oxford: Oxford Univ. Press.

———. 1969. *The Persian Land Reform, 1962–1966.* Oxford: Oxford Univ. Press.

———. 1987. *Qajar Persia.* London: I. B. Tauris.

Landau, Jacob M. 1974. *Radical Politics in Modern Turkey.* Leiden: E. J. Brill.

———. 1981. *Pan-Turkism in Turkey: A Study of Irredentism.* London: C. Hurst.

———, ed. 1984. *Atatürk and the Modernization of Turkey.* Boulder: Westview Press.

"La Question de Cilicie: Discourse pronouncé le 24 Decembre 1920 à la Chambre des Deputés par M. Bellet." 1921. *Extrait du Journal Officiel,* 17–22. Archives du

Quai d'Orsay, RG Levant, Mesopotamie Irak, 1918–1929. Carton 311, vol. 13, dossier 3, series E. Paris, France.

Laqueur, Walter Z. 1957. *Communism and Nationalism in the Middle East.* New York: Praeger.

——. 1969. *The Struggle for the Middle East: The Soviet Union and the Middle East, 1958–1968.* London: Routledge and Kegan Paul.

L'Arabisation du Kurdistan: Les visés racistes du régime Baasiste d'Irak. 1974. Paris: Département a l'Information du Parti Democratique Kurde.

La Solution du probleme Kurde en Irak. 1970. Baghdad: Parti Baas Socialist Arabe.

Lazareff, Pierre, ed. 1961. *Memoires du chah d'Iran.* Translated by Michel Christien and F. Cousteau. Paris: Gallimard.

Le Consul de France à Mossoul. 1929. "Á Son Excellence Monsieur le Minister des Affaires Étrangères." Archives du Quai d'Orsay, RG Levant, Mesopotamie Irak, 1919–1929. May 1, 1918–1931, no. 17, bulletin no. 5, Dec. 9. Paris, France.

Lederer, Ivo I., and Wayne S. Vucinich, eds. 1974. *The Soviet Union and the Middle East: The Post-World War Two Era.* Stanford, Calif.: Hoover Univ. Press.

Leezenberg, Michiel. 2000. "Humanitarian Aid in Iraqi Kurdistan." *Cahiers d'études sur la Méditerranée orientale et le monde Turco-Iranien,* no. 29.

"Le Kurdistan." 1945. *Roja Nû,* no. 61: 1–3.

"Le Mouvement Kurde." 1922. Archives du Quai d'Orsay, RG Levant, Caucause-Kurdistan, 1918–1929. Carton 311, vol. 13, dossier 3, series E, July 28. Paris, France.

"Le Mouvement Kurde, le movement laze, et l'activité de l'opposition en Turquie." 1927. Archives du Quai d'Orsay, RG Levant, Caucause-Kurdistan, 1918–1929. Carton 311, vol. 13, dossier 3, series E, Nov. 2. Paris, France.

Lenczowski, George. 1962. *The Middle East in World Affairs.* Ithaca: Cornell Univ. Press.

——. 1978. *Iran under the Pahlavis.* Stanford, Calif.: Hoover Univ. Press.

"Le Parti Communiste Irakien et la question nationale Kurde." 1959. *Orient,* no. 9: 151–54.

Les Archives de la Préfecture de la Police. 1874–1887. Musée de la Préfecture de la Police, RG Constantinople, box A/335. Paris, France.

"Letter from Sheikh Mahmoud Barzinji to His Excellency the High Commissioner for Iraq." 1930. Copy of British Documents, Institut Kurde de Paris, Sept. 17. Paris, France.

"Lettre de Bedr Khan, Sec. General de la Comité de l'Independence Kurde." 1920. Archives du Quai d'Orsay, RG Levant, Caucause-Kurdistan, 1918–1929. Carton 311, vol. 13, dossier 3, series E, Mar. 14. Paris, France.

"Lettre de Jesse à Curley." 1925. "Kurds and Turks: Last Bonds of Friendship Destroyed," *Baghdad Times,* Mar. 10. Archives du Quai d'Orsay, RG Levant,

Mesopotamie Irak, 1919–1929. Vol. 13, dossier 2, series E, no. 77. Paris, France.

"Lettre de Seyid Ahmed, délégué Kurde au Conference du Paix." 1919. Archives du Quai d'Orsay, RG Levant, Caucause-Kurdistan, 1918–1929. Carton 311, vol. 12, dossier 3, series E, Oct. 4. Paris, France.

"Lettre de Sheikh Abdul Qader à son excellence General Agha Petros." 1922. Archives du Quai d'Orsay, RG Levant, Caucause-Kurdistan, 1918–1929. Carton 311, vol. 13, dossier 3, series E, Apr. 5. Paris, France.

Lettre ouverte de Parti Democratique du Kurdistan Iranian au chef de la revolution, l'Ayatollah Khomeini. 1979. Tehran: KDPI.

"Lettre sur le mouvement Kurde." 1922. Archives du Quai d'Orsay, RG Levant, Mesopotamie Irak, 1919–1929. Carton 311, vol. 13, dossier 3, series E, no. 134/6, July 28. Paris, France.

L'Irak revolutionnnaire, 1968–1973: Le Rapport politique adopté par le Huitième Congres Regional du Parti Arabe Socialiste Baas Irak. 1974. Baghdad: Parti Arab Socialist Baas.

Loeffler, Reinhold. 1986. "Economic Changes in a Rural Area since 1979." In *The Iranian Revolution and the Islamic Republic,* edited by Nikki R. Keddie and Eric Hooglund, 93–109. Syracuse: Syracuse Univ. Press.

Longrigg, Stephen H. 1956. *Iraq, 1900–1950: A Political, Social, and Economic History.* Oxford: Oxford Univ. Press.

Lustick, Ian S. 1993. *Unsettled States, Disputed Lands: Britain and Ireland, France and Algeria, Israel and the West Bank-Gaza.* Ithaca: Cornell Univ. Press.

Lustig, Michael Jennings. 1987. "The Muhajirat and the Provisional Government in Kermanshah, 1915–1917." Ph.D. diss., New York Univ.

Máiz, Rámon. 2003. "Politics and the Nation: Nationalist Mobilization of Ethnic Differences." *Nations and Nationalism* 9, no. 2: 195–212.

Majd, Mohammad Gholi. 2000. "Small Landowners and Land Distribution in Iran, 1962–71." *International Journal of Middle East Studies* 32, no. 1: 123–53.

Malmîsanij, and Mahmud Lewendî. 1993. *Li Kurdistana Bakur û li Turkiyê Rojnamegeriya Kurdî, 1908–1992.* Ankara: Öz-Ge Yayınları.

Mamosta Cheikh Ezzedine Hosseini et la situation politique en Iran et au Kurdistan d'Iran. 1984. Paris: Bureau Politique de Mamosta Cheikh Ezzedine Hosseini.

Marcus, Aliza. 1994. "City in the War Zone." *Middle East Report* (July-Aug.): 16–19.

Mardin, Şerif. 1973. "Center-Periphery Relations: A Key to Turkish Politics?" *Daedalus* 102, no. 2: 169–89.

Margulies, Ronnie, and Ergın Yıldızoğlu. 1987. "Agrarian Change." In *Turkey in Transition: New Perspectives,* edited by Irvin Cemil Schick and Ertugrol Ahmet Tonak, 269–92. Oxford: Oxford Univ. Press.

Marr, Phebe. 1985. *The Modern History of Iraq.* Boulder: Westview Press.

Marten-Finnis, Suzanne. 1995. "Collective Memory and National Identities, German and Polish Memory Cultures, the Forms of Collective Memory." *Communist and Post-Communist Studies* 28, no. 2: 255–61.

Martin, Vanessa. 1989. *Islam and Modernism: The Iranian Revolution of 1906.* London: I. B. Tauris.

McAdam, Doug, John McCarthy, and Mayer N. Zald. 1996. "Introduction: Opportunities, Mobilizing Structures, and Framing Processes—Toward a Synthetic, Comparative Perspective on Social Movements." In *Comparative Perspectives on Social Movements,* edited by Doug McAdam, John McCarthy, and Mayer N. Zald, 1–24. Cambridge: Cambridge Univ. Press.

McAdam, Doug, Sidney Tarrow, and Charles Tilly. 1997. "Toward an Integrated Perspective on Social Movements and Revolution." In *Comparative Politics: Rationality, Culture, and Structure,* edited by Mark Irving Lichbach and Alan S. Zuckerman, 142–72. Cambridge: Cambridge Univ. Press.

McDowall, David. 1988. *The Alevi Kurds.* London: Minority Rights Group.

———. 1997. *A Modern History of the Kurds.* London: I. B. Tauris.

MEDYA Güneşi. 1988. No. 6 (Nov.-Dec).

"Memorandum from Barzani to the Iraqi Government." 1966. Translated and reprinted in *Kurdish Journal* 3, no. 4: 16–20.

"Memorandum Presented by the Kurdish 'Razkari' Party in Iraq to the Conference of Foreign Ministers in Moscow." 1946. Copy of documents from War Department, Institut Kurde de Paris, July. Paris, France.

Menashri, David. 1988. "Khomeini's Policy Toward Ethnic and Religious Minorities." In *Ethnicity, Pluralism, and the State in the Middle East,* edited by Milton J. Esman and Itamar Rabinovich, 215–29. Ithaca: Cornell Univ. Press.

Meskoob, Shahrokh. 1992. *Iranian Nationality and the Persian Language.* Translated by Michael C. Hillman. Washington, D.C.: Mage Publishers.

Middle East Watch. 1993. *The Anfal Campaign in Iraqi Kurdistan: The Destruction of Koreme.* New York: Human Rights Watch.

Milani, Mohsen M. 1988. *The Making of Iran's Islamic Revolution: From Monarchy to Islamic Republic.* Boulder: Westview Press.

Al-minhaj al-thiqafi al-markazi. 1990. Baghdad: Dar al-Howriya.

Miran, Serdar Hamid, and Karîm Mustafa Sharezahr. 1986. *Diwanî Hajî Qadirî Koyî.* Arbil (Hawlêr), Iraq: Emîndarêtî Gishtiy Roshinbîrî û Lawanî Nawchey Kurdistan.

Moghadam, Fatemeh E. 1996. *From Land Reform to Revolution: The Political Economy of Agricultural Development in Iran, 1962–1979.* London: I. B. Tauris.

Mojab, Shahrzad, and Amir Hassanpour. 1995. "The Politics of Nationality and Ethnic Diversity." In *Iran after the Revolution: Crisis of an Islamic State,* edited by Saeed Rahnema and Sohrad Behdad, 229–50. London: I. B. Tauris.

Momeni, Jamshid A., ed. 1977. *The Population of Iran: A Selection of Readings.* Shiraz, Iran: Pahlavi Populations Center and East-West Population Institute.

"Monsieur de France, haut commissaire de la République Française en Orient à son excellence Monsieur Mitterand, president du conseil, ministre des affairs étrangères." 1920. Archives du Quai d'Orsay, RG Levant, Caucause-Kurdistan, 1918–1929. Carton 311, vol. 12, dossier 3, series E, Feb. 22. Paris, France.

Monterserat, Michael. 1959. "L'Affaire de Mossoul." *Orient,* no. 9: 23–30.

Moore, Henry Clement. 1970. *Politics in North Africa: Algeria, Morocco, and Tunisia.* Boston: Little, Brown.

Morsalvand, Hassan. 1995. *Ostad-e Kabine-ye Kudeta-ye Sevum-e Esfand-e 1299.* Tehran: Chapkhane-ye Sayeh.

Moslem, Mehdi. 1999. "Ayatollah Khomeini's Role in the Rationalization of the Islamic Government." *Critique,* no. 14: 75–92.

Mottahedeh, Roy. 1985. *The Mantle of the Prophet.* New York: Pantheon Books.

Moutafchieva, Vera P. O. 1988. *Agrarian Relations in the Ottoman Empire in the 15th and 16th Centuries.* Boulder: Univ. Press of Colorado.

Moynihan, Daniel. 1993. *Pandaemonium: Ethnicity and International Politics.* Oxford: Oxford Univ. Press.

Moynihan, Daniel, and Nathan Glazer, eds. 1985. *Ethnicity: Theory and Experience.* Cambridge: Harvard Univ. Press.

Munch, Richard. 2001. *Nation and Citizenship in the Global Age: From National to Transnational Ties and Identities.* London: Palgrave.

Nader, George A. 1995. "Interview with President Ali Akbar Rafsanjani." *Middle East Insight* 11, no. 5: 6–14.

Nagel, Joane. 1980. "The Conditions of Ethnic Separatism: The Kurds in Turkey, Iran, and Iraq." *Ethnicity* 7, no. 3: 279–97.

Najambadi, Afsaneh. 1987a. "Depolitisation of a Rentier State: The Case of Pahlavi Iran." In *The Rentier State,* edited by Hazem Beblawi and Giacomo Luciani, 211–27. London: Croom Helm.

———. 1987b. *Land Reform and Social Change in Iran.* Salt Lake City: Univ. of Utah Press.

Nasseri, Iraj Tanhatan. 1980. "The Muhajirat and the National Government of Kermanshah, 1915–1917." Ph.D. diss., Univ. of Edinburgh.

Natali, Denise. 1999. "International Aid, Regional Politics, and the Kurdish Issue in Iraq after the Persian Gulf War." Abu Dhabi: Emirates Center for Strategic Studies and Research.

The National Development Plan: 1970–1974. 1971. Baghdad: Government Press.

Nattagh, Nima. 1986. *Agricultural and Regional Development in Iran, 1962–1978.* Cambridgeshire: Middle East and North African Studies Press.

"Nejadî Sasanî Kurd bun û Fars nebûn." 1958. *Hetaw,* no. 134–38: 1.

Nezan, Kendal. 1993. "The Kurds under the Ottoman Empire." In *A People Without a Country*, edited by Gerard Chaliand, 11–37. New York: Olive Branch Press.

Nikitine, Basil. 1956. *Les Kurdes*. Paris: Éditions d'Aujourd'hui.

Nuseibeh, Hasam Zab. 1956. *The Ideas of Arab Nationalism*. Ithaca: Cornell Univ. Press.

O'Ballance, Edgar. 1973. *The Kurdish Revolt, 1961–1970*. London: Faber and Faber.

Ökçün, A. Gündüz. 1968. *Türkiye İktisat Kongresi: 1923 İzmir*. Ankara: Ankara Üniversitesi Siyasal Bilgiler Fakültesi Yayınları.

Olson, Robert. 1989. *The Emergence of Kurdish Nationalism and the Sheikh Said Rebellion (1880–1925)*. Austin: Univ. of Texas Press.

———. 1992a. "Battle for Kurdistan: The Church-Cox Correspondence Regarding the Creation of the State of Iraq, 1921–1923." *Kurdish Studies* 5, no. 1–2: 29–44.

———. 1992b. "The Creation of a Kurdish State in the 1990s?" *Journal of South Asian and Middle Eastern Studies* 15, no. 4: 1–25.

Omid, Homa. 1994. *Islam and the Post-revolutionary State in Iran*. London: St. Martin's Press.

Onis, Ziya. 1991. "Political Economy of Turkey in the 1980s: Anatomy of Unorthodox Liberalism." In *Strong State and Economic Interest Groups: The Post-1980 Turkish Experience*, edited by Metin Heper, 27–40. Berlin: Walter de Gruyter.

———. 1995. "Turkey in the Post-Cold War Era, in Search of Identity." *Middle East Journal* 49, no. 1: 48–68.

O'Shea, Maria T. 1991. "Greater Kurdistan: The Mapping of a Myth?" In *Kurdistan: Political and Economic Potential*, edited by Maria T. O'Shea, 1–26. London: Geopolitics and International Boundaries Research Centre.

Owen, Roger. 1981. *The Middle East in the World Economy*. London: Methuen.

Özoğlu, Hakan. 2004. *Kurdish Notables and the Ottoman State: Evolving Identities, Competing Loyalties, and Shifting Boundaries*. Albany: State Univ. of New York Press.

Özok, Tijen Yalçın. 1990. *Southeastern Anatolian Tribes During the Turkish Nationalist Struggle*. İstanbul: Boğaziçi Univ.

Pacha, Sherif. 1919. "Memorandum sur les revendications du peuples Kurdes." Paris: Imprimerie A. G. Hoir.

Parla, Taha. 1981. *The Social and Political Thought of Ziya Gökalp, 1876–1924*. Leiden: E. J. Brill.

Parvin, Manoucher, and Majid Taghavi. 1986. "A Comparison of Land Tenure in Iran under the Monarchy and under the Islamic Republic." In *Post-revolutionary Iran*, edited by Hooshang Amirahmadi and Manochar Parvin, 168–82. Boulder: Westview Press.

Paşa, Ihsan Nouri. 1986. "La Revolte de Agridagh: Ararat." Geneva: Éditions Kurdes Genève et Atelier P.V.

Peker, Mumtaz. 1996. "Internal Migration and the Marginal Sector." In *Work and Occupation in Modern Turkey,* edited by Erol Kahveci, Nadir Sugur, and Theo Nichols, 7–37. London: Mansell Publishers.

Pelletiere, Stephen C. 1984. *The Kurds: An Unstable Element in the Persian Gulf.* Boulder: Westview Press.

Perinçek, Doğu. 1989. *Abdullah Öcalan ile Görüşme.* İstanbul: Günay Yayıncılık Ticaret ve Sanayi A.Ş.

Peteet, Julie. 2000. "Refugees, Resistance, and Identity." In *Globalizations and Social Movements,* edited by John A. Guidry, Michael Kennedy, and Mayer N. Zald, 183–209. Ann Arbor: Univ. of Michigan Press.

Petry, Jeff. 1993. "The Construction of Karen Nationalism: American Baptists in Burma." *Ethnic Studies Report* 11, no. 1: 64–92.

Pope, Nicole, and Hugh Pope. 1997. *Turkey Unveiled: Atatürk and After.* London: John Murray.

Poujol, Hélène. 1999. "Alevism et construction identitaire en Turquie: Entre stigmatisation, mobilisation, et violence." Master's thesis, École des Hautes Études en Sciences Sociales.

"President: Islamic Culture, Most Important Pillar of Iranian Identity." 1998. *Tehran Times,* Apr. 22, 1.

Program and Constitution of the Kurdistan Democratic Party of Iran. 1981. Paris: KDPI.

Qader, Sheikh Abdul. 1922. "À Son Excellence General Agha Petros." Archives du Quai d'Orsay, RG Levant, Mesopotamie Irak, 1919–1929. Carton 211, vol. 13, dossier 3, series E, Apr. 5. Paris, France.

Qani' [Muhammed Abdul Qader]. 1979. *Diwanî Qani'.* Sulaimaniya: Chapkhaney Zanko Suleymanî.

"Qawmî Kurd layqî Jian." 1943. *Nishtiman,* no. 7–9: 7.

Rahnema, Saeed, and Sohrad Behdad, eds. 1995. *Iran after the Revolution: Crisis of an Islamic State.* London I. B. Tauris.

Rajaee, Bahram. 2000. "The Politics of Refugee Policy in Post-revolutionary Iran." *Middle East Journal* 54, no. 1: 44–63.

Ramazani, K. Rouhallah. 1975. *Iran's Foreign Policy, 1941–73: A Study of Foreign Policy in Modernizing Nations.* Charlottesville: Univ. Press of Virginia.

Ramazanoğlu, Huseyin. 1985. *Turkey in the World Capitalist System.* Aldershot, Hants, England: Gouer Publishing.

Ramsdan, Sonyel Salahi. 1989. *Atatürk: The Founder of Modern Turkey.* Ankara: Turkish Historical Society Printing House.

Raouf, Wafik. 1984. *Nouveau régard sur le nationalism Arab, Ba'ath, et Nasserism.* Paris: L'Harmattan.

"Rapport du Comité Central du Parti Communiste Irakien." 1959. *Orient,* no. 9: 175–81.

Rashid, Ali. 1994. "De-privatisation Process of the Iranian Economy after the Revolution of 1979." In *L'Économie de l'Iran Islamique: Entre l'état et le marché*, edited by Thierry Colville, 37–68. Tehran: Institut Français de Recherche en Iran.

Report by the Majesty's High Commission on the Finances, Administration, and Condition of Iraq for the Period from October 1, 1920, to March 31, 1922. 1922. Baghdad: Government Press.

Resistance to the Huge Military Attack on Kurdistan and to the Repression of Workers and Students. 1981. Komala Document Series no. 5. Uppsala, Sweden: Esmail Sharifzade Publications.

Review of the Civil Administration of Mesopotamia. 1920. London: His Majesty's Stationery Office.

"Review of the Civil Administration of Mesopotamia." 1922–1923. In *Al-Iraq Yearbook*. Baghdad: Al-Iraq Press.

Rigoni, Isabelle. 1998. "Les Mobilisations des Kurdes en Europe." *Revue Européene des Migrations Internationals* 14, no. 3: 203–23.

Rittenberg, Libby, ed. 1998. *The Political Economy of Turkey in the Post-Soviet Era.* Westport, Conn.: Praeger.

Roberts, Gwilym, and David Fowler. 1995. *Built by Oil.* Reading, Berkshire, England: Ithaca Press.

Rondot, Pierre. 1958. "La Nation Kurd en face des movements Arabs." *Orient,* no. 9: 90–96.

———. 1959. "Quelques opinions sur les relations Arabo-Kurdes dans la Republique Irakienne." *Orient,* no. 9: 51–58.

Rose, Gregory. 1983. "Velayat-e Faqih and the Recovery of Islamic Identity in the Thought of Ayatollah Khomeini." In *Religion and Politics in Iran: Shi'ism from Quietism to Revolution,* edited by Nikki R. Keddie, 166–88. New Haven: Yale Univ. Press.

Ross, H. Pierre. 1959. "L'Irak devant la reforme agraire." *Orient,* no. 9: 81–93.

Ruhani, Baba Mardukh, and Majed Mardukh Ruhani. 1992. *Taríkh-e Moshaheer-e Kord.* Vol. 3. Tehran: Shorush Press.

Sader, Makrem. 1982. "Le Développement industriel de l'Irak." In *Industrialization et changements sociaux dans l'Oriente Arabe,* edited by Par A. Bourgey and J. P. Bertrand, 237–44. Beirut: Centre d'Études et de Récherches sur le Moyen Orient Contemporain.

al-Said, Nuri (Prime Minister, Office of the Council of Ministers). 1930. "To the British Resident." Copies of British Documents, Institut Kurde de Paris, RG 371 14523, no. 2957, Oct. 24. Paris, France.

Sakallıoğlu, Umit Cizre. 1998. "Rethinking the Connections Between Turkey's Western Identity Versus Islam." *Critique* 12: 3–8.

Salmanzadeh, Cyrus. 1980. *Agricultural Change and Rural Society in Southern Iran.* Cambridge: Middle East and North African Studies Press.

Samii, Abbas. 1996. "The Shah and the Kurds, 1955–1975." *Namah* 4, no. 1: 1–4.

Saracoğlu, Ruşdu. 1994. "Liberalization of the Economy." In *Politics in the Third Turkish Republic,* edited by Metin Heper and Evin Ahmet, 63–75. Boulder: Westview Press.

Sayan, Celal. 1987. "La Construction de l'état-nation Turc et le mouvement national Kurde (1918–1938)." Master's thesis, Univ. of Paris VIII et Univ. of Paris I.

Schick, Irvin Cemil, and Ertugrul Ahmet Tonak, eds. 1987. *Turkey in Transition: New Perspectives.* Oxford: Oxford Univ. Press.

Schirazi, Aghar. 1997. *The Constitution of Iran: Politics and the State in the Islamic Republic.* Translated by John O'Kane. New York: I. B. Tauris.

Şener, Cemal. 1994. *Atatürk ve Aleviler.* İstanbul: Ant Yayınları.

Sershomari-ye omumi-ye nofus va maskan. 1996. Natayej-e Tafsili. Tehran: Jomhuri-ye Islami-ye Iran, Sazman-e barnameh va bujeh-ye merkez-e Amar-e Iran.

Set Up Peasants' Unions to Wipe Out Derebegayeti. 1981. Komala Document Series no. 6. Uppsala, Sweden: Esmail Sharifzade Publications.

Shaker, Sallama. 1995. *State, Society, and Privatization in Turkey, 1979–1990.* Washington, D.C.: Woodrow Wilson Center Press.

Shamsul, A. B. 1997. "The Economic Dimension of Malay Nationalism: Identity Formation in Malaysia since 1988." *Developing Economies* 35, no. 2: 240–61.

Shankland, David. 1996. "Islam, Secularists, and the Alevis: Dynamics and Dilemmas Confronting the New Coalition Government." *Islamic World Report* 1, no. 3: 102–14.

Shaw, Stanford J., and Ezel Kural Shaw. 1997. *History of the Ottoman Empire and Modern Turkey.* Vol. 2. Cambridge: Cambridge Univ. Press.

Sherzad, A. 1991. "The Kurdish Movement in Iraq, 1975–1988." In *The Kurds: A Contemporary Overview,* edited by Philip G. Kreyenbroek and Stephan Sperl, 134–69. London: Routledge.

Silopi, Zinar. 1969. *Doza Kurdistan.* Beirut: Stewr basim-evi.

Simko, Ismail Agha. 1921. "To Babekr I Selim Agha, Qaimaqam of Qala Diza." Translation of letter. Copy of British Documents, Institut Kurde de Paris, RG 371/6397, 138842, June–July. Paris, France.

Şimşir, Bilal N., ed. 1973. *İngiliz Belgelerinde Atatürk (1919–1938).* Vol. 1. Ankara: Türk Tarih Kurumu Basımevi.

———. 1975. *Documents diplomatiques Ottomans, 1886–1893.* Vols. 1–2. Ankara: Türk Tarih Kurumu Basımevi.

Şivan, Dr. [Sait Kırmızıtoprak]. 1997. *Kürt Millet Hareketleri ve Irak'ta Kürdistan İhtilali.* Stockholm: APEC.

Sluglett, Peter. 1976. *Britain in Iraq, 1914–1932*. London: Ithaca Press.

Smith, Anthony D. 1987. *The Ethnic Origins of Nations*. Oxford: Basil Blackwell.

———. 2002. "Dating the Nation." In *Ethnonationalism in the Contemporary World: Walker Connor and the Study of Nationalism*, edited by Daniele Conversi, 53–71. London: Routledge.

Sökefeld, Martin, and Susanne Schwalgin. 2000. "Institutions and Their Agents in Diaspora: A Comparison of Armenians in Athens and Alevis in Germany." Paper presented at the sixth European Association of Social Anthropologists conference, Kraków, July 26–29.

Soran, Zinar. 1996. "Kûrt Teali Cemiyeti ya Diyarbekirê (Komeleya Pêşket na Kurdan ya Diyarbekirê—1918)." *Çira* 5: 18–27.

Stansfield, Gareth R. V. 2003. *Iraqi Kurdistan: Political Development and Emergent Democracy*. London: Routledge Curzon.

Steinbach, Udo. 1991. "The European Community, the United States, the Middle East, and Turkey." In *Strong State and Economic Interest Groups: The Post-1980 Turkish Experience*, edited by Metin Heper, 103–16. Berlin: Walter de Gruyter.

Stork, Joe. 1979. "Oil and the Penetration of Capitalism in Iraq: An Interpretation." In *Oil and Business in Iraq*, 38–77. Louvain la-Neuve: Centre de Récherches sur le Monde Arabe Contemporaine.

———. 1989. "Class, State, and Politics in Iraq." In *Power and Stability in the Middle East*, edited by Berch Berberoglu, 31–54. London: Zed Books.

Sugar, Peter F., ed. 1997. *Nationality and Society in the Habsburg and Ottoman Empire*. Hampshire, England: Variorum.

Sultan, Ja'far. Howreman tribes, Afrasiab Beg Rustam Sultan Zada, Mustafa Beg Salari Jang Ja'far Sultan Zada, and Badir Khan (Sultani tribe). 1930. "To General Secretary of the League of Nations Through the High Commissioner for Iraq." Copy of British Documents, Institut Kurde de Paris, RG 371/14523, Oct. 9. Paris, France.

Tabrizi, Khosro. 1927. "Nejad va tebar-e Safaviyeh." *Ayandeh* 2, no. 3: 357–59.

"Talabani Remarks from Historic Visit to Kirkuk." 2003. *Kurdistan Nuwe*, Apr. 14. Translated at http://www.kurdishmedia.com by Kamal Mirawdeli.

Tapper, Richard L. 1988a. "Ethnicity, Order, and Meaning in the Anthropology of Iran and Afghanistan." In *Le Fait ethnique en Iran et en Afghanistan*, edited by Jean-Pierre Digard, 21–34. Paris: Éditions du CNRS.

———. 1988b. "History and Identity among the Shahsevan." *Iranian Studies* 31, no. 3–4: 84–108.

———, ed. 1983. *The Conflict of Tribe and State in Iran and Afghanistan*. New York: St. Martin's Press.

Tavahodi, Kalimullah. 1980. *Harakat-e Tarikhi-ye Kurd beh Khorasan*. Mashhad, Iran: Kooshesh.

Telegram from the High Commissioner, Baghdad. 1921. "To Political Officer, Sulaimaniya." Copy of British Documents, Institut Kurde de Paris, RG 371/63976, 138842, no. 950/S, Aug. 19. Paris, France.

"Télégramme Confidentielle de Georges Picot." 1919. Archives du Quai d'Orsay, RG Levant, Caucause-Kurdistan, 1918–1929. Carton 311, vol. 12, dossier 3, series E, Oct. 8. Paris. France.

"Télégramme de Monsieur Gouraud." 1921. Archives du Quai d'Orsay, RG Levant, Caucause-Kurdistan, 1918–1929. Carton 314, vol. 26, dossier 1, series E, Nov. 29. Paris, France.

Télégramme de 22 chiefs du tribu et les notables Kurdes. 1920. "À la Sec. General de la Conference de la Paix." Archives du Quai d'Orsay, RG Levant, Caucause-Kurdistan, 1918–1929. Carton 311, vol. 12, dossier 3, series E. Paris, France.

"Télégramme de Gouraud." 1921. Archives du Quai d'Orsay, RG Levant, Caucause-Kurdistan, 1918–1929. Carton 314, vol. 26, dossier 1, series E, Nov. 29. Paris, France.

Thomas, Lewis V. 1952. "Recent Developments in Turkish Islam." *Middle East Journal* 6, no. 1: 22–40.

Tiryakian, Edward A., and Neil Nevitte. 1985. "Nationalism and Modernity." In *New Nationalisms of the Developed West,* edited by Edward A. Tiryakian and Ronald Rogowski, 57–86. Boston: Allen and Unwin.

Togan, S., and V. N. Balasubramanyam. 1996. *The Economy in Turkey since Liberalization.* London: Macmillan.

Tonak, Ahmet Ertuğrul, and Irvin Cemil Schick. 1987. *Turkey in Transition: New Perspectives.* Oxford: Oxford Univ. Press.

Toprak, Binnaz. 1981. *Islam and Political Development in Turkey.* Leiden: E. J. Brill.

"Translation of Letter from Ismail Agha Simko to Babekr I Selim Agha, Qaimaqam of Qala Diza." 1921. Copy of British Documents, letter FO 371/6397, pp. 109–10, Institut Kurde de Paris, July. Paris, France.

Treaty of Alliance Between Great Britain and Irak. 1925. London: His Majesty's Stationery Office.

The Trial of a Mischievous Landowner in the People's Tribunal. 1981. Komala Document Series no. 4. Uppsala, Sweden: Esmail Sharifzade Publications.

"Trouble in Kurdistan: Suleymaniyah Shaikh's Treachery." 1919. *Basrah Times,* May 28, 1.

Tunay, Muharrem. 1993. "The Turkish New Right's Attempt at Hegemony." In *The Political and Socioeconomic Transformation of Turkey,* edited by Atila Eralp, Muharrem Tunay, and Birol Yesilada, 11–30. Westport, Conn.: Praeger.

"Turkiye û al û gorî ferhengî." 1993. *Sirwa* (Aug.): 4–5.

Turquie: OCDE études économiques, 1984/85. 1985. Paris: OCDE/OECD.

12 September in Turkey: Before and After. 1982. Ankara: Angün Kardeşler Printing House.

"Two Years After." 1968. *Kurdica,* no. 1: 6.

Unal, Unver. 2000. "La Citoyenneté Turque et le question Kurde." Master's thesis, Univ. Lumiére Lyon 2.

Uriel, Dann. 1969. *Iraq under Qassem: A Political History, 1958–1963.* Tel Aviv: Praeger.

Vali, Abbas. 1993. *Pre-capitalist Iran: A Theoretical History.* London: I. B. Tauris.

———. 1994a. "Genèse et structure du nationalism Kurde en Iran." *Peuples Mediterranéens,* no. 68–69: 143–64.

———. 1994b. "Nationalism and Kurdish Historical Writing." *New Perspectives on Turkey* 14: 23–51.

———. 1995. "The Making of Kurdish Identity in Iran." *Critique* 7: 1–22.

van Bruinessen, Martin. 1992. *Agha, Shaikh, and State: The Social and Political Structures of Kurdistan.* London: Zed Books.

———. 1998. "The Kurds and Islam." In *Islam de Kurdes,* 13–35. Paris: Institut National de Langues et Civilisations Orientales.

———. 2001. "Aslını inkar eden haramzadedir!" *Études Kurdes,* no. 3: 7–40.

Vaner, Semih. 1988. "Un premier état des lieux." *Cahiers d'Études sur la Mediterranée Orientale et le Monde Turco-Iranien,* no. 5: 3–22.

Vanley, Ismet S. 1993. "Kurdistan in Iraq." In *A People Without a Country,* edited by Gerard Chaliand, 138–93. New York: Olive Branch Press.

Verdery, Katherine. 1993. "Whither Nation and Nationalism." *Daedalus* 122, no. 3: 37–46.

"Visiting French Senator Expresses Support for Kurds' Aspirations." 2003. *Kurdistan Observer,* Jan. 27.

Weaver, Sally M. 1986. "Struggles of the Nation-State to Define Aboriginal Ethnicity in Canada and Australia." In *Minorities and Mother Country Imagery,* edited by Gerald L. Gold, 182–210. Newfoundland: Institute of Social and Economic Research.

Whittleton, Celine. 1989. "Oil and the Iraqi Economy." In *Saddam's Iraq: Revolution or Reaction?* edited by CADRI, 54–72. London: Zed Books.

William, Alonso. 1995. "Citizenship, Nationality, and Other Identities." *Journal of International Affairs* 48, no. 2: 585–99.

Williams, Brackette F. 1989. "A Class Act: Anthropology and the Race to Nation Across Ethnic Terrain." *Annual Review of Anthropology* 18: 401–44.

"Wutarêikî Shaykh Said pêshawa-yî enqelabî-yî milatî-yî Kurd." 1943. *Nishtiman,* no. 7–9: 1.

"Xemasi." 1998. *Çira,* no. 13: 62–63.

Yalçin-Heckmann, Lâle. 1990. "Kurdish Tribal Organisation and Local Political

Processes." In *Turkish State, Turkish Society,* edited by Andrew Hale and Nükhet Sirman, 292–315. London: Routledge.

Yasemi, Rashid Ghulam Reza. 1937. *Kurd va peyvastegi-ye nejadi va tarikhi.* Tehran: Chapkhane-ye Naqshe Jehan.

Yassin, Borhanedin A. 1995. *Vision or Reality? The Kurds in the Policy of the Great Powers, 1941–1947.* Lund, Sweden: Lund Univ. Press.

Yavari-d'Hellencourt, Nouchine. 1988. "Ethnies et ethnicité dans les manuels scolaires Iraniennes." In *Le Fait ethnique en Iran et en Afghanistan,* edited by Jean-Pierre Digard, 247–65. Paris: Éditions du CNRS.

Yavuz, M. Hakan. 1995. "The Patterns of Political Islamic Identity: Dynamics of National and Transnational Loyalties and Identities." *Central Asian Survey* 14, no. 3: 341–72.

———. 1998. "Turkish Identity and Foreign Policy in Flux: The Rise of Neo-Ottomanism." *Critique* 12: 19–41.

———. 1999. "Search for a New Social Contract in Turkey: Fethullah Gulen, the Virtue Party, and the Kurds." *SAIS Review* 19, no. 1: 114–43.

———. 2001. "Five Stages of the Construction of Kurdish Nationalism in Turkey." *Nationalism and Ethnic Politics* 7, no. 3: 1–24.

———. 2002. "The Politics of Fear: The Rise of the Nationalist Action Party (MHP) in Turkey." *Middle East Journal* 56, no. 2: 200–221.

Yegen, Mesut. 1998. "The Turkish State Discourse and the Exclusion of Kurdish Identity." *Middle East Studies* 32, no. 2: 216–29.

Yerasimos, Stéphane. 1987. "The Monoparty Period." In *Turkey in Transition: New Perspectives,* edited by Irvin Cemil Schick and Ertugal Ehmet Tonak, 66–100. Oxford: Oxford Univ. Press.

Yesilada, Birol. 1993. "Turkish Foreign Policy Toward the Middle East." In *The Political and Socioeconomic Tranformation of Turkey,* edited by Atila Eralp, Muharrem Tunay, and Birol Yesilada, 169–92. Westport, Conn.: Praeger.

Yousif, Abdul-Salaam. 1991. "The Struggle for Cultural Hegemony During the Iraqi Revolution." In *The Iraqi Revolution of 1958: The Old Social Classes Revisited,* edited by Robert Fernea and William Louis, 172–96. London: I. B. Tauris.

Zabih, Sepehr. 1966. *The Communist Movement in Iran.* Berkeley and Los Angeles: Univ. of California Press.

Zarcone, Thierry. 1998. "Note sur quelques shaykh soufis Kurdes contemporains et leurs disciples à Istanbul." In *Islam de Kurdes,* 109–23. Paris: Institut National des Langues et Civilisations Orientales.

Zekî, Muhammed Amin. 1931. *Kurd û Kurdistan.* Mahabad, Iran: Entesharat Seyidiyan.

Zekî, Rashid (délégué de Souleimanieh du Kurdistan du Sud). 1919. "À Monsieur le Haute Commissarie du Glorieux Governement Francaise à Beyrouth."

Archives du Quai d'Orsay, RG Causase-Kurdistan 1918–1922. Carton 311, vol. 13, dossier 3, series E, July 6. Paris, France.

"Zemanî Kurdî." 1940. *Gelawêj,* no. 2: 1–7.

Zeynelabidin, Zinar. 1998. "Medrese Education in Northern Kurdistan." In *Islam de Kurdes,* edited by L'Équipe de Recherche Interdisciplinaire sur le Sociétés Méditerranéennes Musulmanes (ERISM), 39–58. Paris: Institut National des Langues et Civilisations Orientales.

Zimmerman, Ann. 1994. "Kurdish Broadcasting in Iraq." *Middle East Report* 24, no. 4: 20–21.

Zürcher, Erik Jan. 1991. *Political Opposition in the Early Turkish Republic.* Leiden: E. J. Brill.

Index